AMERICAN MUSEUM
GUIDES
FINE ARTS

Tom L. Freudenheim, Consultant Editor

**Cover Photograph Courtesy of
The SOLOMON R. GUGGENHEIM MUSEUM**

COLLIER BOOKS
MACMILLAN PUBLISHING COMPANY
New York

A Quarto Book

European Art © 1983 by
Quarto Marketing Ltd. and Peter Frank

First published in the United States by
Macmillan Publishing Company, Inc.
866 Third Avenue
New York, NY 10022
Collier Macmillan Canada, Inc.

Library of Congress Cataloging in Publication Data
Main entry under title:

American museum guides.

Includes indexes.
Contents: [1] Fine arts/Tom Freudenheim, editor
—[2] Sciences/Paul Hoffman, editor.
1. Museums—United States. 2. Museums—United States
—Directories. I. Freudenheim, Tom L. II. Hoffman,
Paul, 1956.–
AM11.A64 1983   069'.025'73   83-13604

ISBN 0-02-541450-X (v. 1)
ISBN 0-02-097680-1 (pbk. : v. 1)
ISBN 0-02-552020-2 (v. 2)
ISBN 0-02-097710-7 (pbk. : v. 2)

10 9 8 7 6 5 4 3 2 1

Produced and prepared by
Quarto Marketing Ltd.
212 Fifth Avenue
New York, NY 10010

Editor: Bill Logan
Editorial Assistant: Richard Selman
Designer: Richard Boddy
Design Assistant: Mary Moriarty
Cover Design: Abby Kagan

Typesetting: BPE Graphics, Inc.
Printed and bound in the United States by
Interstate Book Manufacturers, Inc.

American Museum Guides: Fine Arts is also published in
a hardcover edition by Macmillan Publishing Company.

CONTENTS

CHAPTER THREE
ASIAN ART
by CAROL BIER
PAGE 59

• Art Institute of Chicago • Asian Art Museum of San Francisco •
• Brooklyn Museum • Cincinnati Art Museum •
• Cleveland Museum of Art • Denver Art Museum •
• Detroit Institute of Arts • Freer Gallery of Art •
• Isabella Stewart Gardner Museum • Kimbell Art Museum •
• Los Angeles County Museum of Art •
• Jacques Marchais Center for Tibetan Art •
• Metropolitan Museum of Art • Minneapolis Institute of Arts •
• Museum of Fine Arts, Boston • Nelson-Atkins Museum of Art •
• Newark Museum • Philadelphia Museum of Art •
• Seattle Art Museum • Walters Art Gallery •
• Yale University Art Gallery •

CHAPTER FOUR
EUROPEAN ART
by PETER FRANK
PAGE 85

• Art Institute of Chicago • Museum of Fine Arts, Boston •
• Isabella Stewart Gardner Museum •
• William Hayes Fogg Art Museum, Harvard University •
• Cleveland Museum of Art • Frick Collection •
• Los Angeles County Museum of Art •
• Norton Simon Museum of Art at Pasadena •
• J. Paul Getty Museum •
• Henry E. Huntington Library and Art Gallery •
• Metropolitan Museum of Art • National Gallery of Art •
• Nelson-Atkins Museum of Art • Philadelphia Museum of Art •
• John and Mabel Ringling Museum of Art •
• Toledo Museum of Art •

INTRODUCTION

by
TOM L. FREUDENHEIM

The extraordinary strength and variety of American art museums is a result of the unique history of this field in our country. Our museums originated in a variety of ways. Civic ventures for public enlightenment (e.g., Metropolitan Museum of Art), adjuncts to great colleges and universities (e.g., Yale University Art Gallery), and compulsively-generated personal collections (Isabella Stewart Gardner Museum), as well as combinations of these, have meant that there are major art museums all across the land. The resulting breadth and depth of their collections is impressive, as are the buildings in which the art is housed. Imagination, energy, and a strong commitment to quality are evident beyond the actual works of art, communicated as well through splendid installations, sensitive conservation practices, and ambitious architectural projects, many of which suggest a rethinking of the museum's role and of its visual impact on the visitor and the community.

In addition, today's art museum frequently offers programs and a variety of other activities that take us far beyond the realm of the "picture gallery" origins of so many public and private collections. The current "special exhibition trend" of numerous art museums, now encompassing much more than the showing of their own holdings, is not a new phenomenon. But this enlarged aspect of the museum's function has gradually tended to overshadow many of the other things that the museum does. Certainly the interest in bor-rowed art has tended to concentrate fervent public attention on the museum—with an intensity outdone only by the occasional astro-nomically priced work of art, whose monetary value gives it an iconic value that may outweigh the aesthetic admiration it draws.

There seems to be general agreement about the five basic func-tions of the museum: to collect, to preserve, to exhibit, to study, and to educate. Yet this attitude was not always prevalent, and public orientation was minimal in many of our institutions in the last century. Thus an English writer in 1904 defined a museum as "a collection of the monuments of antiquity or of other objects interesting to the scholar and the man of science, arranged and displayed in accordance with scientific method."[1] By 1933, in a study on the arts in American life, Frederick P. Keppel and R. L. Duffus observed that "the idea that the public is more important than the exhibits is certainly new, and it is this idea that distinguished the museum of the present day from that of half a century ago.... Our great contemporary museums, especially those specializing in the arts, now deserve to be ranked with our schools and colleges as institutions of learning.[2]

If this half-century-old observation seems prescient, we would do well to remember that the intervening years have been the ones of greatest growth for our art museums. The older and larger museums turned into world leaders in their field, while many new museums were founded. The quality of collections has been continually upgraded, while numerous private assemblages were absorbed into public institutions by gift and bequest. New fields of interest, such as American, African and Oceanic art, photography and film, have become the subjects of attention in museums. New ways of interpreting their educational functions have enlarged on the programs conducted by most museums, in response to questions, and perhaps even doubts, about the inherent eloquence of works of art. New audiences, target audiences, and other specifics have gradually replaced the generalized view of someone called the "museum visitor." Moreover, tangentially related museum activities, such as eating and shopping, with their attendant facilities, are now considered essential to the operation of the art museum. Jacques Barzun has observed that "the spread during the past fifty years not only of receptivity to art as such, but also of tolerance for it is in fact amazing; indeed, it is unexampled in the history of our civilization."[3]

THE AMERICAN MUSEUM GUIDE—FINE ARTS must be understood against such a background, for this volume attempts to refocus the visitor/reader toward the core of the art museum: *its collections.* Our approach is through various fields of specialization within museums, and we are aware of the concerns of "the scholar and the man of science." But our aim is to assist the non-specialist in relating to some of the excitement that is generated by understanding the museum through its *specific* collection strengths, rather than seeing the museum in a romantic haze as a splendid public attic.

This is a time of impermanence, even in museums, which are charged with articulating permanence. The public has been invited to view spectacular temporary exhibitions of a wide variety, emphasizing in yet another manner how quickly we move around the world and how adroitly we are able to move art treasures as well. This guide, on the other hand, emphasizes the museum's stability, because it discusses collections, and in general deals with works that are usually on view. The various sections have been written by scholars who are specialists in their fields, knowledgeable both about the art itself, and about the various museums, their collecting histories, idiosyncrasies, and the relative importance of the collections to the field as a whole.

Because this is not a guide to every American art museum, the format deserves some explanation. Each section is organized around a field of collecting, often analagous to a curatorial department or division in an art museum. While the major thrust of the section is to discuss the most significant collections in that field, with some detailed comments on the collection and its importance, there has also been an attempt to include some major resources that may be relatively less familiar even to sophisticated museum travelers. The selection does not pretend to exhaust the number of excellent collections in existence, occasionally presenting a smaller but exciting collection instead of a large, well-known one. And of course, some of our largest museums have several major collections, and therefore they are discussed in more than one section. There is no attempt to give a cross-section account of American museums, since this has been done in other books. Rather, through a specialist's eyes, the reader will be resensitized to the pleasures awaiting him in the museum, and will be excited by the choices discussed. These choices were made jointly by the editor and the various scholar-authors.

There has been an effort to include works that are generally on public view, but even those works may occasionally be out of the museum on loan, or in a conservation laboratory for examination or treatment. Works on paper, such as drawings and photographs, are not permanently displayed, in order to assure their long lives. Visitors wanting to see such works are advised to contact the museum's appropriate curatorial department in advance of a visit, in order to make an appointment to view works on paper. Such advance notice, or perhaps an inquiry, is also suggested for the visitor who wants to see a specific work of art, in order to ascertain that it is, in fact, on exhibition. In addition, in this age of budgetary difficulties, museum hours (and admission fees) may change, and some museums may open certain galleries on a rotating schedule, so that is also worth checking prior to setting out on an excursion.

But the merits of such an excursion will hopefully be enticing to readers of this guide. Even in New York City, with museums that house treasures far beyond what this volume could encompass, the interest ranges from several major areas of the giant Metropolitan

Museum of Art all the way to the excellent small Jacques Marchais Center for Tibetan Art. Typically, while the large older cities on the East Coast generally boast great encyclopedic museums, there are major collections elsewhere as well. These include extraordinary resources such as The Phillips Collection and Dumbarton Oaks in Washington, where the various Smithsonian museums and National Gallery frequently appear most visible. But they may also include important museums a bit farther afield, such as Connecticut's New Britain Museum of American Art, or the Addison Gallery of American Art in Andover, Massachusetts.

It is also important to remember that major collections of great variety are housed in virtually every corner of the country. Thus Buffalo and Minneapolis are home to the Albright-Knox Art Gallery and Walker Art Center respectively, and both of these are pivotal museums for seeing contemporary art. The history of photography cannot be fully studied without the resources of Rochester's International Museum of Photography as the George Eastman House. Nor does any place in this country present antiquities in so splendid and appropriate a setting as the J. Paul Getty Museum in Malibu. From seeing the ancient past at Princeton University's Art Museum, to understanding Asian art at the Seattle Art Museum; from learning to feel the background and importance of Native American art at the Buffalo Bill Historical Center in Cody, Wyoming, to being immersed in Baroque art at the Ringling Museum in Sarasota—it is almost the entire country that beckons for visits to major art museums.

Goethe suggested that "the contemplation of works of art" enables us "to keep a high and unattainable ideal alive in the mind, . . . to fix as best we can a hierarchy of standards by our judgment of what the artist has accomplished, to seek earnestly what is perfect, to point out the fountainhead as well to the amateur as to the professional, to elevate his standpoint, [and] to make history and theory, criticism and practice aim for the same goal . . ."[4] This guide is, of course, only a means of suggesting opportunities for such an experience. But if that potential is exploited, then this volume serves its purpose.

TOM L. FREUDENHEIM
DIRECTOR
WORCESTER ART MUSEUM, 1983

NOTES

1. Murray, David, *Museums, Their History and Use* (Glasgow, 1904), Volume I, p. 1.
2. Keppel, Frederick P., and Duffus, R. L., *The Arts in American Life* (New York, 1933), p. 63.
3. Barzun, Jacques, *The Use and Abuse of Art* (Princeton, 1974), pp. 10-11.
4. Gage, John, editor, *Goethe on Art* (Berkeley, 1980), p. 43.

CHAPTER ONE

AMERICAN ART

by
GILBERT VINCENT

ADDISON GALLERY OF AMERICAN ART

PHILLIPS ACADEMY, ANDOVER, MA 01810. Tel: (617) 475-7515
Hours: Tues–Sat 10 am–5 pm, Sun 2:30–5 pm, closed Mon, holidays and August.
Admission: Free.
Publications: Christopher Cook has written seven mini-catalogues which cover much of the collection. They describe the 50th Anniversary exhibitions of 1981, $4. each.
Reproductions: Postcards of selected art works from the collection.
Research: Library open to staff.

The Addison Gallery of American Art is unique among American art museums in that it is an integral part of a secondary school, Phillips Academy. Located on the main lawn of the campus, the Addison is housed in a handsome Georgian Revival structure that opened in 1931. The collection, for many years under the astute leadership of Bartlett Hayes, Jr., includes important paintings, sculpture and graphics that span the whole development of American art from the colonial period to the present.

The early portraits include choice examples by John Smibert, John Singleton Copley, Gilbert Stuart and Samuel F. B. Morse, a graduate of the class of 1805. The Hudson River School is well represented, and the small oil sketches for Thomas Cole's *Voyage of Life* series at Utica and the National Gallery are usually on view.

Some of the finest art dates from the late nineteenth century. *The White Monk* is a pivotal masterpiece in George Inness' oeuvre, between his Hudson River School landscapes and the altered vision of his later painterly images. Painted in his meticulous American style in Italy in the 1870s, the scene is a view from the Villa Barberini at Albano.

Among Andover's works by Winslow Homer, *Eight Bells* is probably the most famous, but equally noteworthy are *Kissing the Moon* and *New England Country School.* The artist's *West Wind* is a masterful study of browns and the lonely watch of a woman looking at high surf. Thomas Eakins's *Salutat* is one of his studies of boxers and *Professor Henry A. Rowland* boasts not only Eakins's distinctive psychic intensity but also elaborate scientific notations on the frame.

Works by The Eight include Maurice Prendergast's *Float at Low Tide—Revere Beach,* one of his sparkling, mosaiclike watercolors, and John Sloan's *Sunday Morning—Women Washing Their Hair,* one of his powerfully authentic views of common life in the city. *Manhattan Bridge Loop* is one of Edward Hopper's constructed cityscapes, empty but for a single figure at the far left. Also related to the city but elegant in a delightful way and referring to American folk art in its wooden construction is *Seated Woman.*

THE BROOKLYN MUSEUM

EASTERN PARKWAY, BROOKLYN, NY 11238. Tel: (212) 638-5000
Hours: Wed–Sat 10 am–5 pm, Sun 12–5 pm, holidays 1–5 pm, closed Mon–Tues.
Admission: Suggested contribution $2 adult, $1 student; free to children under 12 and senior citizens.
Publications:
  John I. H. Baur, Sarah Faunce, Linda S. Ferber, *Masterpieces of American Painting from the Brooklyn Museum.* 1976, $6.
  The Brooklyn Museum: American Paintings. 1979, $9.95.
Reproductions: Numerous posters, prints, postcards and slides from the collection and special exhibitions.
Research: Art reference library is open to those with specific need by appointment only.

The Brooklyn Museum, housed in an impressive classical structure designed by the important firm of McKim, Mead and White, is a venerable institution with an important American collection. The American period rooms, dating from 1715 to the present, are probably the most complete representations of all the important style periods gathered in any single institution.

Among the more unusual eighteenth-and early-nineteenth-century portraits by John Singleton Copley, Ralph Earl, Charles Willson Peale and Gilbert Stuart are *John Haskins* and *Mrs. John Haskins* by Joseph Badger and *Deborah Hall* by William Williams. Dressed in a salmon-pink dress and standing in a formal garden with a pet squirrel, the young woman projects an unusually elegant air for the daughter of Benjamin Franklin's first printing partner, especially when one thinks of Poor Richard's advice about frugality. There are exceptional portraits from the nineteenth century by Daniel Huntington, Charles Ingham and Henry Inman.

The collection has works by all members of the Hudson River School. One of the most dramatic examples is Albert Bierstadt's *A Storm in the Rocky Mountains—Mt. Rosalie.* Thomas Cole's *A View of the Two Lakes and Mountain House, Catskill Mountains* shows the famous resort hotel and the locale of so many Hudson River School landscapes. Jasper Cropsey's panoramic *Bareford Mountain, West Milford, New Jersey* is an unusual and successful contrast of yellow and green in the artist's oeuvre. The landscapes by George Inness represent his entire career from the careful delineation and distant perspective of *On the Delaware River* to his late, painterly visions in *Montclair Landscape.*

Among the genre paintings are John Quidor's humorous *The Money Diggers,* a burlesque of an incident in Washington Irving's *Tales of a*

George Bellows.
Pennsylvania Station Excavation,
Oil on canvas, 1909

Traveller, George Caleb Bingham's image of a popular western competition, *Shooting for Beef,* and William Sidney Mount's reminiscence of a hot, summer day on the farm, *Boys Caught Napping.* Eastman Johnson's *A Ride for Liberty—The Fugitive Slaves* shows a black family bareback on a galloping horse, the tense faces actively capturing their dangerous situation. His *Not at Home* is another world, one with established conventions yet a sense of humor and a comfortable established culture. Light floods across the furniture and gilded frames of a Victorian parlor as an anonymous woman rapidly climbs the stairs in the relative dark of a hallway. William Merritt Chase's *In the Studio* is a similar if more exotic interior, the artist's famous studio on 10th Street, depicted with the painterly brush and light palette of American Impressionism. There are also notable works by other American Impressionists, particularly Childe Hassam, Willard Metcalf, Theodore Robinson and John Twachtman.

Winter Landscape: Washington Bridge is one of the most outstanding of seven paintings by Ernest Lawson at Brooklyn. Other works by The Eight include four portraits by Robert Henri, *Haymarket* by John Sloan and William Glackens's *Nude with Apple,* as well as several of his well-known street scenes. Painted in the same tradition of city scenes is George Bellows's

Pennsylvania Station Excavation, a powerful study of brown cubic forms rising above a snow-covered pit containing smoking pile drivers.

THE CORCORAN GALLERY OF ART
17TH STREET AND NEW YORK AVENUE, NW,
WASHINGTON, DC 20006. Tel: (202) 638-3211

Hours: Tues–Sun 10 am–4:30 pm, closed Mon.

Admission: Free.

Publications:

Edward J. Nygren, Peter C. Marzio, *Of Time and Place: American Figurative Art from the Corcoran Gallery of Art.* 1981, $15.

Dorothy W. Phillips, *A Catalogue of the Collection of American Paintings in the Corcoran Gallery of Art Vol. I.* 1966, $7.50.

———*A Catalogue of the Collection of American Paintings in the Corcoran Gallery of Art Vol. II.* 1973, $10.

Reproductions: An extensive selection of posters, prints, postcards and slides drawn from the permanent collection and special exhibitions. Catalogue available.

Research: Library, prints and drawings room, and curatorial reference material available to scholars. Appointments necessary.

The Corcoran Gallery of Art is a museum that not only includes a school but actively supports avant-garde art, photography and the work of Washington-area artists. A private institution, it is something of a rarity in this federal city. Founded in 1869 by local philanthropist William Wilson Corcoran, the museum has a superb collection of American art from Corcoran's original holdings and a continuing acquisitions program. It is particularly noted for its nineteenth-century landscape and genre paintings as well as portraits by John Smibert, the Peale family, Eastman Johnson, Thomas Eakins and John Singer Sargent. Total works amount to about 800 paintings, 250 sculptures and over 3,000 works on paper that are as comprehensive as the more ballyhooed collections at the Metropolitan and Boston.

Outstanding among the early portraits by Robert Feke, Christian Gullager, John Wollaston and the Peales is William Jennys's *Woman with a Fan,* an anonymous face that emphasizes our contemporary image of the reserve and determination of early New Englanders without becoming a caricature.

One of the most important history paintings is Samuel F. B. Morse's *The Old House of Representatives.* Designed by Benjamin Latrobe and now called Statuary Hall, the room was considered to be one of the most beautiful and correct neoclassical interiors in the world. Morse was careful in reproducing the difficult, curving perspective and painted miniature portraits of most of the members.

The works of the Hudson River School are well represented. Thomas Cole's *The Departure* and *The Return* are important allegorical landscapes, but most impressive is Frederic E. Church's *Niagara Falls.* Over seven feet long, it is painted with such fidelity and detail that on first viewing, the eminent British critic and writer, John Ruskin, thought the painted rainbow was a reflection from a window. One almost feels oneself flowing over the edge with the swirling water in the foreground until one recognizes that the nearby branch is actually an entire tree trunk, whereupon the scale is instantly magnified tenfold. Albert Bierstadt's striking *The Last of the Buffalo*, a sculptural composition of an Indian rider spearing a buffalo on the open plains, was intended to symbolize the end of the Plains Indian culture, but also came to symbolize the end of the popularity of the Hudson River School when it was refused for the American exhibition at the 1890 Paris Exposition.

Thomas Eakins's *The Pathetic Song* is considered one of his major full-length portraits. George Bellows's *Forty-two Kids*, a joyous representation of boys swimming from a New York City dock, is perhaps the most popular of all the works related to the Ashcan School. Marsden Hartley's *Berlin Abstraction* is an important example of the early avant-garde movement among American artists before World War I. The *Ground Swell* by Edward Hopper, with his characteristic simplification of form, is an image of a catboat on Cape Cod Bay that forms an interesting modern counterpart to the National Gallery's *Breezing Up*, Winslow Homer's study of virtually the same subject.

THE DETROIT INSTITUTE OF ARTS
5200 WOODWARD AVENUE, DETROIT, MI 48202. Tel: (313) 833-7900
Hours: Tues–Sun 9:30 am–5:30 pm, closed Mon, Christmas, New Year's.
Admission: Suggested contribution; fee for some special exhibitions.
Publications:
　　Frederick J. Cummings, *Selected Works from The Detroit Institute of Arts*. 1982, $25.
Reproductions: Good selection of posters and postcards, mainly of the collection.
Research: Research library open to public Mon–Fri 9 am–5 pm. The 75,000 volumes emphasize European art history.

The Detroit Institute of Arts is a massive building housing a collection intended to represent all the arts of civilization. Among the many areas, the American section is probably the strongest. It covers the entire span from the seventeenth century to the present and includes many examples of superlative quality.

Among the outstanding works is a version of John Singleton Copley's *Watson and the Shark* and Washington Allston's *The Flight of Florimel*, an early Romantic landscape derived from Spenser's *Faerie Queene. Paddington Passage* is an unusual, picturesque landscape by Benjamin West that represents the West family and friends taking an excursion on the roof of a passenger barge as it glides through a park filled with strollers and horseback riders. West's bucolic countryside is strikingly different from Frederic E. Church's dramatic landscape *Cotopaxi*. Inspired by Alexander von Humboldt's description of "the most beautiful and the most terrible of the American volcanoes," Church traveled to South America to witness the sight for himself. Intended as a pendant to *The Heart of the Andes* at the Metropolitan, the painting represents the awesome might of nature and depicts the volcano from afar, a dark, threatening blast of smoke coming from its top while the sun spreads an orange-red light across the sky.

The movements of American genre painting are well represented by such works as John Quidor's *The Embarkation from Communipaw,* Winslow Homer's *The Four Leaf Clover,* Thomas Eakins's *The Courtship* and William Sidney Mount's *Banjo Player. Trapper's Return* by George Caleb Bingham is the second version of the painting *Fur Traders,* displayed at the Metropolitan Museum.

Nocturne in Black and Gold: The Falling Rocket may be considered James A. M. Whistler's most famous painting. It was John Ruskin's 1877 review of this work, in which he accused the artist of "flinging a pot of paint in the public's face," that caused Whistler to sue for libel. The details of the trial, transposed to his own advantage, are recounted in Whistler's *The Gentle Art of Making Enemies.*

Among works by The Eight, *Promenade* by Maurice Prendergast, part of a four-part mural series owned by John Quinn, and *Wake of the Ferry* by John Sloan stand out. There are also important works by the Stieglitz circle. Charles Sheeler's *Home Sweet Home* is a carefully composed, realistic study of hooked rugs and eighteenth-century American country furniture in the artist's house. Charles Demuth's *Building Abstraction-Lancaster* is a double image of a water tower and factory united by the diagonal force lines of the Futurists but frozen into an abstraction of great clarity and precision.

THE FINE ARTS MUSEUMS OF SAN FRANCISCO

LINCOLN PARK, SAN FRANCISCO, CA 94121. Tel: (415) 558-2881
GOLDEN GATE PARK, SAN FRANCISCO, CA 94121. Tel: (415) 558-2887
Hours: Wed–Sun 10 am–5 pm, closed Mon–Tues, some holidays.
Admission: $1 adults, $.50 senior citizens and children 5–18, free to children under 5; free first Wednesday each month.
Publications:
   F. Lanier Graham, *Three Centuries of American Painting.* 1971, $6.98.
   E.T. Richardson, *American Art: An Exhibition from the Collection of Mr. & Mrs. J. D. Rockefeller III.* 1976, $4.95.
Reproductions: Posters, prints, postcards of the collection.
Research: Library for the staff.

The largest collection of historic American art west of Chicago is located in the M. H. de Young Memorial Museum. In 1977, the American Galleries were opened with the combined works of the de Young and the California Palace of the Legion of Honor. More than doubled in size in 1978 by a gift of 175 paintings from John D. Rockefeller, III, the museum has paintings, sculptures and graphics representative of American art from 1720 to 1950.

Among several portraits by John Singleton Copley, *Mrs. Daniel Sargent* is the most memorable. Another remarkable painting is John Vanderlyn's *Marius on the Ruins of Carthage.* A powerful, brooding image, the work was Vanderlyn's first classical subject and was so admired by Napoleon that he awarded it a gold medal in the Paris Salon of 1808.

Frederic E. Church's *Rainy Season in the Tropics* depicts a rainbow over the rough chasm of a waterfall. In the foreground is a road and a section of tropical vegetation painted with Church's distinctive botanical accuracy. His *Sacramento Valley in Spring* is a fitting subject for San Francisco and shows a vista of the placid, flat valley bottom with luminous, storied clouds.

Raphaelle Peale's *Blackberries,* a fruit-laden branch resting in a small, porcelain dish, is a wonderful contrast in its neoclassical simplicity to William Michael Harnett's *After the Hunt* and John F. Peto's *Still Life with Pitcher, Candle and Books.* A remarkable image in the tradition of trompe l'oeil painting is Alexander Pope's *Trumpeter Swan,* the single form of the white bird hanging head down on a dark-green door.

William Hahn.
Sacramento Railroad Station,
(detail) Oil on canvas, c. 1874

The Pension Agent by Eastman Johnson shows his love of the rich browns of seventeenth-century Dutch painting. The subject accentuates not only the anecdotal sentimentality of Victorian genre painting but also the poignancy of a generation that witnessed the Civil War. In contrast is Grant Wood's stylized section of a farmhouse entitled *Dinner for Threshers,* with its clear precise details.

Marjorie Henri is a wonderful portrait of Robert Henri's wife, a long, elegant figure in black with a defiant look and a brilliant crown of red hair. The pose and composition are similar to society paintings by John Singer Sargent and William Merritt Chase, but the broad strokes of paint and dark tonalities are Henri's own.

The de Young also has a notable collection of American sculpture from William Rush's small, wooden *Winter,* a cherub sitting on blocks of ice, to Beniamino Bufano's *Torso.*

THOMAS GILCREASE INSTITUTE OF AMERICAN HISTORY AND ART

1400 N 25 WEST AVENUE, TULSA, OK 74127. Tel: (918) 582-3122

Hours: Mon–Sat 9 am–5 pm, Sun and holidays 1–5 pm, closed Christmas.
Admission: Free.
Publications:
    Patricia Broder, *Great Paintings of the Old American West.* 1979, $12.98.
    Fred Myers, *Art Treasures of Gilcrease Museum.* 1982, $20.
    Paul Rossi, David Hunt, *Art of the Old West.* 1971, $22.95.
Reproductions: Selection of posters and postcards pertaining to the collection.
Research: Library open by appointment. It includes genealogical, hispanic and Native American documents, as well as much on the Old West.

The Thomas Gilcrease Institute of American History and Art was founded in 1942 to preserve the story of man in the Western Hemisphere. The collection includes art, artifacts, rare books and documents that range from Central American jades and the papers of Cortez to major holdings of the works of Thomas Moran, Frederic Remington and Charles Russell. Thomas Gilcrease, who was part Indian, discovered oil on the family ranch and began buying art in 1912. His private gallery and library were purchased by the city of Tulsa in the early 1950s and opened to the public in 1955.

The art collection is important in quality and quantity. There are fifty-eight works by Remington, including examples of most of his sculpture, eighty-eight works by Russell, 484 by George Catlin, 1,065 works by Thomas Moran and the entire studio of William Robinson Leigh. Notable among Remington's paintings are *The Coming and Going of the Pony Express*, a representation of the running change of horses by express riders in the unique service that lasted less than two years but entered American folklore on a permanent basis, and *Stampeded by Lightning*, a dramatic image of horse, rider and longhorn cattle in the artist's green-black night tonalities. Paintings by Russell include *Jerked Down*, an accurate depiction of roping cattle, *Running Buffalo*, an historic re-creation of the famous hunt involving Buffalo Bill, General Sherman and Grand Duke Alexis of Russia, and *Bronc for Breakfast*, an amusing memory of an unbroken horse plunging through the cook's campfire. Works by Moran comprise some of his original water-colors made on the Hayden Expedition in 1871 and used by Hayden in his successful application before Congress to create the Yellowstone National Park, the first national park in the world. Particularly impressive finished oil paintings are *Shoshone Falls on the Snake River* and his magnificent *Pueblo of Acoma, New Mexico*. Among the works of Catlin are an early watercolor of Red Jacket and a superb portrait of a chieftain in complete leather garb and headdress, *Mah-to-toh-pa* and *Four Bears*.

The Gilcrease also owns 136 works by Alfred Jacob Miller, the official artist on the 1837 western tour of the eccentric Scottish nobleman, William Drummond Stewart. Miller not only recorded the short-lived tradition of fur traders meeting in the Wind River mountains but painted in a unique Romantic imagery combining the dynamism of the French painter Eugène Delacroix and the sparkling verve of the Rococo Revival style of the 1830s. Outstanding among his oil paintings are *Fort Laramie*, *The Buffalo Hunt* and *Indians on Green River*. Another important collection is the 233 works by the Taos artist Joseph Henry Sharp, as well as major paintings by Oscar Berninghaus, Bert Phillips and Ernest Blumenschein, other Taos residents.

THE METROPOLITAN MUSEUM OF ART
FIFTH AVENUE AT 82ND STREET,NEW YORK, NY 10028.
Tel: (212) 535-7710

Hours: Tues 10 am–8:45 pm, Wed-Sat 10 am–4:45 pm, Sun and holidays 11 am–4:45 pm, closed Mon, Thanksgiving, Christmas, New Year's.

Admission: Suggested contribution $4 adults, $2 children and senior citizens, free to children under 12.

Publications:
   American Paintings: Guide to the Collection. 1962, $.95.
   Marshall B. Davidson, *The American Wing: A Guide*. 1980, $9.95.
   John K. Howat et al., *19th-Century America: Paintings and Sculpture*. 1970, $50.

Reproductions: Extensive selection of prints, posters, postcards and reproductions of sculpture and other works from the collection.

Research: Library open to staff of the museum and other qualified researchers and graduate students with appropriate identification. Most comprehensive art and archaeology collection in Western Hemisphere, including over 210,000 books and 1200 periodicals subscriptions. It covers all areas in which the museum has holdings.

The Metropolitan Museum has one of the best and most representative collections of American art. About 300 works are on permanent exhibition in the American Wing. Temporary exhibitions are also mounted from time to time while new installations will allow for open storage access. First opened in 1924 as an innovative display of period rooms, recently the American Wing has been greatly enlarged to the designs of Kevin Dinkeloo and John Roche and incorporates major examples of American painting, sculpture and decorative arts in one location.

The court is flooded with light from the slanting glass roof and west wall opening onto Central Park and forms a pleasant oasis of green as well as a convenient resting place for visitors. Despite lopsided exterior walls and a confusing imbalance of proportion and axes, the court contains important architectural fragments and choice examples of American sculpture. The neoclassical, ashlar facade of the United States Branch Bank, built on Wall Street between 1822 and 1824, fills the center of the north wall. Across the court, beside the main entrance, is a polychrome Art Nouveau loggia designed by Louis Tiffany for his house in Oyster Bay, Long Island, about 1905. The stepped arches, iridescent blue glass tiles and ceramic capitals composed of poppies on long stalks strike a rich, colorful and exotic note in contrast to the austere, monochrome bank facade. What was originally the loggia door is now a superb, stained-glass window in the inimitable Tiffany style that depicts a view of Oyster Bay although it came from a New York townhouse. Other fragments include a staircase from Louis Sullivan's Chicago Stock Exchange Building, a stained-glass triptych window from Frank Lloyd Wright's Avery Coonley playhouse built in Riverside, Illinois, in 1912, and a Beaux Arts mantlepiece from the palatial Cornelius Vanderbilt house on Fifth Avenue and Fifty-Seventh Street that incorporates mosaics by John LaFarge and two caryatids by Augustus St. Gaudens.

The large, free-standing sculpture placed about the courtyard is intended to represent a brief history of sculpture in America. The earliest works are Carrara marble nudes in the neoclassical style by Hiram Powers *(California)* and Erastus Dow Palmer *(The White Captive)*. America's end-of-the-century admiration for the culture of the Italian Renaissance is reflected in George Grey Barnard's powerful and Michelangelesque *Struggle of the Two Natures in Man*. In contrast, Paul Manship's elegant *Dancer and Gazelles* follows the stylized classicism popular in the early twentieth century.

The American paintings are on the second floor of the new wing in the Joan Whitney Payson Galleries. Once the exact rooms are located, it is difficult to orient oneself without a floor guide. The collection is arranged more or less chronologically, but one is most likely to start halfway through and miss some areas. It is best to begin with the Colonial painting in Room 217 and follow the numerical progression of rooms.

George Caleb Bingham.
Fur Traders Descending the Missouri,
Oil on canvas, c. 1845

The eighteenth century room contains John Smibert's companion pieces, *Francis Brinley* and *Mrs. Francis Brinley and Her Son Francis,* two of the finest examples of the English Baroque style in colonial portraiture. While Brinley's pose is derived probably from a mezzotint of Sir Isaac Newton—a common sort of borrowing in American portraits—the view of Boston in the background, said to be the view from Brinley's country house in Dorchester, is one of the earliest American landscapes. Smibert came to Newport, Rhode Island, with George Berkeley as one of the faculty members for a projected college in Bermuda. The year he painted the Brinleys, Smibert became the most important portrait painter in New England.

John Singleton Copley, America's self-taught artistic genius, painted *Mrs. John Winthrop* at the height of his powers a year before he left for England, a new career and a new style. As in the best of his colonial portraits, Copley not only captures the forthright character of his sitter but his remarkable technical ability presents a textural richness of contrasts.

The late-eighteenth- and early-nineteenth-century gallery displays works by Benjamin West and some of his many students. The son of a Quaker innkeeper, West left Pennsylvania for training in Europe, settled in London in 1762, became history painter to King George III within ten years and president of the Royal Academy in the 1790s. One of the leading figures in

European artistic circles, West opened his house and studio with never failing generosity to a succession of American students. His allegorical *Omnia Vincit Amor* represents the idealistic Great Style of the European academies that eighteenth-century artists and theoreticians believed to be the most difficult, creative and admirable type of painting.

The effect of West's example and training can be seen in John Trumbull's *Sortie Made by the Garrison of Gibraltar.* Other students such as Gilbert Stuart affirmed the popular taste for portraits. Stuart adopted the loosely brushed style of the contemporary London portraitists and returned to the United States in 1793 to transform American portraiture. His portrayals of the first five presidents, particularly George Washington, have become our popular visual images of the men.

The gallery representing painting from 1812 to 1840 displays the growing diversity of subject matter in American art. Raphaelle Peale's exquisite *Still Life with Cake* captures some of the precision and illusionism of Dutch still life painting, but the distinctive spareness of the image suggests a combination of Neoclassical bas-reliefs and the simplified nature of American life. The same plain but balanced sense of classicism is the dominant characteristic of George Caleb Bingham's *Fur Traders Descending the Missouri,* a study of a French fur trapper and his half-Indian son. Working in Missouri, Bingham captured the character and dignity of everyday American life on the edge of the frontier in many of his genre paintings, but never more powerfully than in this one.

The interest in commonplace America is evident in the work of William Sidney Mount. A native of Long Island, Mount painted his neighbors in both genre scenes and portraits that revealed certain essential human traits with an intimacy and humor that transcends his narrow geographic bounds. Mount's *Cider Making* records a familiar country pastime but also celebrates the victory of William Henry Harrison in the 1840 election.

Thomas Cole's *View from Mount Holyoke, Massachusetts, after a Thunderstorm,* now generally called *The Oxbow,* is one of the outstanding landscapes in the Early Hudson River School gallery. A self-taught artist who had a seminal position in the popularization of landscape painting in America, Cole depicts the oxbow on the Connecticut River near Northampton, contrasting the wilderness on Mt. Holyoke with the well-tended valley farmlands below and the dark thunderclouds with the clear sparkling air left with the storm's passing. The same highly composed technique, but with a narrower perspective, can be seen in Asher B. Durand's *The Beeches,* one of a series of what have been termed "tree portraits" that he painted in 1840s and 1850s.

In the adjoining room are examples of the Late Hudson River School. The difference in scale from the previous room is immediately striking. There are enormous canvases and small ones. The small, precise views with an atmospheric quality that has given rise to the term Luminism are the works of such men as Fitz Hugh Lane, Martin J. Heade and John F. Kensett. Heade's *The Coming Storm* with its still atmosphere and black sky with blacker water reflects the exactness and intensity of the Luminists' study of natural light. In contrast, Albert Bierstadt's *The Rocky Mountains, Lander's Peak* and Frederic E. Church's *The Heart of the Andes* capture the operatic aggrandizement of another group of artists who counterbalanced quiet intensity with the scale, complexity and color of landscapes on a grand scale.

The entrance to the following gallery frames Winslow Homer's *Searchlight on Harbor Entrance—Santiago de Cuba,* and his work fills the entire room. Trained as a lithographer and illustrator, Homer began painting in oil during the Civil War. His first major work, *Prisoners from the Front,* while its subject matter reveals his background as an illustrator, is a wonderful series of character studies in the poses, clothes and facial expressions. *Snap the Whip,* painted while the nation was undergoing a rediscovery of its history during the Centennial, is a nostalgic image of rural childhood. Homer slowly but consistently altered his painting technique and subject matter. Fascinated with the struggle of man against nature, as in *The Gulf Stream,* Homer ended his days on Prout's Neck, a peninsula in Maine, where he painted the elemental forces of nature without reference to man.

The large L-shaped room lying between the old American Wing and the new galleries contains a selection of paintings from 1780 to 1880 that complements or parallels the paintings in the smaller galleries. The exhibition is intended to change periodically except for Emanuel Leutze's *Washington Crossing the Delaware.* Conceived in the idealizing tradition of history painting, the work seemingly records one moment at the outset of the Battle of Trenton, yet Leutze created an imaginary scene to symbolize Washington's determination, courage and leadership at undertaking the dangerous crossing and completely surprising the British and Hessians.

The long balcony overlooking the mezzanine contains works by Homer's contemporaries. Equal in distinction is the Philadelphia painter Thomas Eakins. A masterpiece of his early career, *Max Schmitt in a Single Scull,* is one of the finest genre scenes in nineteenth-century art with its careful perspective, interplay of horizontal and vertical lines, straightforward portrayal of the Schuylkill River and intense depiction of light.

The center of the balcony contains the Richard J. Schwartz display of sculpture and paintings of the American West, particularly the well-known *Bronco Buster* and *Comin' Through the Rye* by Frederic Remington. At the north end are paintings in the trompe l'oeil tradition by William Michael Harnett and John F. Peto.

Down the staircase and along the mezzanine are a diverse but notable collection of late-nineteenth- and early-twentieth-century paintings. A variety of works by the expatriate John Singer Sargent offer examples of his multifaceted and amazing talents. Among his portraits is the famous *Madame X,* which caused a scandal in Paris when first exhibited, and brought about Sargent's removal to London. The artist gave the painting to the Metropolitan near the end of his life, noting that he considered it the best work he had ever done. Less notorious but equally interesting as a character study is *Mr. and Mrs. I. N. Phelps Stokes.* Mary Cassatt's *Lady at the Tea Table,* much admired by the French artist Edgar Degas, is a beautifully painted study of upper-class formality. Similar works in the

Impressionist style are Julian Alden Weir's *The Red Bridge* and Childe Hassam's *Avenue of the Allies, Great Britain, 1918.* The American paintings come to a close with works by Edward Hopper, Reginald Marsh, Milton Avery and Andrew Wyeth.

MUSEUM OF FINE ARTS

465 HUNTINGTON AVENUE, BOSTON, MA 02115. Tel: (617) 267-9300
Hours: Tues, Thurs–Sun 10 am–5 pm, Wed 10 am–10 pm, closed Mon, Christmas eve and day, New Year's, July 4th. West Wing only: Thurs–Fri 5–10 pm.
Admission: $3.50 adults, $2.50 adults Thurs–Fri 5–10 pm, $2.50 senior citizens, free to children under 17 and members; free Sat 10 am–12 pm.
Publications:
> Jonathan Fairbanks,*Copley, Stuart, West in America and England.* 1976. $5.95.
> William H. Gerdts and Theodore E. Stebbins, Jr., *"A Man of Genius" The Art of Washington Allston, 1779–1843.* 1979, $19.95.
> Martha J. Hoppin, *William Morris Hunt: A Memorial Exhibition.* 1979, $7.95.
> Perry T. Rathbone, *American Paintings in the Museum of Fine Arts, Boston.* 1968, $33.
> Carol Troyen, *The Boston Tradition: American Paintings from the Museum of Fine Arts, Boston.* 1980, $19.95.

Reproductions: Large selection of posters, postcards, prints, slides from the collection and special exhibitions.
Research: Main library open to public; reference libraries of specific departments available to students and scholars by appointment.

The American collection at the Museum of Fine Arts in Boston has a size and scope that rivals the American Wing at the Metropolitan. The collection has a number of acknowledged masterpieces but is strongest in the art of the Colonial and early Federal periods: for example, there are 60 Copleys, 15 Allstons and 9 Smiberts.

A selection of the best colonial portraiture is interspersed with examples of American furniture. John Singleton Copley's portrait of Paul Revere is located often at the end of a corridor glistening with examples of early American silver including examples from Revere's own hands. Painted about five years before Revere's famous ride, the portrait avoids any hint of grandeur and shows a stolid, broad figure dressed in the work clothes of the day holding a rococo teapot much like one in a nearby case. Revere's steady gaze suggests the look of creative thought as well as the look of someone just disturbed at work. The life-like imagery—particularly the reflection of Revere's fingers on the the teapot—is a wonder of technical ability.

Some of Copley's other portraits are hung in the Chippendale-style furniture galleries or in the base of the rotunda. Within the museum's collection one can follow the full development of Copley's style from his early, primitive portraits such as *Mrs. Joseph Mann,* completed when he was fifteen years old, to the emergence of his mature style about 1758 in *Mary and Elizabeth Royall* to his distinctive and realist portraits on the eve of his departure for England, such as *Mr. and Mrs. Isaac Winslow.* Copley's portraits have an immediate appeal in their austere beauty; there is a straight-forwardness and simplicity about them that seems to embody the simple cultural values of Boston's eighteenth-century mercantile society. By

John Singleton Copley.
Mr. and Mrs. Issac Winslow,
Oil on canvas, 1774

happenstance of the Revolution, some of Copley's sitters acquired more than local prominence. One unfamiliar with Boston history can look at the faces of Samuel Adams, General Joseph Warren, John Hancock or Mercy Otis Warren to discover traces of the character that brought them renown.

The depth of Copley's self-training can be seen in comparing his work to nearby examples by Joseph Blackburn, who had a brief but strong impact on the young Copley. An English emigrant who was successful in Boston, Portsmouth and Newport in the 1750s, Blackburn painted such delicate rococo portraits as *Isaac Winslow and His Family,* the same man later painted by Copley. Blackburn returned to England in 1764. Copley's realistic images, careful modeling and exact renditions of different textures stand in contrast to Blackburn's flatter and somewhat artificial images.

A second interesting comparison can be made with Copley's later works after he left Boston and settled in London. His portrait of Winslow Warren, Mercy Otis Warren's son, has the idealized grandeur, softer shading and looser brushwork of the current London style. Copley was also able to delve into history painting. His *Watson and the Shark,* painted for a Lord Mayor of London, is part portrait, part contemporary event raised to a grand scale within the tenets of academic artistic theory and far beyond the means and artistic intentions of his Boston patrons.

Another resident artist represented by over thirty portraits is Gilbert Stuart. Born in Rhode Island, trained in London and working there, in Dublin, in New York and in Philadelphia before settling in Boston in 1805, Stuart is best known for his portraits of American presidents, particularly George Washington. The original of the "Athenaeum Head," an unfinished life study that served Stuart, his daughter Jane and many others as the source for innumerable copies is now shared between the National Portrait Gallery and Boston, which exchange it every two years. The museum retains one of Stuart's own replicas of the "Athenaeum Head" as well as a full-length portrait *Washington at Dorchester Heights,* based on the artist's "Lansdowne" portrait now at the Pennsylvania Academy of the Fine Arts. Among other Federal period worthies recorded by Stuart is a portrait of Paul Revere, completed almost forty-five years after the Copley and an interesting contrast in technique as well as age. Among the more remarkable early-nineteenth-century portraits is John Neagle's *Pat Lyon at the Forge.* Lyon, an immigrant from London, was falsely imprisoned for theft by the officers of a Philadelphia bank. Working his way to eventual prominence and wealth from his early disgrace and poverty, Lyon commissioned his portrait a few years before his death but preferred to commemorate his origins as a blacksmith rather than the successful engineer he had become. Through the window is an anecdotal reminder of the tower of the Walnut Street Prison. Such a reversal of position is not often encountered in grand portraiture.

The collection of landscape painting spans the leading figures of the nineteenth century. The museum's first purchase was Washington Allston's *Elijah in the Desert,* a large, brownish-gray study of a desolate rocky landscape with the small, blue-coated figure of Elijah in the foreground receiving "bread and flesh" from the ravens. Provocative and mysterious is Allston's small *Moonlit Landscape.* Unusually fine examples of the Hudson River School includes Thomas Doughty's *New Hampshire Lake,* Thomas Cole's *Sunset in the Catskills,* Worthington Whittredge's *Old Home by the Sea,* Asher B. Durand's *Lake George, New York* and John F. Kensett's *Cliffs at Newport, R.I., Low Tide.* The sizable collection from Maxim Karolik of paintings by Martin J. Heade includes all aspects of his career from an early portrait to his late flower studies. Heade's intense study of light in its outlining of detail and of different atmospheric conditions can be seen by contrasting the limpid clarity of his *Lake George,* the misty translucence of *Newburyport Marshes* and the glowering dark overcoming the sunlit shore in *Approaching Storm: Beach Near Newport.* Albert Bierstadt was the first artist to represent the dramatic mountains and long vistas of the American West. His *Thunderstorm in the Rocky Mountains,* first exhibited in New York during the Civil War, established the artist's immense popularity and the style of vast, detailed, panoramic landscapes that he painted until his death in 1902. Maxim Karolik added over two dozen works in addition to those already owned by the Museum, including *Storm in the Mountains,* a swirling vortex of clouds reminiscent of J. M. W. Turner, and a number of smaller works including the particularly beautiful *Wreck of the Ancon in Loring Bay, Alaska,* a luminous study in gray but for the vivid yellow wheel house and black stack of the stranded vessel.

The museum's collection is as impressive in nineteenth-century genre painting as in landscape. Henry Sargent, a Boston student of West's, eventually abandoned his painting career to become a merchant. He never lost his artistic interests, however, and in 1820 painted *The Dinner Party,* a record of a Wednesday Evening Club meeting in his dining room, and *The Tea Party,* an elegant gathering that may also represent his house. The paintings are relatively large in scale, and while the refinement of the participants leaves little anecdotal interest, the scenes are rare and fascinating representations of Federal manners and interiors.

The museum purchased works by Winslow Homer as early as the 1890s. *Long Branch, N.J.* portrays fashionable parasoled ladies on the windswept cliff leading down to bathing houses and beach at this popular mid-nineteenth-century resort. What strikes the viewer is the strong sense of colors seemingly intensified by and reflecting a brilliant summer sun and the rush of summer wind as it billows the ladies' dresses. From the subject of Long Branch Homer has turned to the essence of what drew and still draws so many people to the Atlantic coast—the bright and distinctive summer weather.

Increased academic training in the nineteenth century encouraged figure drawing, and as artists became more adept, the scale of the human form increased in genre painting. This partly explains the difference in Homer's work of the 1880s and 1890s, particularly his *Fog Warning,* a quiet but dramatic representation of the dangers of being lost in the fog, and *The Lookout—"All's Well."*

Among the many works of John Singer Sargent, Boston possesses one of the most distinctive portraits in American art, *The Daughters of Edward Darley Boit.* Painted in the Parisian apartment of Sargent's friend, the American painter Edward D. Boit, the large, square canvas captures the essential personality traits of the four children in a combination of pose, glance and position. The enormous blue and white Chinese vases, cherished family possessions that traveled the ocean with the Boits almost like pets, unsettle the expected scale but, in conjunction with the Chinese rug, give essential color to the otherwise black, brown and white color scheme. The composition is a masterpiece of abstract balance, one that enlarges the scope of the painting well beyond the bounds of four properly attired Victorian children.

Mary Cassatt, the expatriate Philadelphian, was a contemporary of Sargent but worked directly with the French Impressionists in Paris. *A Cup of Tea,* exhibited at the Impressionist Exhibition of 1880, is a direct representation of Cassatt's life. The setting is a dutifully proper parlor at the Cassatt's summer home in Marly-le-Roi, while the style is the flattened perspective and the loosely brushed and colorful technique of the then revolutionary Impressionists.

Childe Hassam is another Impressionist well represented in the museum collection. His dark-toned, realist work *Boston Common at Twilight* offers a teling comparison to *Grand Prix Day,* painted just a year later when he adopted the technique of the Impressionists. He was a native of Boston and friend and compatriot to a group of painters conservatively influenced by Impressionism known as the Boston Group. These artists, including Edmund C. Tarbell, Joseph DeCamp and Frank Benson, were centered around the museum's school, and the museum has a sizable collection of their work.

NATIONAL GALLERY OF ART

4th STREET AND CONSTITUTION AVENUE, NW,
WASHINGTON, DC 20565. Tel: (202) 737-4215
Hours: Winter: Mon–Sat 10 am–5 pm, Sun 12–9 pm.; Summer: 10 am–9 pm, Sun 12–9 pm. Closed Christmas and New Year's.
Admission: Free.
Publications:
  American Paintings: An Illustrated Catalogue. 1980, $8.75.
  John Walker, The National Gallery of Art. 1978, $60.
  John Wilmerdint, Important Information Inside: The Still-Life Paintings of John F. Peto. 1982, $14.95.
Reproductions: A selection of posters, postcards and slides from the collection and special exhibitions.
Research: Reference and circulating library open to graduate students, visiting scholars, and other researchers by special permission. Circulation desk open Mon–Fri 9 am–5 pm; stack open all week. Library includes American art from post-Columbian era to present.

The American collection, including twentieth-century realist work, is displayed in thirteen galleries in the original building, while an additional installation on the ground floor contains the Garbisch collection of American folk art. The museum has a total of about 1,000 American paintings, many of which are outstanding.

The American galleries are arranged chronologically beginning with Room 60. The first four rooms are largely devoted to early portraiture. Particularly powerful is Copley's *Epes Sargent,* where the impasto of the veins and wrinkles of the right hand and the worn marble plinth are so evocative of Sargent's old age. The beginning of his smoother finish and greater elegance inspired by moving to London is evident in the group portrait of himself, his wife, children and father-in-law, *The Copley Family.* Another famous group portrait is Edward Savage's *The Washington Family* showing the Washingtons, the two Custis children and the faithful servant Billy Lee. Other portraits by such artists as John Trumbull and Charles Willson Peale include forty-two works by Gilbert Stuart. *The Skater* is the masterpiece of his English years. The fluid brushwork and shimmering surface demonstrate the technique that Stuart used to transform American portraiture.

Among the landscape paintings, Frederic E. Church's *Morning in the Tropics* is a distinctive rendition of a steamy tropical river with the exacting detail of South American flora and fauna in the foreground. Recognizably American in the red and yellow colors is Jasper Cropsey's vista, *Autumn on the Hudson River.* Equally American in subject is George Inness' ambiguous

Winslow Homer.
Breezing Up,
Oil on canvas, 1876

representation of settlement, industry and the American wilderness. *The Lackawanna Valley* presents a view across a stump-covered field to a train carrying coal cars. The train heads into a rural setting of fields and trees; behind it is a factory, roundhouse and village set on the edge of a treeless valley. While a handsome landscape, there is a powerful suggestion of the destructive transformation the railroad is heralding for the wilderness. The collection of George Catlin's paintings at the gallery includes over twenty works entitled *The Voyages of Discovery of LaSalle.* The series was commissioned by Louis-Philippe of France for his gallery of history paintings at Versailles, and retrieved by Catlin after the revolution of 1848.

The Biglin Brothers Racing is one of the best of Thomas Eakins's early rowing paintings. His *Baby at Play* is a careful study of the preliminary human rational processes in his young niece. There are two major oils by Winslow Homer. *Breezing Up* is a joyous representation of young boys sailing a catboat on one of those memorable ocean days when the wind is blowing and the air reaches its clearest and brightest intensity. *Right and Left* is something of a visual joke on the viewer. The painting presents a powerful black, white and gray image of two large ducks arranged on a scale not unlike Audubon's work. The right duck has a strangely contorted shape that seems inexplicable until one notices a speck of orange on the horizon and realizes that a hunter is shooting the ducks and aiming directly at the viewer.

The American appreciation of objective reality may have reached one of its finest expressions in the work of William Michael Harnett, here represented by his exquisite still life *My Gems.* Painted in a softer style and with a sense of melancholy for discarded objects is John F. Peto's *The Old Violin*. The gallery owns nine works by James A. M. Whistler. A recent gift is *Wapping-on-Thames*, one of Whistler's early works in the French Realist style that uses his artist friend Alphonse Legros and his mistress Jo Hiffernan to frame the complex but artistic tangle of fishing boats, nets and masts on the edge of the Thames. *The Woman in White* is another early work, light in color with large areas of color painted without gradations from one to another. It was a revolutionary technique in the 1860s, but one that led the artist to his mature style of harmonious near abstractions. A painter strongly influenced by Whistler but never as innovative is Thomas Dewing, who created delicate, muted tonal studies of women.

The portrait of *Mrs. Adrian Iselin* demonstrates why John Singer Sargent was such a successful society portraitist, yet when one sees his genre paintings such as *Street in Venice* there comes a wish that he had devoted less time to his fashionable sitters. His watercolors are equally superb.

NATIONAL MUSEUM OF AMERICAN ART
SMITHSONIAN INSTITUTION, 8TH AND G STREETS, NW, WASHINGTON, DC 20560. Tel: (202) 357-2108
Hours: Sun–Sat 10 am–5:30 pm, closed Christmas.
Admission: Free.
Publications:
Andrew J. Cosentino, *The Paintings of Charles Bird King (1785–1862)*. 1977, $8.
George Gurney, *Cast and Recast: The Sculpture of Frederic Remington*. nd, $6.50.
Sheldon Reich, *Alfred H. Maurer (1868–1932)*. 1973, $4.75.
John Walker, *The National Gallery of Art*. 1978, $60.
Reproductions: Posters, postcards and slides of much of the collection and special exhibitions.
Research: Library open to graduate and postgraduate students and qualified researchers Mon–Fri 10 am–5 pm. Includes Inventory of American Painting Executed before 1914. There is a Scholar's Research Program promoting research in history of American art, open to doctoral and postdoctoral scholars. Archives of American Art accessible to public on microfilm.

The National Museum of American Art is part of the Smithsonian Institution. Located several blocks north of the main museum complex on the mall, it shares the massive Greek Revival edifice of the old Patent Office with the National Portrait Gallery.

The collection is unusual and provocative, in part because it developed haphazardly but also because of the erudition and scholarly interests of its late director Joshua Taylor, who allowed the museum to explore a number of byways of American art history. Bequests over the years have resulted in 445 paintings by George Catlin, 150 contemporary paintings collected by William T. Evans between 1890 and 1910, and the largest collection anywhere of Albert Pinkham Ryder's paintings.

Some of the notable works in the collection are Benjamin West's *Self-Portrait* at age eighty-one and Charles Bird King's handsome images of a group of Indian chiefs, *Young Omaha, War Eagle, Little Missouri and Pawnees*, one of only a few survivors from the collection destroyed in the

Smithsonian fire of 1865. Frederic E. Church's *Aurora Borealis* represents the large scale and theatrical panorama of mid-nineteenth-century American landscape painting. The small size of the ice-bound schooner beneath the enormous sky of flickering, luminous blue, red and white veils was intended to symbolize the puniness of man before the magnificence and power of nature. A fine example of late-nineteenth-century academic genre painting is Gari Melcher's evocation of religious piety among the Dutch peasantry in *The Sermon*.

Unusual specific collections consist of the Doris M. MacGowan Gallery, a specially constructed room for miniatures. There is also a display devoted to American artists in Italy and representative objects from the Florentine studio of the Neoclassical sculptor Hiram Powers. One can see his plaster casts and painting models as well as finished marbles, such as his masterpiece *The Greek Slave*. The paintings by George Catlin are the ones he exhibited in London and Paris in the 1840s. A mixture of finished portraits and oil sketches in a simple style with strong colors, the works are fascinating as a record of a long-vanished way of life.

The sixteen paintings by Albert Pinkham Ryder from the John Gellatly collection are a must for anyone interested in American Symbolism. The paintings are small in size and as hermetic as the artist. Although carefully conserved, they are shadows of the original image, as Ryder used bitumen in his paint and added thin layer after layer of pigment over many years. Ryder's most evocative imagery is based around the sea. His *Flying Dutchman*, the ghostly image sailing on the horizon above a storm-tossed boat, evokes the mystery of the sea and the unknown. There are also literary subjects such as *King Cophetua and the Beggar Maid* and empty, haunting little pastorals such as *Landscape with Trees and Cattle*. The portraits by Romaine Brooks form a twentieth-century counterpart to Ryder.

Among the Hudson River School landscapes are Thomas Moran's colossal *The Grand Canyon of the Yellowstone* and *Cliffs of Upper Colorado River* and Albert Bierstadt's *The Sierra Nevada in California*. Not as grandiose but just as impressive is Samuel Colman's *Storm King on the Hudson*.

The Evans bequest concentrated on such end-of-the-century artists as John Twachtman, Childe Hassam, Thomas Dewing and Abbott Thayer. The museum is also active in prints and drawings exhibitions and has a superb collection assembled by the curator Janet Flint.

THE NEW BRITAIN MUSEUM OF AMERICAN ART

56 LEXINGTON STREET, NEW BRITAIN, CT 06052. Tel: (203) 229-0257
Hours: Tues–Sun 1–5 pm, mornings by appointment for groups; closed Mon.
Admission: Free.
Publications:
　New Britain Museum of American Art, *Catalogue of the Collection*. 1975, $3.
　Theodore E. Stebbins, *Three Centuries of Connecticut Art*, 1981, $3.
Reproductions: A few posters and prints.
Research: Reference library open to public.

Thomas Hart Benton.
Arts of the West,
Tempera with oil glaze, 1932

The New Britain Museum of American Art is a little-known jewel among American museums. Located in a nondescript, stucco house with discreet modern additions on a quiet residential street, the collection equals or surpasses those of many larger museums.

Probably the earliest portrait is John Smibert's *Benjamin Colman* painted in 1739. John Singleton Copley's elegant *Mrs. Lydia Lynde Walter* offers an interesting comparison to *Major Samuel Moody* and *Mrs. Samuel Moody,* the flat, primitive but delicate work of his Boston compatriot Joseph Badger. William Jennys, a folk artist in the Connecticut River valley during the first decade of the nineteenth century, painted the portraits *Mr. William Earle* and *Mrs. William Earle.* Jennys's distinctive modeling gives his sitters a rigid, sculptured, almost mournful countenance that is redolent of Nathaniel Hawthorne's later Romantic interpretation of the troubled New England soul. There are fine portraits by Charles Willson Peale and John Trumbull, and an unfinished head by Gilbert Stuart of Jared Sparks, an early biographer of George Washington and president of Harvard College. One of the most unusual portraits is Samuel Waldo's *Pat, the Independent Beggar.* A painter of New York's business elite in a style simpler but reminiscent of Sully, Waldo created a masterpiece of character study in this painting.

The landscape collection touches on the major artists and movements throughout the nineteenth century. Thomas Cole's *The Clove, Catskills* is an example of the early wilderness views that first brought Cole to public notice. *Haying Near New Haven* by Frederic E. Church, Cole's only pupil, is an early example of Church's attention to detail and high, aerial perpective that he would later use to such advantage in his landscapes of South America. Martin J. Heade's *Ipswich Marshes* and John F. Kensett's *Rondout*

Creek are excellent landscapes in the small, clear Luminist mode of mid-century, where certain still atmospheric conditions are so precisely captured. The museum has three works by George Inness. Two are from his first trip to Italy in the 1850s when he still worked in the style of the Hudson River School; the third, *Late Afternoon Montclair,* has a characteristic mystical mood and soft hazy veils of color.

Childe Hassam's *Le Jour du Grand Prix,* a sparkling depiction of carriages heading past the Arc de Triomph on their way to the famous race, is a later version of the painting in the Boston Museum of Fine Arts and is probably the most impressive work of the American Impressionists in the collection. Theodore Robinson's *Union Square* and Frederick Frieseke's *The Bird Cage* are other beautiful representations of Impressionism.

The collection of works by the Ashcan School is small but choice. Among the five works by Robert Henri, *Spanish Girl of Segovia* is particularly impressive with his broad, free brushstrokes and distinctive dark, fluid eyes. George Luks's *Pals,* an old woman stroking her pet parrot, has all the vivid color and crude, expressive energy of his best works. There are characteristic street scenes by both William Glackens and John Sloan as well as drawings and prints. *French Vaudeville* by Everett Shinn is a late work that depicts his undying love of the gaiety, charm and artificiality of theatrical life.

The Ashcan School, led by Henri and supporting themselves as illustrators, had all studied at the Philadelphia Academy and carried on Eakins's realistic imagery of contemporary city life. Running up against the picturesque aestheticism of the National Academy, they joined with three other artists in 1908 to create an exhibition entitled Eight American Painters that proved a landmark in American art. The other artists were Arthur B. Davies, Ernest Lawson and Maurice Prendergast. The museum owns work by them all, one of the most notable being Prendergast's *Beechmont,* a watercolor painted in his sparkling, mosaiclike dabs of pigment. Although not a member of the Ashcan group, George Bellows employed the same broad, slashing brushstroke and preferred the same type of realism. *The Big Dory* is a particularly vivid example of his work.

In addition to oils and prints by Grant Wood and John Steuart Curry, the museum has an impressive collection of lithographs as well as paintings, drawings and watercolors by Thomas Hart Benton. The major holding is the five murals painted in 1932 for the library of the old Whitney Museum in New York. New Britain acquired them in 1953 and installed them in a special gallery eleven years later. They show Benton, one of the so-called "American Scene" painters of the 1930s, at his best. Benton created his murals, measuring from seven to twenty-two feet in length, as a series of overlapping, interlaced scenes. The elongated, undulating figures move with the rhythmic dynamism the artist saw in American life.

PENNSYLVANIA ACADEMY OF THE FINE ARTS
BROAD AND CHERRY STREETS, PHILADELPHIA, PA 19102.
Tel: (215) 972-7600
Hours: Tues–Sat 10 am–5 pm, Sun 1–5 pm, closed Mon, Christmas, New Year's.

Admission: $2 general, $1.50 senior citizens, $1 students.
Publications:
  Linda Bantel, *William Rush, American Sculptor.* 1982, $19.95.
  Richard Boyle, Frank H. Goodyear, *In This Academy.* 1976, $7.50.
Reproductions: Posters, postcards, slides and prints from collection with special emphasis on children's interests.
Research: Library open to researchers by appointment.

The remarkable character of the High Victorian Gothic building that houses the Pennsylvania Academy of the Fine Arts is surpassed only by the exceptional quality of the collection it contains. Founded in 1805, the academy became one of the most important art institutions in the country throughout the nineteenth century. Functioning as an art museum and art school while mounting annual exhibitions, it has developed a collection that expresses American taste with a specific Philadelphian heritage. There are over fifty works by the Peale family, twenty-seven by Gilbert Stuart, forty-two by Thomas Sully, twenty-three by John Neagle and casts and original sculpture by William Rush. It lacks works by Copley, Cole, Church, Bierstadt, Heade and Whistler, but the diversity and high level of excellence in the collection more than compensates for any lack.

The exhibition galleries are located on the sky-lighted second floor and as the collection is far larger than the space allows and is frequently rotated, it is only possible to describe some of the best-known objects. The public entrance is the main portal on Broad Street. In 1976, the building underwent a thorough and sympathetic restoration both inside and out when the original entrance doors and oak foyer were restored. Two small exhibition rooms lie to the right, but what attracts attention is the massive stone, brass and wood staircase straight ahead. The stairs lead in two runs to the main exhibition areas. The stair hall, as the architect intended, sets the stage for entering the world of art. Rising to a skylight, the stair hall changes from incised sandstone walls to stylized and gilded plaster flowers in relief on a deep red background. Above the cornice, the cove ceiling is a deep blue with silver stars. Natural light floods the space reflecting off the gilding, carving, marble and brass to a dazzling effect.

One of the first American paintings in the permanent collection was Gilbert Stuart's Lansdowne portrait of Washington. This is the original signed and dated commission; the versions at Boston and the National Portrait Gallery are copies by Stuart. The painting shows a full-length Washington in an expansive gesture borrowed ultimately from Imperial Roman sculpture. Favorite son Benjamin West is well represented. The original of *Penn's Treaty with the Indians,* of such inspiration to Quaker artists and school book illustrators, came to the academy in the late nineteenth century. The second of West's revolutionary representations of modern history, the idealized scene represents not only Penn's treaty but the ensuing peace and decades of successful settlement and trade. Less familiar but of great importance to the early nineteenth century are West's two enormous history paintings, *Death on a Pale Horse* and *Christ Rejected.* Although the paintings are the type of high-minded moralism established by eighteenth-century academic theory as the highest endeavor for any artist, twentieth-century Modernism has reversed artistic standards so thoroughly that these works are among the few to be seen hanging in any American museum. With John Vanderlyn's exquisite symbol of feminine beauty, *Ariadne,* and Washington Allston's *Dead Man Restored by Touching the Bones of the Prophet Elisha,* also at the Academy, one sees a rare glimpse of the Great Style in American painting.

Among the many portraits are an unusual series of self-portraits. Largest and most important is Charles Willson Peale's full-length view of himself inviting the viewer into his museum, at that time located on the second floor of Independence Hall. Some of the others are by Rembrandt Peale, Charles Loring Elliot, Henry Inman and George C. Lambdin.

The genre paintings range from John Lewis Krimmel's *Fourth of July in Center Square,* an early view of Federal America, to Edward Hopper's *Apartment Houses.* The high technical ability and sentimentality of late-nineteenth-century academic art is visible in William H. Lippincott's *Infantry in Arms,* a glimpse of upper-middle-class family life, and Daniel Ridgway Knight's *Hailing the Ferry,* an exquisite *plein-air* landscape and picturesque figure study. Enchanting as an example of the Victorian penchant for anecdote and subtle sensuality is *May Day Morning* by Edwin Austin Abbey. An expatriate who settled in England but maintained close ties with the American art world, Abbey was a gifted painter and illustrator who produced carefully researched and beautifully colored historical genre scenes. In strong contrast to the narrative emphasis of Abbey is Winslow Homer's powerful *The Fox Hunt.* A scene suggestive of hardship and death, the strange perspective of red fox and hovering black crows against the snow, even the delicate still life of a few red berries, reminds one of the abstract qualities of Japanese prints and the subject recedes in relation to the beauty of the composition.

In addition to Mary Cassatt's *Young Thomas and His Mother,* two fine examples of American Impressionism are Theodore Robinson's *Port Ben, Delaware and Hudson Canal* and John Twachtman's *Sailing in the Mist.* Late-nineteenth-century portraits include *Lady with White Shawl* by William Merritt Chase and *New England Woman* by Cecelia Beaux. Most unusual is Thomas Eakins's study of Walt Whitman in old age, a smiling bust in gray.

The painters of the Ashcan School began their careers in Philadelphia and the Academy has some notable examples of their work, such as Robert Henri's *Ruth St. Denis in the Peacock Dance* and George Luks's *Polish Dancer,* a broadly painted study in purple, pink, white and gray.

PHILADELPHIA MUSEUM OF ART
BENJAMIN FRANKLIN PARKWAY, PHILADELPHIA, PA 19101.
Tel: (215) 763-8100
Hours: Wed–Sun 10 am–5 pm, closed Mon, Tues and legal holidays.
Admission: $2 adults, $1 children under 18, students, senior citizens.
Publications:
    Theodor Siegal, *The Thomas Eakins Collection.* 1978, $11.95.
    Evan H. Turner, *Philadelphia: Three Centuries of American Art.* 1976, $5.98.

Reproductions: Large selection of prints, posters and postcards.
Research: Library, print and study collections open by appointment.

American art at the Philadelphia Museum is housed on the second floor at the end of the south wing of the sprawling Greco-Roman temple built in the 1920s. The galleries have recently been reopened with a new arrangement that combines paintings and smaller sculpture with the American decorative arts collection. The rooms vary abruptly in light quality and seem crowded on occasion, but they display many objects to advantage.

The room housing colonial painting contains a handsome pair of New York Patroon portraits, *Johannes Ten Broeck* and *Catryna Van Rensselaer Ten Broeck* in their primitive Baroque formality, among other startling works, but it is in a large room painted in Victorian colors and exhibiting groupings of furniture dating from 1835 to 1895 that one finds some of the largest and most important of American paintings. Mary Cassatt's *Woman and Child Driving* uses her sister Lydia and a young niece of Degas as subject. In addition to the loosely brushed and high-keyed color, the asymmetrical composition balanced by strong color areas shows her affinity to the work of Degas and other Impressionists. The dark tones and staring countenance of Thomas Eakins's *Mrs. William D. Frishmuth* suggest an intense and forceful personality quite different from Cassatt's dispassionate portrayal. Mrs. Frishmuth is surrounded by a seemingly artless display of her musical instrument collection, but it is her face and particularly the powerful gesture of her right hand striking and sustaining a single note on the piano that dominates the scene. Thomas Hovenden's *Breaking Home Ties,* the most popular painting at the 1893 Columbian Exposition, depicts a young man's leavetaking of his simple farming family as he sets off to make his way in the world. The sentimental emphasis on the fresh-faced youth, tearful mother, staring younger siblings and faithful dog creates a narrative subject at variance with the concerns of Eakins and Cassatt.

Philadelphia is the birthplace and lifelong home of Thomas Eakins, America's great realist painter of the late nineteenth century, and there is an entire room and hallway arranged with the museum's collection of his work. A devoted pupil of Gérôme, Eakins brought his master's precise eye and figural emphasis to his own study of contemporary life in Philadelphia. Foremost in Eakins's early work are the rowing and boxing paintings represented here by *Pair-Oared Shell.* Influenced by the heightened interest in American history during the Centennial, he painted a genre scene from the early art history of Philadelphia, *William Rush Carving the Allegorical Figure of the Schuylkill.* Eakins' concern with depicting movement is reflected in *The Fairman Rogers Four-in Hand,* a careful depiction of the highly lacquered coach, spinning wheels and well-dressed occupants against a blurred background. There are also drawings, sketches and casts of Eakins's anatomical studies. Most numerous are the portraits from his later career. Particularly eye-catching are *The Concert Singer* and *The Actress,* the reclining figure of Susan Santje gazing at the viewer with a look of both languor and physical exhaustion but dressed in a glowing, flowing reddish-pink swath of a dress.

THE ST. LOUIS ART MUSEUM

FOREST PARK, ST. LOUIS, MO 63110. Tel: (314) 721-0072

Hours: Tues 1:30–8:30 pm, Wed–Sun 10 am–5 pm, closed Mon, Christmas and New Year's.

Admission: Free, to permanant collection. Contribution to special exhibitions required Wed–Sun, free Tues.

Publications:

> Judith A. Barter, *Currents of Expansion: Paintings in the Midwest, 1820–1940.* 1977, $8.95.
>
> Charles E. Buckley, *The Saint Louis Art Museum Handbook of the Collection.* 1975, $12.50.

Reproductions: Postcards and some posters of the collection and related works.

Research: Library open to the public by appointment.

The St. Louis Art Museum is housed in the central portion of the Palace of Art constructed for the Louisiana Purchase Exposition in 1903. The American collection was begun in 1910, but not actively developed until the last thirty years, so that although it is not large, it reflects current standards on the important movements of American art. The holdings range from John Smibert to Ellsworth Kelly. The pair of portraits of Thaddeus Burr and Eunice Denny Burr are two characteristic examples of John Singleton Copley's mature style. Another pair of portraits by Ralph Earl, *Major Moses Seymour* and *Molly Marsh Seymour,* shows the colonial tradition continuing up to the nineteenth century. A still life by John Johnston of Boston depicts a simple grouping of peaches and grapes on the top of a mahogany sideboard. Dated 1810, it is the earliest known American still life. There are others by the more famous still-life painters William Michael Harnett and Martin J. Heade.

The major figures of nineteenth-century landscape are all represented. *The Hudson at Piermont* is a particularly fine Jasper Cropsey with none of the reds and oranges that become too acidic on occasion, and John F. Kensett's *Upper Mississippi* is a beautiful tonal study of the river as it passes through large hills. It resembles the artist's Lake George studies, and is a rare Luminist landscape of the West. Martin J. Heade's *Sunset, Newburyport Marshes* is one of his remarkable series of studies of the salt-marsh haystacks at different times of day and under different weather conditions.

Perhaps best known of all the St. Louis paintings is George Caleb Bingham's *Raftsmen Playing Cards.* The six figures are carefully grouped into a pyramidal formation that is emphasized by a system of diagonals between foreground details and the receding river, and is typical of Bingham's elementary but powerful compositions. The museum also has Bingham's early self-portrait as well as the more complex and perhaps less successful *Jolly Flatboatmen in Port.*

STARK MUSEUM OF ART

712 GREEN AVENUE, ORANGE, TX 77630. Tel: (409) 883-6661.

Hours: Wed–Sat 10 am–5 pm, Sun 1–5 pm.

Admission: Free.

Publications:
 Catalogue of the Western Collection. 1978, $10.
Reproductions: Postcards plus 3 posters, from western collection.
Research: Reference library available upon approval of written request.

A museum second only to the Gilcrease in the quality, size and comprehensiveness of the western-art collection is the little-known Stark Museum of Art in Orange, Texas. Housed in a modern, white-marble cube that opened in 1976, the Stark collection includes works by many of the same artists represented at the Gilcrease. Of particular rarity are the western sketches made by the Canadian artist Paul Kane on a trip in the 1840s from the Great Lakes to the Pacific Northwest. The Stark has a large concentration of work by the Taos school, including Berninghaus, Phillips, Sharp, Blumenschein, Walter Ufer, Eanger Irving Couse and William Victor Higgins, as well as the studio of William Herbert Dunton.

WORCESTER ART MUSEUM
855 SALISBURY STREET, WORCESTER, MA 01608. Tel: (617) 799-4406
Hours: Tues–Sat 10 am–5 pm, Sun 1–5 pm, closed Mon, Thanksgiving, Christmas, New Year's, July 4th.
Admission: $1.50 adults, $1 children under 14 and senior citizens, free to children under 10 and members; free on Wednesdays.
Publications:
 Stephen B. Jareckie, *The Early Republic: Consolidation of Revolutionary Goals, 1776–1826.* 1976, $4.50.
 Dagmar Reutlinger, *The Colonial Epoch in America.* 1975, $4.50.
 Timothy A. Riggs, *The Second Fifty Years: American Art 1826–1876.* 1976. $4.50.
Reproductions: Posters, prints and postcards representing the permanent collection.
Research: Library open to public Tues–Fri 10 am–5 pm, Sun 2–5 pm, except in summer. Largest art reference library in central Massachusetts; strong in areas relating to the collection.

The very best examples of seventeenth-century American portraiture are part of the Worcester Art Museum. A distinguished institution founded in 1896, the museum ranks closely behind the large city museums in size and breadth of collections. The important American art holdings are only a part of its varied and superlative art that spans fifty centuries and all media.

 The earliest American paintings are *John Freake* and *Mrs. Elizabeth Freake and Baby Mary,* long considered the masterpieces of seventeenth-century American art. Few portraits survive from the first century of colonial settlement, but one wishes there were many more if they resembled the Freake paintings. The work of an unknown artist, now referred to as the Freake limner, the paintings are striking depictions of an elegant young couple dressed in carefully detailed finery that little evokes the common vision of gray, dour Puritans. Freake was a successful merchant in Boston who commissioned the portraits shortly before his tragic death from an explosion in 1675. Although he wears an elaborate lace collar and silver-buttoned coat, it is the rich reds and yellows, the laces and ribbons of his wife's costume that are particularly noticeable.

Unknown, American.
Mrs. Elizabeth Freake and Baby Mary,
Oil on canvas, 1671-1674

Thomas Smith is the only named artist in seventeenth-century New England. His presumed self-portrait and another of his daughter Maria Catherine are at Worcester. Whereas the Freake portraits have all the flat, decorative qualities of the medieval tradition, the Smiths introduce Renaissance perspective and simple Baroque formality. The museum also has several portraits by the native-born artist John Badger, a glazier who taught himself to paint and became Boston's leading portraitist between 1748 and 1758. The stiff and simple style of Badger's *Cornelius Waldo* is an interesting contrast to the work of Joseph Blackburn, an itinerant Englishman, using the Rococo style, who quickly eclipsed Badger's popularity. Blackburn's *Col. Theodore Atkinson* has a relaxed elegance and careful depiction of textiles that aided the young John Singleton Copley in his development. Copley soon eclipsed Blackburn, and Copley's portrait *John Bours* has the qualities that have established his art as the finest in the Colonial period.

Another portrait of significant quality is Gilbert Stuart's unfinished half-length of Mrs. Perez Morton. The sitter was important in her own day; called the American Sappho, she was one of a circle of sophisticated Bostonians who, among other efforts, organized the first theater in the city. More interesting today is the chance to see Stuart's painting technique in the broad dashes of brush strokes that quickly define the repositioning of her arms and the fabric of her shawl and dress.

Worcester also has one of the earliest American landscapes. *Looking East from Denny Hill* was painted by Ralph Earl, better known as a portraitist. Earl trained for a short time with Benjamin West in London, but he retained the simplicity of colonial portraiture. On occasion, Earl was commissioned to paint landscapes in which he followed the English topographical tradition and recorded the bucolic beauty of farmland rather than the wilderness scenes that became so popular with the Hudson River School.

Other outstanding works are Samuel F. B. Morse's *Chapel of the Virgin at Subiaco,* a powerful rendition of golden light. Asher B. Durand's *The Capture of Major André* has become the standard representation of the famous Revolutionary incident in which three New York farmers discovered Benedict Arnold's treasonous plans in the heel of André's boot. There is a remarkable sketch by Thomas Eakins of Dr. Samuel D. Gross for his masterpiece *The Gross Clinic* at the Jefferson Medical College, Philadelphia, and an early Childe Hassam of a Boston Street, *Columbus Avenue,* painted in the dark tones of his academic training before he discovered Impressionism.

YALE UNIVERSITY ART GALLERY
BOX 2006, YALE STATION, NEW HAVEN, CT 06520. Tel: (203) 436-0574
Hours: Tues–Sat 10 am–5 pm, Sun 2–5 pm; Thurs 6–9 pm Sept 15–May 15 only;
closed Mon, Thanksgiving, Christmas, New Year's, July 4th.
Admission: Free.
Publications:
    Helen Cooper, *John Trumbull: The Hand and The Spirit of a Painter.* 1982, $19.95.
    Theodore E. Stebbins, Galya Gorokhoff, *Checklist of American Painting at Yale
    University.* 1982, $19.95.
Reproductions: Poster, prints and postcards of selected works in the collection.
Research: Gallery does not maintain reference library. Special arrangements may
be made to use reference material of a specific curatorial department.

The Yale University Art Gallery contains unusual and important holdings
representing art throughout the history of man. The American section is
the largest and most complete, with many superlative examples.

Among the colonial portraits is *John Davenport,* painted in 1670 by an
unknown limner and purchased by the college in 1750. The extreme
delicacy of detail is in the same tradition as the Freake portraits at
Worcester, although not by the same hand. The most ambitious and
probably the first group portrait in America is John Smibert's *Dean
Berkeley and His Entourage (The Bermuda Group),* dating from 1729. It
shows Berkeley, the faculty and wives of a projected college in Bermuda that
was never founded. Foremost in examples of portraits by John Singleton
Copley are *Issac Smith* and *Mrs. Issac Smith,* painted when Copley was at
the peak of his powers in America. Benjamin West's *Agrippina Landing at
Brundisium with the Ashes of Germanicus* is one of the first Neoclassical
paintings, the central group taken directly from a surviving Roman bas-
relief and actual Roman buildings incorporated into the background. The
Philadelphia version was painted a few years later.

In 1831, Yale acquired most of John Trumbull's studio in exchange for a
yearly stipend for the remainder of the artist's life. The agreement included
a separate gallery structure that proved to be the first university art
museum in the Western Hemisphere when it opened in 1832. Included in
the Trumbull collection are his original oil sketches of his "national history"
series, particularly *The Death of Warren* and *The Death of Montgomery,*
brilliant and striking Baroque compositions inspired by Rubens's Marie de
Medici cycle at the Louvre. Never commissioned at full size, the studies
remain as provocative reminders of an ambitious project that was finally
achieved in part as the Capitol Rotunda murals in 1817. Yale also has
Trumbull's superb miniatures of Revolutionary War period worthies.

There are many works by Ralph Earl, including his masterpiece *Roger
Sherman,* an awkward, somber and powerful portrait. Charles Willson
Peale's *William Buckland* is another portrait that particularly evokes the
unique character of the sitter; in this case, the glint of the eyes radiates the
talented creative powers of this remarkable colonial architect.

Some more recent purchases include Frederic E. Church's *Mt. Ktaadn,* a
vast panorama of the majestic Maine landmark in a soft reddish-brown haze
of sunset; Martin J. Heade's *Jungle Orchids and Hummingbirds* from his

John Trumbull.
Death of General Montgomery in the Attack on Quebec,
Oil on canvas, 1788

well-known series; William M. Harnett's *Still Life with Flute, Vase and Roman Lamp*, a small, jewellike painting; and Worthington Whitteredge's *White Birches*, an interior woodland scene.

Winslow Homer's *The Morning Bell* is a precisely composed view of young women workers passing across a bridge to the small New England mill in the background. The picturesque, anonymous figures, strong colors and high contrast of light and dark gives the image a strong, almost nostalgic appeal. Even more precise is Thomas Eakins's *John Biglin in a Single Scull*. More exotic and less anecdotal is John Singer Sargent's *View of Capri*, a figure standing on a rooftop with the echoing shapes of white stuccoed chimney stacks. In contrast to the recreative setting of much of Sargent's work, Robert Henri's *West 57th Street, New York* is a landscape in the city painted in the gray, brown and white tones of an urban winter.

Among the examples by American Impressionists, Willard Metcalf's *Midsummer Shadows* is particularly notable. Painted in broken pigmentation and brushstrokes, it is a study of decrepit barns alongside an elm-shaded dirt road near his summer home in Cornish, New Hampshire. All four of the Edward Hoppers are masterpieces: *Rooms for Tourists* is a night scene of a nineteenth-century house on Cape Cod, *Sunlight in a Cafeteria* is in the theme of his famous *Nighthawks* at the Chicago Art Institute, *Western Motel* is similar to his Brooklyn interiors, and *Rooms by the Sea* presents a glimpse into two empty rooms with an open door where only the ocean is visible. George Bellows's *Lady Jean*, which depicts a young girl in Victorian dress before an antique red cupboard, is similar in quality.

CHAPTER TWO

ANCIENT ART

by
KARLA KLEIN ALBERTSON

THE ART MUSEUM

PRINCETON UNIVERSITY, PRINCETON, NJ 08544. Tel: (609) 452-3788
Hours: Tues–Sat 10 am–4 pm, Sun 1–5 pm (academic year), 2–4 pm (summer),
closed Mon and holidays.
Admission: Free; nominal charge for groups.
Publications: *Record of the Art Museum,* bi-annual. $7.
Reproductions: Postcards of many objects in the collection.
Research: No reference library. University library for use of university commu-
nity and qualified scholars by appointment.

Some people think of New Jersey as the grey area across the Hudson from
New York City; more charitable minds think of Princeton, one of the most
charming university towns in the country. At the center of the campus, the
Art Museum shares a modern building with the Department of Art and
Archaeology and its library. The collections have grown through the gifts of
alumni, supplemented by material from Princeton excavations.

In the 1930s, the university was part of a team of American institutions
that excavated at Antioch-on-the-Orontes, a Hellenistic and Roman city that
flourished from 300 B.C. into the Early Christian period. The site was
enormously rich in figural and geometric mosaic floors. After being carefully raised by the excavators, many were donated by Syria to the participat-
ing museums and colleges in appreciation for their help. The finest share
are installed in the museum and the lobby of the art building.

Composed of cut squares of colored marble, the mosaics brilliantly
decorated the houses of wealthy Antiochenes with intricate patterns and
scenes from mythology. One example set into the floor of the Classical
Gallery depicts a drinking contest between Herakles and the god Dionysos.
Another, also dating from the third century A.D., features Cupid figures
riding on dolphins and continues to fulfill its original function as the floor of
a niched pool placed along one side of the gallery.

Princeton owns a fine bronze statuette of Zeus standing ready to hurl his
thunderbolt that dates from the fifth-century-B.C. Golden Age of Greece. The
portrait of Marcus Aurelius, who ruled the Roman Empire from A.D. 161 to
180, has an expression of dreamy introspection, perhaps natural for a

hardworking man who never had enough time to pursue the philosophical studies he loved best. Several objects on display remind us of the Classical fondness for the theater; a Hellenistic marble relief shows a playwright contemplating the traditional masks for three of his characters. A noteworthy recent acquisition is the life-size bronze head of a woman from the second century A.D.; her hair is arranged in braids covered by a net, and the eyes are inlaid with silver.

THE BROOKLYN MUSEUM
EASTERN PARKWAY, BROOKLYN, NY 11238 Tel: (212) 638-5000
Hours: Wed–Sat 10 am–5 pm, Sun 12–5 pm, holidays 1–5 pm, closed Mon–Tues.
Admission: Suggested contribution $2 adults, $1 students; free to children under 12 and senior citizens.
Publications:
    Robert Steven Bianchi, *Egyptian Treasures.* nd, $10.95.
    Bernard V. Bothmer, *Brief Guide to the Department of Egyptian and Classical Art.* nd, $4.
    John D. Cooney, *Late Egyptian and Coptic Art.* nd, $9.00.
    Emil G. Kraeling, *The Brooklyn Museum Aramaic Papyri: New Documents of the Fifth Century B.C. from the Jewish Colony at Elephantine.* nd, $18.
    Edna R. Russmann, *The Representation of the King in the XXVth Dynasty.* nd, $13.
Reproductions: Numerous posters, prints, postcards and slides from the collection and special exhibitions.
Research: Art reference library open to those with specific need by appointment only.

Although the Brooklyn Museum also holds many fine examples of Near Eastern and Classical art, it is the remarkable depth and quality of the Egyptian collection that must be emphasized. The time span is enormous, nearly five millennia, and the objects exhibit a variety that denies any claims of a single static style for Egyptian art.

As is often the case, the earliest Predynastic pieces somehow appear most "modern," with their simple, expressive images. This is especially true for the buff and red vase with animal decoration covered with a design of marauding aardvarks in silhouette.

Famous as he is, one cannot omit mention of the statuette of Methethy, who was not a pharaoh but an estate administrator. The exquisitely carved features of this busy executive point out the artist's mastery of sculpture in wood as well as hard stone.

The Egyptian artist was no less skillful when dealing with images of women. Lady Thepu was the mother of an artist herself, and the colorful painting taken from her son's tomb shows her as a young and desirable woman. Equally attractive, even in its mutilated state, is the quartzite statue of Pharaoh Akhenaten's daughter, Princess Maket-aten. Both these images are from the XVIIIth Dynasty in the New Kingdom period.

Egyptian art did not decline with the country's waning political power in the ancient world. The head of priest Wesir-wer dates from the fourth, century B.C., immediately before the conquest of Egypt by Alexander the

Great. There is an extraordinary beauty in the carefully structured planes of the face, still presented in a pure native style. By 80 B.C., Hellenistic influence had tempered the Egyptian; this can be seen in the realistic diorite portrait called the Brooklyn Black Head. Nor does Brooklyn's collection stop at the death of paganism, for there are numerous interesting Coptic carvings and textiles from the Early Christian period.

The Brooklyn Museum not only possesses these outstanding objects but has long been deeply involved in the field of Egyptian archaeology. Most of the artifacts mentioned above were purchased through a fund established by Charles Edwin Wilbour, and the exceptionally large and complete Egyptological library at the museum is named in honor of this generous early collector. The institution has been actively engaged in archaeological field work, including excavations in the vicinity of ancient Thebes. Also, the museological expertise of the staff has helped to make the new museum at Luxor one of the most attractive in Egypt.

Unknown, Egyptian.
Lady Thepu,
Paint on gesso, Dynasty XVIII

THE CLEVELAND MUSEUM OF ART

11150 EAST BOULEVARD AT UNIVERSITY CIRCLE,
CLEVELAND, OH 44160. Tel: (216) 421-7340

Hours: Tues, Thurs, Fri, 10 am–6 pm, Wed 10 am–10 pm, Sat 9 am–5 pm, Sun 1–6 pm; closed Mon, Thanksgiving, Christmas, New Year's, July 4th.

Admission: Free.

Publications:

Sherman E. Lee, *The Handbook of the Cleveland Museum of Art.* 1978, $10.
The Bulletin of the Cleveland Museum of Art. $10.

Reproductions: Posters, prints, postcards and slides from the collection and special exhibitions.

Research: Reference library open to members, visiting curators, faculty and graduate students with identification.

Nothing could be more remote from the Cleveland jokes of nightclub comedians than the reality of cultural Cleveland with its often-praised symphony, ballet and museum of art. The last of these contains one of the best ancient-art collections in the country. Founded in the nineteenth century through the munificence of three local benefactors, the museum has continued to build a strong endowment with further bequests.

The policy of the Department of Ancient Art has been to buy only objects of the finest quality for permanent display. This is far from the practice at some large museums where the mediocre majority of works may remain submerged in storage rooms forever. Consistently excellent curatorial direction coupled with this availability of funds has resulted in the many unique or exceptional pieces present in this collection, only some of which can be highlighted here. The Near Eastern, Egyptian and Classical objects are beautifully displayed in one quiet, well-planned suite of rooms. The collection, although extensive, is not overwhelming and can be covered in an enjoyable hour of study.

It is difficult to focus on only a few objects in a group characterized by such high quality. The tendency is to mention the most famous or historically important, while a visitor is more likely to be beguiled by the small charming pieces he comes across in between. Entering the ancient galleries through a section devoted to Near Eastern art, it is impossible to ignore the basalt statuette of a Hittite Priest-King in pointed cap dating to around 1600 B.C. It is a one-of-a-kind possession for the museum, thus important both archaeologically and art historically. Nearby is a dazzling array of Persian metalwork in bronze and silver covering a time span of almost 2,000 years. Mostly luxury tableware, the pieces display the skillful workmanship, richness of detail and use of animal forms typical of the Eastern empires.

In the Egyptian section, one of the oldest works, an alabaster sculpture from the First Dynasty of the frog goddess Heqat, somehow contrives to make a most modern impression with its simple lines. These rooms are filled with many fine wall reliefs. Some, like the picture of four Nome gods bearing offerings, arrest the eye with their vivid original color; others, such as that of the King's Scribe Amenhotep from the XIXth Dynasty, are superbly carved. Among the portraits, note the under-life-size limestone head of the Fifth Dynasty pharaoh Weserkaf and the striking Greco-Egyptian funerary painting from the Faiyum of a noble woman.

The smaller of the two rooms devoted to Classical art contains a pleasant mixture of very fine vases and objects from the minor arts—terracottas, jewelry, bronzes and glass. Of the former, a rare, white-ground *lekythos,* or oil jar, by the painter Douris depicts Atalanta, an independent-spirited woman of Greek mythology. Several bronze mirrors from sixth- and fifth-century Greece use the human figure as a support for their polished surfaces. Even more striking is the Etruscan *cista* handle formed by two helmeted men carrying the body of a third. Among the examples of Greek and Roman sculpture is a charming statue in marble of a young woman wearing a high-waisted Greek dress called a *chiton.* The small bronze figure of a standing athlete was created in Greece during the fifth century B.C., the golden age of Classical sculpture represented in this country by very few original works.

The absence of preserved fabrics from ancient contexts leaves us with a fairly sterile idea of early standards regarding luxurious or even comfortable interior decoration. Only in the dry Egyptian climate were some of these wool and linen tapestries saved from destruction. Cleveland has formed an exceptional collection of these fragments from the Late Roman and Early Christian periods, which are displayed in a separate gallery devoted to textiles and objects of Early Western art. While some, like that of a plump little Nereid, look back to pagan mythological themes, a large wool tapestry of the Virgin enthroned presents the Christian iconography of the future. Also in this section is a unique series of carvings depicting the adventures of Jonah and a statuette of the Good Shepherd with one of his sheep across his shoulders, both popular motifs in the new religion. All of these works emphasize the fact that there was no sharp break but rather a gradual transition from Classical art to that of the Byzantine period.

THE J. PAUL GETTY MUSEUM

17985 PACIFIC COAST HIGHWAY, MALIBU, CA 90265.

Tel: (213) 459-2306

Hours: Sept. 15–June 15; Tues–Sun 10 am–5 pm, closed Mon. June 15–Sept. 15: Mon–Fri 10 am–5 pm, closed Sat–Sun. No admission after 4:30 pm.

Admission: Free. Reservations are required for those arriving by car; pedestrians not admitted, must use taxi, bicycle, public bus.

Publications:

Jiri Frel, *Greek Portraits in the J. Paul Getty Museum.* 1982, $16.95.
————, *Painting on Vases in Ancient Greece.* 1979, $5.75.
————, *Roman Portraits in The J. Paul Getty Museum.* 1982, $16.95.
————, *Classical Antiquities in the J. Paul Getty Museum.* 1983, $20.

Reproductions: Large selection posters, slides, postcards from the collection and special exhibitions. Reproductions of popular antiquities, to size.

Research: New research center being created with a focus on art history to be used by scholars in the humanities engaged in interdisciplinary research. International information retrieval systems. Open to interested persons with defined goals by arrangement.

Spectacular is the best word for the Getty Museum; it describes not only the contents of the museum but its physical structure and even its view over the coast at Malibu. *Controversial,* however, might be another good word. The museum is the child of the late J. Paul Getty, and, like any rich heiress who can have whatever she wants, she often makes others jealous. With funds generated by the largest museum endowment in the country, the Getty can afford to acquire the finest pieces appearing on the art market and spend whatever is necessary for their care and preservation.

As early as the 1930s, Mr. Getty began to gather works of ancient art, but he was particularly fond of Classical statuary, which makes up the nucleus of the present collection. He purchased many figures from well-known European collections, some of which were started in the Renaissance. Since his death, the curatorial staff has continued to make major acquisitions.

It is impossible to discuss the collection without first examining the beautiful structure that was built to house it. The trustees hoped that the building would "be a statement in itself," and it certainly speaks to us of Mr. Getty's interest in Classical civilization. He had been particularly fascinated

Lysippos. (attribution)
Statue of a Victorious Athlete,
Bronze, 4th century B.C.

by the plans of the sumptuous Roman Villa dei Papiri at Herculaneum, a building which was buried by Vesuvius in A.D. 79 and rediscovered in the eighteenth century. The building at Malibu is a reconstruction of this villa. Upon entering, the visitor passes through two peristyle courtyards open to the sky and adorned with the statuary, reflecting pools and botanical plantings appropriate to an aristocratic dwelling of the first century. Almost everything in view is a direct copy of something found in Italy. Note especially the interior use of multicolored marble to duplicate ancient floor and wall veneer designs. Credit must be given to the combination of scholarly and technological effort that turned a dream of reconstructing the past into a modern reality.

Most of the ancient art is on display in the rooms that open off the Inner Peristyle on the ground floor. The Hall of Aphrodite holds numerous Classical representations of the goddess of love. There are well-polished, life-size versions in marble and a tiny, transparent one in rock crystal. Aphrodite crouches in her bath, attempting to conceal herself, or flaunts her body as the mood strikes her. One of the beautiful pieces in this group, the Mazarin Venus, is named for a former owner: the prime minister of Louis XIV of France. Until quite recently, the common practice was to have missing portions of a figure restored; in this case, the museum has left the seventeenth-century restorations in place. The taste then was for completeness, whereas curators now prefer to conserve objects and add only for structural soundness. In the same room is an Attic grave relief of the sixth century B.C. that is carved with a touching scene between two youths, one of whom gently binds the head of his dying companion.

A nearby gallery holds the Getty Bronze, a recent acquisition that received much publicity when it arrived. Many ancient Greek sculptors preferred to work in bronze, but few life-size examples survive, since in times of crisis bronze would be melted down to reuse as weapons, coinage or fresh materials for statues. Some pieces, such as this standing athlete, survived as part of the cargo of ancient shipwrecks. Its style is reminiscent of that of the famous sculptor Lysippos who was active in the fourth century B.C. This room also contains a marble head of Achilles from the architectural sculptures of the Temple of Athena Alea at Tegea, possibly the creation of Skopas, another great sculptor of that period.

Across the atrium are three unique statues of terracotta from the late fourth century B.C. Orpheus, the enchanting musician of mythology, sits between two sirens, half-female monsters known for their singing. Clay was often used for large sculpture in southern Italy because of the absence of good carving stone; the excellent preservation of these figures suggests they were placed in a tomb.

In the Mosaic Gallery, a seated statue of Cybele depicts the Eastern mother goddess who became popular in Roman religion. The homely face on the figure, however, is the portrait of a Roman matron. Well-born women often had themselves portrayed in the guise of a favorite deity.

The circular Temple of Herakles was specially constructed for one of Mr. Getty's most prized statues, a marble Herakles from Hadrian's Villa at Tivoli, which was formerly in the Lansdowne Collection in England. The young but muscular hero is shown carrying his two emblems, the club and lion skin.

THE METROPOLITAN MUSEUM OF ART
FIFTH AVENUE AT 82ND STREET, NEW YORK, NY 10028.
Tel: (212) 535-7710
Hours: Tues 10 am–8:45 pm, Wed–Sat 10 am–4:45 pm, Sun and holidays 11 am–4:45 pm, closed Mon, Thanksgiving, Christmas, New Year's.
Admission: Suggested contribution $4 adults, $2 children and senior citizens, free to children under 12.
Publications:
> Vaughn E. Crawford et al., *Assyrian Reliefs and Ivories in The Metropolitan Museum of Art*. 1980, $3.95.
> Henry G. Fischer, *Ancient Egyptian Calligraphy: A Beginner's Guide to Written Hieroglyphs*. 1979, $10.
> William C. Hayes, *The Scepter of Egypt: A Background for the Study of Egyptian Antiquities in The Metropolitan Museum of Art*
> > *Volume I: From the Earliest Times to the End of the Middle Kingdom*. 1953, $18.50.
> > *Volume II: The Hyksos Period and the New Kingdom*. 1959, $18.50.

Anna Marguerite McCann, *Roman Sarcophagi in The Metropolitan Museum of Art.* 1978, $25.
Gisela M. A. Richter, *The Sculpture and Sculptors of the Greeks.* 1971, $42.50.
———, *Attic Red-Figured Vases: A Survey.* 1958, $22.50.
Reproductions: Extensive selection of posters, prints, postcards, slides and reproductions of sculptures and other works from the collection.
Research: Library open to staff of the museum and other qualified researchers and graduate students with identification. Most comprehensive art and archaeology collection in Western Hemisphere, including 210,000 books and 1200 periodicals subscriptions. It covers all areas in which museum has holdings.

There is no collective body of ancient art at the Metropolitan; the past is, rather, carefully parceled out between the independent departments of Egyptian, Near Eastern, and Greek and Roman Art. But proximity does not breed similarity. The departments differ considerably in curatorial attitude and museological style, although one assumes that their respective staff members nod when they pass one another in the hall. All three sections have vast amounts of material, from the world-renowned objects on display to multitudinous items in subterranean storage.

No one could fail to be dazzled by the attractive reinstallation of the Egyptian collection, completed in June of 1983. The galleries are arranged to present the highlights of this most important collection in chronological order from the Predynastic to Coptic periods.

Smaller objects are integrated into colorful mixed-media groupings within well-labeled plexiglass cases. The results are instructive in a painless way and will hold the attention of child and adult alike. These areas are punctuated by galleries containing selections of the museum's beautiful facsimile drawings of Egyptian wall paintings, by special sections devoted to gold objects, mummy cases and sculpture and by permanent architectural installations such as the mastaba tomb of Perneby.

The Sackler Wing, which houses the Temple of Dendur, may be one of the most pleasant spots to sit and think in New York, with its cool combination of stone, water and light. The temple itself is a small one from the Roman period, donated by the Egyptian government in return for U.S. help in the salvage operations occasioned by the construction of the Aswan Dam. Yet it provides an environmental link between the diverse objects in this section and their original home near the Nile.

The Department of Egyptian Art is proud of its wealth in excavated material with recorded histories and of its own finds from the Metropolitan excavations of 1907–1939. The latter include magnificent statues of the female Pharaoh Hatshepsut from her funerary temple at Deir el Bahri constructed during Dynasty XVIII of the New Kingdom. These sculptures, many in red granite on a colossal scale, show this enterprising woman in the regalia and false beard customary for male rulers. A seated statue of Horemheb, who became the last king of this same dynasty, is considered one of the Metropolitan's finest Egyptian pieces for its exquisite carving. Although a military officer at the time of this portrait, he has chosen to be depicted as a peaceful, almost effeminate-looking, scribe with scroll in lap.

Some visitors may be more charmed by Egyptian craftsmanship in the minor arts. The heavy stone sculptures seem quite permanent, but nothing can surpass gold for sheer immortality. The pectoral, or chest ornament, of Princess Sit Hathor Yunet has two solar falcons flanking the cartouche of her father, the Pharaoh Sesostris II of Dynasty XII. The front of the pendant is skillfully inlaid with minute pieces of lapis lazuli, turquoise, garnet and carnelian. Even more spectacular is the jewelry of the three wives of Thutmose III; the massive golden headdress worn by one wife was certainly the definitive solution to everyday hairstyling problems.

Entire books can be, and have been, written about this collection. The later Egyptian periods are as interesting artistically as the more powerful days of the great pharaohs. Do not fail to examine the fine group of second century A.D. funerary portraits from the Faiyum that bring us literally face to face with the ancient people of Roman Egypt.

The Metropolitan's Near Eastern department was at various times incorporated with Egyptian and Islamic antiquities but has enjoyed its present independence since 1963. The department has a good fifty years of excavation experience at major sites such as Ctesiphon, Nimrud, Nippur, Hasanlu and Lagash. There are also renovations under way on the exhibition facilities of this section, although the Raymond and Beverly Sackler Gallery, which houses Assyrian art, has remained open. This room contains much of the material from Nimrud in Iraq, which ranges from immense human-headed bulls from the gateway of Ashurnasirpal II's palace to delicate carved ivories in mixed Assyrian, Syrian and Phoenician styles.

Open in Spring of 1984, a new, long gallery running between the Assyrian room and the Islamic section of the museum will display examples from other ancient Near Eastern civilizations—Sumerian to Sasanian. The third millenium B.C. is represented by the stolid, dark stone figure of Gudea, a governor in the Sumerian city of Lagash. Also in the new gallery will be other important groups of ivories from Acem Hüyük in Anatolia and Hasanlu and Ziwiyeh in Iran. One of the most impressive treasures among the Sasanian silver is a near life-size head of a king with luxuriously curling hair and bulbous crown.

Any visitor who has had lunch at the Metropolitan has unavoidably seen part of the museum's Greek and Roman collection. After bearing left from the main lobby, it is necessary to pass through the Roman gallery and down a long hall lined with smiling Cypriote statues to reach the cafeteria. These large limestone figures that exhibit traces of Greek, Near Eastern and Egyptian influence are a part of the Metropolitan's early history. They were acquired by the young museum in 1873 as part of thousands of Cypriote objects that had been gathered by the adventurous General Luigi Palma di Cesnola. Later, as director of the museum, he supervised the move to its present quarters on Fifth Avenue.

Of the three ancient departments, Greek and Roman could be called the most traditional in its presentation of its holdings. Although the displays may be less enticing, the galleries contain classical works of the highest quality and the greatest significance for art history. The "New York Kouros," for example, is one of the earliest extant pieces of life-size Greek sculpture in stone, an art that seems to have sprung up suddenly full-grown in the late seventh century B.C. Also in the galleries on the main floor of the South Wing are many more bronzes, works of major sculpture, objects from the Mediterranean Bronze Age and a selection of Etruscan antiquities.

Other galleries on the second floor are devoted exclusively to the department's outstanding collection of Greek vases. Among the earliest are the enormous funerary vases dating from the eighth century B.C.; these served as grave markers in the early Athenian cemeteries and are appropriately decorated with mourners and the laying out of the dead. Almost every great vase painter has his work represented in these galleries; one of the best-known masterpieces is the late sixth-century B.C. red-figure krater by Euphronios, on which Sleep and Death are shown lifting the body of the deceased hero Sarpedon.

Occupying a gallery near the lobby on the main floor, the Metropolitan's collection of Roman art includes the greatest assemblage of wall paintings outside of Italy. The murals once decorated the rooms of ancient villas at Boscoreale and Boscotrecase near Mt. Vesuvius; they depict monumental figures as well as architectural elements and charming rustic scenes.

MUSEUM OF ART AND ARCHAEOLOGY
UNIVERSITY OF MISSOURI-COLUMBIA, 1 PICKARD HALL, COLUMBIA, MO 65211. Tel: (314) 882-3591
Hours: Tues–Sun 12–5 pm, closed Mon, national holidays and university holidays.
Admission: Free.
Publications:
> *Muse, the Annual of the Museum of Art and Archaeology,* $5.
> Osmund Overby, *Illustrated Museum Handbook: A Guide to the Collection in the Museum of Art and Archaeology.* 1982, $10.

Reproductions: Prints, posters and postcards of objects in the collection. Reproductions of some objects; hand-pulled prints from old Japanese woodblocks.
Research: Small reference library available for use by appointment.

This small but excellent university museum has recently expanded on its original academic purpose to become a regional museum for central Missouri. Located geographically on the interstate halfway between larger institutions in St. Louis and Kansas City, its presence may seem to the out-of-state traveler as unexpected as a ruby in a cornfield. The museum began as a small study collection for students, housed, at one time, in the general library. In 1967, the museum began to publish its own impressive annual, *MUSE,* devoted to discussions of individual artifacts and current excavations. The real transformation occurred in 1976, when the collections were moved to their present quarters in the former chemistry building on a historic campus quadrangle.

Ancient art is this museum's great strength, reflecting the national importance of the university's Department of Art History and Archaeology, whose faculty members serve as museum advisors. This gives the museum a distinctive flavor; the content runs not to large statues but to the exciting finds of objects from everyday life that delight the archaeologist's heart and prove most instructive for our knowledge of the past.

A simple pottery Shrine Group, ca. 800 B.C., from the Moabite people in Jordan may have been used during worship in a home or small sanctuary and provides evidence regarding religious practices in Biblical times. A decorated cylindrical *pyxis* from the Mycenaean period in Greece was used for cosmetics and, in fact, closely resembles a modern powder box. The carved stone stele from Crete depicting a warrior gives an accurate idea of fighting equipment in early Greece, and a bronze shield blazon with horse's head represents another device for decorating the armor of that period. Two examples of what we would call "novelty vases" are molded in the shape of female heads. One from fifth-century Athens with decorated headdress and painted eyes is actually a ceramic jug topped with a pouring spout; the other lovely head with softly gathered hair is part of a group of green Roman lead-glazed pottery. Glance also at the many other examples of Greek, Cypriote and Palestinian pottery and at the recently excavated objects from an ancient glass factory at Jalame near Haifa in Israel.

MUSEUM OF FINE ARTS

465 HUNTINGTON AVENUE, BOSTON, MA 02115. Tel: (617) 267-9300
Hours: Tues, Thurs–Sun 10 am–5 pm, Wed 10 am–10 pm, closed Mon, Thanksgiving, Christmas eve and day, New Year's, July 4th. West Wing only: Thurs–Fri 5–10 pm.
Admission: $3.50 adults, $2.50 adults Thurs–Fri 5–10 pm, $2.50 senior citizens, free to children under 17 and members; free Sat 10 am–12 pm.
Publications: Gallery guides.
> George Chase, revised by Cornelius Vermeule, *Greek, Etruscan, and Roman Art: The Classical Collections of the Museum of Fine Arts, Boston.* 1972, $3.75.
> Mary Comstock, Cornelius Vermeule, *Greek, Etruscan and Roman Bronzes in the Museum of Fine Arts, Boston.* 1971, $35.
> Cornelius C. Vermeule, Mary Comstock, *Greek and Roman Portraits, 470 B.C.–A.D. 500, Museum of Fine Arts, Boston.* 1972, $1.50.

Reproductions: Large selection of posters, prints, postcards, slides from the collection and special exhibitions.
Research: Main library open to public; reference libraries of specific departments available to students and scholars by appointment.

This museum has one of the country's legendary departments of Egyptian antiquities. The genesis of the collection was in their own excavations carried on for more than forty years at Giza near Cairo and far to the south in the Sudan. From the former site comes the majestic standing figure of Mycerinus, pharaoh of Dynasty IV and builder of the third of the great pyramids at Giza. He is shown with his queen in a double, or pair, statue that was to become a common type in Egyptian art. There is a striking contrast between the formality of the royal pose and the intimacy of the couple's own relationship, expressed by the wife's arms encircling her husband. From slightly earlier in the Fourth Dynasty, the bust of Vizier Ankh-haf portrays the overseer of the second great pyramid with remarkable naturalism. It is almost like having the man—somewhat tired, serious but very competent—present in person. This amazing verisimilitude is achieved by adding detail with plaster and paint over the basic limestone.

It is interesting to compare Ankh-haf with the Greco-Egyptian "Boston Green Head," made over 2,000 years later, when realism was once again in fashion. The accurate translation to stone of these dignified features reminds one of Roman portraits of the Republican period.

Within the Department of Classical Art are important objects of the Mediterranean Bronze Age, contemporary in date with the early years of the New Kingdom in Egypt. From the Minoan civilization, almost devoid of three-dimensional sculpture, the museum is fortunate to have a small ivory carving of the Cretan mother goddess with her writhing snakes and other accessories added in gold.

The early Iron Age in Greece is usually called the Geometric period after the angular style of decoration used on vases. This type of painting is also found on the unusual Boeotian bell-doll of the eighth century B.C. Her legs

Unknown, Etruscan.
Woman playing Lyre,
paint on terracotta, ca. 475 B.C.

form the clappers under the bell of her patterned dress. Whether plaything or cult object, the Alice-in-Wonderland neck and small, outlined breasts give this terracotta figure a very stylized appearance.

The Classical collections at the MFA include marvelous examples in every medium, whether lovely pieces of marble sculpture such as the fourth century B.C. head of a maiden from Chios or small tours de force of the miniaturist's art on coins and gems. From the latter realm comes the diminutive gold sculpture of Victory driving a two-horse chariot, complete in every detail down to the tiny reins. Actually one of the world's most elaborate earrings, it may originally have adorned the statue of a goddess.

From the wonderful array of Greek vases, some examples in the earlier black-figure technique depict genre scenes, such as the water jar with women filling their jugs at a fountain house or the shoemaker's workshop on a storage jar. Most, however, feature the exploits of various gods and heroes. The great sixth century B.C. artist Exekias painted the amphora with Dionysos seated among his grape-gathering satyrs. On a later hydria by the Chiusi Painter, Herakles has an acrobatic wrestling match with the fish-tailed Triton. A truly ambitious composition on a hydria of the later sixth century shows Achilles on a chariot dragging the body of his enemy Hector around the walls of Troy. Similar mythological themes were used in the red-figure style, which dominated fifth century vase painting. A bell krater by the Pan Painter shows poor Actaeon attacked by his own dogs on the orders of the goddess Artemis.

The Museum of Fine Arts has equally outstanding objects from the Etruscan civilization of Italy. Funerary art is represented by two brightly painted terracotta plaques dating to the first half of the fifth century B.C. that may come from the necropolis at Vulci. A man playing the double flute is shown with the reddish-colored skin reserved for male figures, while on another a female musician with lighter skin holds a seven-stringed lyre.

Roman pottery is generally less celebrated than the painted Greek vases that are a staple of every museum. Fulfilling the obvious need for "dishes" were molded wares, most notably the red Arretine pottery that flourished in the Augustan period. When removed from a mold, the outside of the characteristic bowls was decorated with graceful figures and patterned borders. Although unpainted, the pieces are covered with a lustrous red finish that is most attractive. Boston's large collection of Arretine ware includes not only the finished products but examples of molds and the figural stamps that were used to create them.

The Romans continued the Greek practice of decorating gems with designs in intaglio and refined the later Hellenistic invention of cameo carving. For the latter, skilled artists carved banded chalcedonies so that figures in relief and background were of contrasting colors. The MFA owns several exceedingly large and handsome cameos of sardonyx, one depicting a winged Victory driving her chariot, another, known as the "Marlborough gem," the marriage of Cupid and Psyche.

THE ORIENTAL INSTITUTE MUSEUM OF THE UNIVERSITY OF CHICAGO

1155 E. 58TH STREET, CHICAGO IL 60637. Tel: (312) 753-2474

Hours: Tues–Sat 10 am–4 pm, Sun 12–4 pm, closed Mon and holidays.

Admission: Free.

Publications: General and scholarly publications on Near East include:

William J. Murnane, *United With Eternity: A Concise Guide to the Monuments of Medinet Habu.* 1980, $8.

Ann Louise Perkins, *The Comparative Archaeology of Early Mesopotamia.* 1949, 1977, $14.

Reproductions: Prints, postcards and reproductions of Near Eastern objects in the collection.

Research: Research library available for use to Oriental Institute members and visiting scholars. Large collection covers art, archaeology, language, history of ancient Near Eastern civilizations; strongest in Egyptology and Mesopotamian archaeology and language.

"Oriental" in the case of this museum refers to the Near, rather than the Far, East. This institution is occupied not only by curators but also by archaeologists and philologists who teach at the University of Chicago, well-known for its distinguished Department of Near Eastern Languages and Civilizations. The founder of the Oriental Institute, James Henry Breasted, remains one of the great names of Egyptology. Chicago fieldwork continues on the banks of the Nile, where they have conducted a monumental epigraphic survey for sixty years, at Nippur in Iraq, and at many other sites throughout the Middle East. Preparation for the institute's Assyrian Dictionary began in the 1920s, and the project is still going strong.

With this type of background, it is no surprise to find the museum's collections rich in archaeological contexts, the majority of which were recorded during their own excavations. The objects are displayed in long galleries, broken up by partitions into alcoves. One section is devoted to Egyptian antiquities, others to artifacts from various Near Eastern civilizations. The recently renovated Mesopotamian Hall holds many treasures, including the famous Bismaya head, named for the city in Iraq where it was unearthed. This beautiful gypsum sculpture was created in the late third millenium B.C. at one of the rare moments when Mesopotamia was unified under a single ruler, Sargon of Akkad. The eyes, inlaid in the manner of earlier Sumerian works, give a startlingly lifelike appearance to the face.

Many of the objects are connected with the religious practices that played such an important part in Mesopotamian life. The small bronze statuette of a Babylonian deity with four faces keeps an eye, or two, on all comers.

Some exhibits are spectacular in their impact, such as the reconstruction of the great processional gateway of Babylon from the sixth century B.C. In an area poor in stone the pylons were constructed of colorful glazed bricks with animals in relief. Other cases hold rows of tiny cylinder seals with samples of their impressions, used to mark and identify possessions. Some have continuous abstract patterns; others elaborate mythological scenes.

Also fascinating are the displays in the Iranian Hall, which contains many limestone sculptures and reliefs from the Oriental Institute excavations at Persepolis, the capital of the Persian Empire under Darius and Xerxes. The colossal head of a bull was part of an architectural element in the Hundred-Column Hall, which functioned as the throne room of the palace.

In all of the galleries, intermingled with works of tremendous aesthetic quality, are simple everyday objects—the basic finds of archaeological exploration—that perhaps tell us the most about the life of ancient Near Eastern peoples. To our benefit, the Oriental Institute demonstrates a welcome marriage of art and scientific research.

THE TOLEDO MUSEUM OF ART
2445 MONROE STREET AT SCOTTWOOD AVENUE,
TOLEDO, OH 43697. Tel: (419) 255-8000
Hours: Tues–Sat 9 am–5 pm, Sun 1–5 pm, closed Mon and national holidays.
Admission: Free.
Publications: Book, exhibition catalogues and periodicals include:
   "Art of Egypt, Part 1", *Museum News*. 1971, $1.
   A Guide to the Collection. 1976, $3.95.
Reproductions: Prints, posters, postcards and slides from the collection and special exhibitions.
Research: Glass Study Room, Print Study Room, Art Reference library open to public; museum affiliates and visiting scholars may borrow.

Behind the Ionic colonnades of this low, elegant neoclassical building is a fine sampling of works from various ancient cultures and one of the best comprehensive glass collections, ancient to modern, in the United States. The design of the building creates the right atmosphere for the presentation of objects from the past. The principal gallery for the ancient material is a large skylit room with its roof supported by four Doric columns. Through the double doors on one side, visitors can look into a circular concert hall, designed in the manner of a Hellenistic open-air theatre.

Near Eastern, Egyptian and Greek and Roman works are displayed within the single gallery and can be examined at leisure in half an hour or so. Noteworthy among the pieces from earlier cultures are a XIXth Dynasty limestone relief from Egypt of the royal scribe Amenhotep and his wife, three granite statues of the Egyptian lion-headed goddess Sekhmet from Karnak, and a third millennium B.C. alabaster head of a woman from the Sumerian city of Khafaje near Baghdad, Iraq. A selection of Greek vases, ranging over a thousand years from the Mycenaean to the Hellenistic period, fill central glass cases. The statue of a young athlete, which stands in the center of the room, is a rare surviving example of sculpture in bronze from the Classical era. The museum continues to add to its ancient collection; the very fine Roman marble heads of Venus and the Emperor Lucius Verus were acquired during the 1970s. Children will enjoy the Roman dress military helmet of silver with gilt ornament, and lovers of jewelry the exotic second-century A.D. limestone relief of the lady Ummabi from the caravan city of Palmyra in Syria.

Its wealth in early glass, however, is what transforms this ancient collection from the pleasant to the outstanding. Toledo was a glass-making town, and it was glass money provided by Edward Drummond Libbey that built the museum and purchased the vast collection in this medium. At the back of the ancient art gallery is the entrance to the attractive museum-within-a-museum that houses thousands of fragile objects, from the first Egyptian and Near Eastern core-formed vessels to modern art glass. Most nonspecialists will be astounded to discover the variety of glass-handling techniques already in use in the Roman period and by the beauty of the decorative and utilitarian objects they produced. Glass was formed into pendants for jewelry, blown into head-shaped molds for flasks, used to encase gold-leaf pictures of early Christian saints and engraved with mythological scenes.

VIRGINIA MUSEUM OF FINE ARTS

BOULEVARD AND GROVE AVENUE, RICHMOND, VA 23221.
Tel: (804) 257-0844
Hours: Tues–Sat 11 am–5 pm, Sun 1–5 pm, closed Mon.
Admission: Suggested contribution $1, free to members, senior citizens, students.
Publications:

> Marit Jentoft-Nilsen, *Ancient Portraiture: The Sculptor's Art in Coins and Marble.* 1980, $3.50.
> Margaret Ellen Mayo, *The Art of South Italy: Vases from Magna Graecia.* 1982, $24.50.
> Helen Scott Townsend Reed. *Ancient Art in The Virginia Museum.* 1973, $10.95.

Reproductions: Posters, prints, postcards and slides from the collection and special exhibitions.
Research: Reference library open to public Mon–Fri 9 am–5 pm. Major strengths are decorative arts throughout the world, and oriental collections.

In the not-too-deep South, the Virginia Museum in Richmond provides a lovely setting for a recently gathered but well-diversified collection of ancient art. There has been an attempt to purchase representative pieces in all media from Near Eastern, Egyptian and Classical art. The results are attractively displayed in galleries clustered around the tranquil Mediterranean Court, with a central pool and supporting Doric columns.

The dramatically lit Egyptian section has a good selection of freestanding and relief sculpture. A limestone False Door Stele from the Old Kingdom tomb of Princess Inti reflects an interesting funerary practice; it was thought that the spirits of the dead were able to penetrate these nonopening portals in their passage to the next world. In certain cases, animals also

Unknown, Roman.
Caligula,
Marble, 1st century A.D.

shared in the life beyond; the museum owns a group of figural coffins for their small mummies. One example in gilded wood and bronze was intended to hold the body of a sacred ibis, the bird associated with Thoth.

Virginia is fortunate to have several excellent pieces from the Mediterranean Bronze Age. Created circa 2300 B.C., the Cycladic *Seated Harp Player* of marble is a small masterpiece of early sculpture. The composition is more complex than the usual Cycladic figures clutching the midriff, yet the artist has caught the essence of the little musician with only a few smooth curves. Later—circa 1500 B.C.—and far "busier" in design is the gold Mycenaean disk with a central rosette surrounded by snaky threads.

In the Hellenistic period, gold was used to form the wreaths and sprays of grain deposited in tombs of the wealthy. The shining ears of wheat on display are remarkable for their successful imitation of nature. Light also reflects off the lustrous red and black gloss of well-fired Attic vases. On obverse and reverse, a black-figure amphora attributed to the Swing Painter features groups of horses. One side shows an interesting frontal perspective on a quadriga, while on the other two animals fight over a fallen companion.

From the first century A.D. comes the museum's fine statue of the notorious Emperor Caligula, looking deceptively nice in his flowing toga. In fact, this emperor's reputation was so bad that his images were systematically destroyed after his death, which makes the survival of this full-length portrait even more exceptional.

The bronze figure of a wind-blown Lar, or traditional Roman household god, is typical of the stylistic classicism that prevailed in the Augustan period. By the third century A.D., many foreign religions, including Christianity, competed for followers in the Empire. One of the most popular was the worship of the Persian god Mithras, whose central cult scene is depicted on a relief in the museum. On the panel, the god sacrifices a bull, whose blood will bring fertility to the earth.

THE WALTERS ART GALLERY
600 NORTH CHARLES STREET, BALTIMORE, MD 21201.
Tel: (301) 547-9000

Hours: Tues–Sun 11 am–5 pm, closed Mon, Thanksgiving, Christmas eve and day, New Year's, July 4th.
Admission: $2 adults, $1 senior citizens and students, free to children under 18 and members; free on Wednesdays.
Publications:
Jeanny Vorys Canby, *The Ancient Near East in The Walters Art Gallery.* 1974, $4.
Dorothy Kent Hill, *Greek and Roman Metalware.* 1976, $3.50.
Reproductions: Prints, posters, postcards and reproductions from the collection.
Research: Reference library open to public by appointment.

The Walters Art Gallery is a fine example of a peculiarly American type of personal museum, whose collections are based upon the taste and fortunes of a single individual or family. Begun by William T. Walters, a nineteenth-century railroad magnate, the collections were expanded by his son Henry, who branched off into new areas of acquisitions. The ancient art is now on view in stunning new galleries that have been justly applauded for their marvelous use of direct and indirect lighting to set off objects.

In 1899 Henry Walters began to buy classical antiquities to round out his father's acquisitions. By 1902, he had become a major owner of ancient art through his purchase of the entire collection of Don Marcello Massarenti, a priest serving at the Vatican. The group included marble sculptures, small bronzes and terracotta figurines, but, most important, there was a series of seven magnificent Roman sarcophagi of the late second and early third centuries A.D., which are among the best-known pieces in the Walters today.

Excavated in 1885 from the burial chambers of a noble Roman family, three of the sarcophagi depict scenes from the life of the god Dionysos, whose cult had become entwined with classical beliefs about the afterlife and immortality. One shows vignettes from the god's childhood, another his Asiatic Triumph surrounded by uninhibited followers, and a third Dionysos's encounter with his future bride, Ariadne. In the skillful hands of certain Roman workshops, these utilitarian items were embellished with reliefs sculpted with the greatest artistry, foreshadowing the funerary commissions of the Middle Ages and the Renaissance.

The Massarenti Collection also included Etruscan objects from Praeneste in Italy, among them cylindrical bronze *cistae*. These toiletry boxes, like the bronze mirrors with which they must have been used, are covered with finely engraved episodes from the lives of classical deities. In 1910, Walters acquired an unusual Etruscan casket of the seventh century B.C., carved from a single section of ivory tusk. The body of the object is decorated with bands of animals, a chariot procession and mythological scenes in the Orientalizing style; the lid is crowned by a striding winged sphinx. Later research revealed that the casket had originally come from the famous Regolini-Galassi Tomb at Caere in Etruria, most of whose contents are in the Vatican Museum.

Henry Walters was fond of small, exquisitely crafted things, particularly Greco-Roman bronzes. This accounts for the museum's profusion of outstanding examples. The earliest are very spare in design, such as the eighth-century B.C. seated man from the Greek Geometric period. Later examples are more suave and polished; a Celtic Jupiter stands beneath a mysterious emblem of what appear to be radiate croquet mallets. Walters was also attracted by Greek and Greco-Persian gems used as seals in ancient times. The detail of the engraving on these tiny semi-precious stones is wondrous.

In the area of major Classical sculpture, the Walters has a lovely marble statue of a young satyr, rhythmically curving to balance his hipshot stance. The work is a Roman copy, but the lost bronze original is attributed to Praxiteles, a style-setting sculptor of the fourth century B.C. In addition, the museum possesses a large collection of Egyptian sculpture, both large and small, in stone, wood and bronze.

It is impossible to leave the Walters without considering briefly their holdings in Early Christian art. The "Rubens Vase," carved from a single luminous piece of honey-colored agate, has been dated to around 400 A.D. The vase utilizes classical style and designs that lingered into the Late Antique period. A deeply undercut grape-leaf motif stands out above the body polished to porcelain thinness; there are horned satyrs' heads on the shoulders. Although it passed through the hands of many wealthy and famous individuals, its ownership by Peter Paul Rubens has given the vase its permanent appellation.

Turning from the worldly to the sacred, the Hamah Treasure of twenty-two silver liturgical objects was found near Antioch in Syria. The complete altar service includes chalices, candlesticks, plates, and crosses; inscriptions on the pieces indicate that they were presented by a single family to a church dedicated to the Eastern saints Sergius and Bacchus in the sixth century A.D.

Unknown, Roman.
Procession of Bacchus to India,
(detail) Marble, 2nd century A.D.

CHAPTER THREE

ASIAN ART

by
CAROL BIER

THE ART INSTITUTE OF CHICAGO
MICHIGAN AVENUE AT ADAMS STREET, CHICAGO, IL 60603.
Tel: (312) 443-3600
Hours: Mon–Wed 10:30 am–4:30 pm, Thurs 10:30 am–8 pm, Fri 10:30 am–4:30 pm, Sat 10:30 am–5 pm, Sun and holidays 12–5 pm, closed Christmas.
Admission: Discretionary. Suggested contribution $4 adults, $2 children, senior citizens, students, free to children under 6; free Thursdays.
Publications:
John Maxon, *The Art Institute of Chicago.* 1970, 1977, $6.95.
Everett & Anne McNear, *Persian and Indian Miniatures from the McNear Collection.* 1974, $5.
Reproductions: Selection of posters, postcards, prints and slides from selected exhibitions.
Research: Library open to museum affiliates, visiting scholars and curators. Collection is strong in history of art and architecture.

Recent renovation and reinstallation of the Asian art galleries at the Art Institute of Chicago permit frequent changes in exhibitions drawn from the permanent collections. Individual galleries are devoted to the display of particular arts, such as the Clarence Buckingham Gallery of Japanese prints. The Ryerson Collection of Chinese and Japanese books is a rare resource, and an exceptional collection of Chinese and Indian jades ranges from the Sung (A.D. 960–1279) and Ming (A.D. 1368–1644) dynasties to the finely carved translucent products of seventeenth-century Mughal India.

There are also specialized collections of Chinese bronzes, Korean painting and a choice selection of silver jewelry from Bhutan, India and Tibet. Exquisite Persian and Indian miniatures show exceptionally fine brushwork, used to express the most minute details of intricate narrative scenes illustrating literary and historical works.

Among the arts of South Asia, there is an unusual collection of terra cottas from Sri Lanka, dating from prehistoric times to the twelfth century A.D.

Rotating displays from the permanent collections are designed to bring out particular aspects of the arts of Asia and are often specifically focused. One recent exhibition, for example, compared impressions and variations to

Unknown, Nepalese.
Krishna's Marriage to Kalinda,
Colors on paper, ca. 1770-1800

show subtle color changes, redrawings and afterthoughts that went into the production of Japanese prints.

ASIAN ART MUSEUM OF SAN FRANCISCO, THE AVERY BRUNDAGE COLLECTION

GOLDEN GATE PARK, SAN FRANCISCO, CA 94118.
Tel: (415) 558-2993.
Hours: Sun–Sat 10 am–5 pm, closed Christmas.
Admission: $2 adult, $.50 senior citizens, children 5–17; free first Wednesday each month.
Publications:
> Rene-Yvon Lefebvre d'Argente, *Bronze Vessels of Ancient China in The Avery Brundage Collection.* 1977, $10.
> ———, *Chinese Jades in The Avery Brundage Collection.* 1977, $10.
> ———, *Chinese, Korean, and Japanese Sculpture in The Avery Brundage Collection.* 1974, $65.

Reproductions: Limited selection of postcards.
Research: Reference library open to public Mon–Fri 1–4:30 pm.

The Asian Art Museum of San Francisco is formed around the extensive collection of Asian art donated to the city of San Francisco by the late Avery Brundage, Olympic champion and for many years president of the International Olympic Committee. His frequent travels to the Far East inspired him to collect the arts of India, Cambodia, Thailand, Burma, Tibet, Nepal, Iran, China, Japan and Korea. Over the years, he acquired paintings and sculpture, as well as bronzes, ceramics and lacquerware. He wanted his collection, which soon amounted to more than 10,000 works of art spanning 6,000 years of Asian history, to serve as a bridge of knowledge between East and West.

Roughly half the collection is Chinese, which is reflected in the layout and arrangement of the exhibition space in the museum. The first-floor galleries are devoted to the arts of China and are arranged chronologically. The second floor has its galleries arranged geographically to represent the arts of Iran, Korea, Japan, India, Southeast Asia and the Himalayan regions. Floor-to-ceiling windows on each floor look out over the Japanese tea garden in Golden Gate park—a perspective that complements the art.

Unknown, Japanese.
Fudō Myō-ō,
Ink/colors/gold on silk, 13 c. A.D.

Objects within each gallery are grouped together aesthetically and effectively to convey stylistic unity in any one period. The visitor may thus encounter the juxtaposition of a moody dark painting of a Buddha on silk hung behind a gleaming bronze statue of a seated Buddha executed in a similar style.

THE BROOKLYN MUSEUM

EASTERN PARKWAY, BROOKLYN, NY 11238. Tel: (212) 638-5000.
Hours: Wed–Sat 10 am–5 pm, Sun 12–5 pm, holidays 1–5 pm, closed Mon–Tues.
Admission: Suggested contribution $2 adults, $1 students; free to children under 12 and senior citizens.
Publications:
    Lois Katz, *Asian Art.* nd, $3.95.
    Robert Moes, *The Brooklyn Museum: Japanese Ceramics.* nd, $5.
    Hisao Sugahara, *Japanese Ink Painting and Calligraphy.* nd, $4.50.
Reproductions: Numerous posters, prints, postcards and slides from the collection and special exhibitions.
Research: Art reference library open to those with specific need by appointment.

The Brooklyn Museum deserves brief mention for an especially good collection of modern Japanese ceramics and prints that complements historical developments in these media, also well represented in the collections. One of the finest collections in the United States of the Qajar art of Iran, includes several nineteenth-century oil paintings on canvas, and lavishly decorated lacquerware objects, both categories of Iranian art that represent a synthesis of Oriental and Occidental traditions.

CINCINNATI ART MUSEUM

EDEN PARK, CINCINNATI, OH 45202. Tel: (513) 721-5204.
Hours: Tues–Sat 10 am–5 pm, Sun 1–5 pm, closed Mon and holidays.
Admission: $2 adults, $1 senior citizens, children 12–18, $.25 children 3–11, free on Saturdays.
Publications: None.
Reproductions: Posters, prints, postcards and slides from the collection and special exhibitions.
Research: Reference library open to museum members, students, visitors; Circulating library open to museum affiliates. Strong in Oriental prints, Persian art and carpets.

The holdings of Asian art in the Cincinnati Art Museum concentrate on high points of Asian civilizations. Several gorgeous ritual bronzes of the Shang Dynasty, for example, are characterized by their highly stylized designs, and there is fine Buddhist sculpture, elegantly carved in stone and painted, dating from the greatest period of Buddhist expansion in China in the sixth century A.D. From the height of Chinese painting in the fourteenth century come several exquisite paintings of the Yüan Dynasty. Related contemporary and later works of art from Iran are also displayed, including beautiful samples of calligraphy and ceramics that illustrate different techniques of underglaze and overglaze painting from the height of production in the twelfth through thirteenth centuries. These are complemented by other works of art from the Islamic world and antecedents in Southwest Asia, comprising one of the major collections of ancient Near Eastern art in the United States.

THE CLEVELAND MUSEUM OF ART

11150 BOULEVARD AT UNIVERSITY CIRCLE,
CLEVELAND, OH 44160. Tel: (216) 421-7340.
Hours: Tues, Thurs, Fri, 10 am–6 pm, Wed 10 am–10 pm, Sat 9 am–5 pm, Sun 1–6 pm; closed Mon, Thanksgiving, Christmas, New Year's, July 4th.
Admission: Free.
Publications:
Pramod Chandra, *Tuti-Nama: (Tales of a Parrot)*. 1976, $30.
Joellen DeOreo, Marjorie Williams, *Introduction to the Arts of Korea*. nd, $.25.
Sherman E. Lee et al., *Eight Dynasties of Chinese Painting*. 1981, $30.
Sherman E. Lee, *Japanese Decorative Style*. 1961, $5.95.
Marjorie Williams, *Escape from the Dusty World: Chinese Painting*. 1981, $4.
Reproductions: Posters, prints, postcards and slides from the collection and special exhibitions.
Research: Reference library open to members, visiting curators, faculty and graduate students with identification.

The arts of Asia at the Cleveland Museum of Art form a collection of international importance, particularly in the areas of Chinese painting, Indian and southeast Asian sculpture, and the arts of Islam.

Its premier strength lies in the permanent collection of Chinese painting, which virtually documents the whole history of this major art form. Allied to intellectual history more directly than other artistic traditions, Chinese painting serves as the visual expression of philosophical currents. Painters were usually scholars as well. Dominant among the works are landscape paintings, in which the relationship of man and nature is explored.

Painters of the Northern Sung dynasty (960–1279 A.D.) came to be considered classical models for later generations of artists. Their works are characterized by muted colors of ink and ink washes on silk or paper in three standard formats: handscroll, hanging scroll and album leaf. Portrayal of atmospheric elements was important, with human activities absorbed into the *gestalt* of the natural environment. Streams and mountains as well as palaces and pavilions are frequently represented among mists and clouds.

Paintings of the later Yüan dynasty (1279–1368 A.D.) show a transition from concerns with the relaxed, classical mood to the expression of internal feeling, a transformation reflected too in developments in philosophy and politics. The work of literati at this time manifested both political and a personal awareness as well as ideals of natural harmony. Painting assumed an important role in the visual expression of ideas. Zhao Meng-fu (1254–1322) is thought to be one of the greatest artists of this period. His painting of a "Bamboo, Rocks and Lonely Orchids", exemplifies the more personal attitudes expressed in Yüan painting. His careful brushstrokes evoke classical tradition, but personal expression is evident in his reductive choice of natural scenery.

Somewhat later, Wu Pin (ca. 1568–1626) was a central figure active in the revival of monumental landscape painting in the style of earlier painters of the classical era. His work and that of his contemporaries was also influenced by the social and political turmoil of late Ming times, wrought in part by the conquest of China by the Manchus and in part by the influx of Western ideas introduced by the Jesuits. Painting in China in the seventeenth century thus exhibits a classicizing tendency in which the works of old masters were studied in an effort to renew underlying principles of composition and philosophy. Modern influences are obvious, in the naturalism with which hills, streams, mountains and rivers, are rendered.

But the museum is not strong in Chinese painting alone. The Textile Department has had an unusually active history, developing one of the most important collections of ancient and medieval textiles in the world. This interest is based upon the recognition of the major importance of the textile arts in the development of decorative styles in all media in the East as well as in the West. In some ways the textile industry may be considered the major industry of the preindustrial age, and the extent and variety of the textile collections here bear witness to this fact.

Sculpture from India and Southeast Asia comprise other areas of the arts of Asia particularly well developed at the Cleveland Museum. Early Buddist sculpture from Gandhara shows the influence of Greek and Roman figural traditions, especially in the rendering of drapery folds, but native Indian traditions still shine forth in the iconographic distinguishing details, and in the figural styles of Mathura and Amaravati. With the refined elegance of sculpture from the Gupta period, Indian art reached its classical phase, the infuence of which dominates the development of religious art in other parts

Mughal School, Indian.
Tuti-nama (Tales of a Parrot),
Ink/color/gold on paper, ca. 1560

of Asia, all of which are represented in this superb collection. A statue of Krishna Govardhana from Cambodia in the first half of the sixth century, for example, illustrates the early synthesis of Indian and Cambodian styles. Bronze images of the Hindu gods are also borne of this classical tradition; their influence may be traced in the arts of India and surrounding regions to the north and east. The strength of the collection of Southeast Asian art from the sixth to thirteenth centuries allows a rare opportunity to observe development of sculptural styles associated with religious architectures.

From later periods of Indian art come the famous manuscript illustrations which accompanied literary and historical works of the Mughal dynasty. Of particular importance is the almost complete manuscript of the "Tuti-nama" or "Tales of a Parrot," which is replete with 211 extraordinary minatures painted with ink and gold on paper during the reign of the emperor Akbar around 1560 A.D. Other works of the sixteenth and seventeenth centuries are well represented in the collection, including several attributed to Basawan.

Islamic art at Cleveland has also received international acclaim. The finely crafted brass objects inlaid with silver, produced by Muslim craftsmen in the thirteenth to fifteenth centuries, strongly influenced subsequent European production. A large prayer niche from a sixteenth-century monument in Isfahan, Iran, decorated in ceramic tile mosaic, exemplifies the combined use of Arabic calligraphy, floral ornament and geometric pattern that is so characteristic of religious art throughout the Islamic world.

Japanese art is represented by several examples of early ceramic sculpture as well as more monumental wood sculptures from the classical, Heian period and later. Of special interest are a few portraits carved at a time when naturalism was first attempted in Japan, in arts of the Kamakura period (twelfth and thirteenth centuries). Hanging scrolls and handscrolls as well as six-fold screens reveal Japanese interest in seasonal landscapes and figural narrative. And major artists of the Ukiyo-e school of the Edo period are also represented by their paintings and woodblock prints.

DENVER ART MUSEUM
100 WEST 14TH AVENUE PARKWAY, DENVER, CO 80204.
Tel: (303) 575-2793.

Hours: Tues–Sat 10 am–4:30 pm, Wed 10 am–8 pm, Sun 1–5 pm, closed Mondays.
Admission: Suggested contribution $2.50 adults, $1.50 students and senior citizens; free to children under 12 and members.
Publications:
  Guide to the Denver Art Museum. 1982, $6.50.
Reproductions: Selected prints, slides and postcards.
Research: Library facilities open to those who make prior arrangements with curatorial department.

———————————

Especially renowned for its arts of the Edo period, the museum has a long handscroll depicting the procession of a Japanese lord escorting a Korean envoy in 1711 and woodblock prints by Isoda Koryusai and Ando Hiroshige, two of the most important Japanese woodblock artists of the nineteenth century. Established traditions of Japanese art are complemented by excellent holdings of modern painting and ceramics.

The arts of other areas are also on view. Carved relief sculpture and statuary from Hindu temples include guardian figures as well as deities of the Hindu pantheon such as Vishnu, Shiva and Parvati. And an early standing Buddha dating from the second to third century A.D. represents religious art of the Kushan Dynasty, while a stone head of Shiva exemplifies Cambodian sculpture of the twelfth century. One section of a mural painting executed in ink and color on plaster dates from the Ming Dynasty and depicts Buddhist celestial beings, *apsarases,* among the clouds. Important works introducing the art of the Ancient Near East and Islamic lands are also represented.

THE DETROIT INSTITUTE OF ARTS
5200 WOODWARD AVENUE, DETROIT, MI 48202. Tel: (313) 833-7900.
Hours: Tues–Sun 9:30 am–5:30 pm, closed Mon, Christmas, New Year's.
Admission: Suggested contribution; fee for some special exhibitions.
Publications: None.
Reproductions: Good selection of posters and postcards, mainly of the collection.
Research: Research library open to public Mon–Fri 9 am–5 pm. The 75,000 volumes emphasize European art history.

———————————

The Detroit Institute has a fully computerized catalogue system, but personal attention is very evident on the part of curators for the exhibition of objects in their care. The arts of Asia are a major component of the Detroit collections and consist of works produced in China, Japan, India, Iran and the Near East. Materials are displayed carefully to bring out visual relationships that might not otherwise be apparent, relating, for example, a pattern enameled on Mamluk glass to a similar design executed in silk embroidery.

Several items in the collection are outstanding. An extraordinary Kamakura painting in ink and watercolor, for example, depicts Buddha of the Western Paradise. Amida Buddha is enthroned, surrounded by Bodhisattvas and other divine and semi-divine beings; scenes from the life of the Buddha, in the borders, are outlined with tiny flakes of gold leaf.

The *Tale of Genji,* a Japanese novel written by a woman in the eleventh century, inspired for centuries literary and aesthetic tastes at the imperial court and provided subjects popularly illustrated. Scenes from its narrative are shown on three hanging scrolls painted in the early Edo period that bear the seal of Taketsugu, who was active in the middle of the seventeenth century. There is also an excellent selection of eighteenth- and nineteenth-century Iranian art, preserving a synthesis of Islamic and pre-Islamic traditions.

FREER GALLERY OF ART
SMITHSONIAN INSTITUTION
NATIONAL MALL AT JEFFERSON DRIVE AND 12TH STREET, SW, WASHINGTON, DC 20560. Tel: (202) 357-2104.
Hours: Sun–Sat 10 am–5:30 pm, closed Christmas.
Admission: Free.
Publications:
> Esin Atil, *Art of the Arab World.* 1975, $20.
> *The Freer Gallery of Art, Vol I: China.* 1971, 1981, $30.
> *Vol II: Japan.* 1972, 1981, $30.
> *Masterpieces of Chinese and Japanese Art - Freer Gallery of Art Handbook.* 1976, $5.
> John A. Pope et al., *The Freer Chinese Bronzes, Vol I.* 1967, $45.
> Rutherford J. Gettens, *The Freer Chinese Bronzes, Vol II.* 1969, $30.

Reproductions: Prints, posters, postcards and slides from the collection and special exhibitions.
Research: Open to public weekdays 10 am–4:30 pm; comprehensive Oriental collection, half the books in Oriental languages.

The Freer Gallery of Art is devoted mainly to the arts of Asia. One of the finest collections of Oriental art in the world, it also has an important group of American works from the late nineteenth and early-twentieth centuries. Its collections of ancient bronzes and jade, Buddhist sculpture, Chinese painting, Japanese paper screens and Islamic art are of world renown.

The core of the collection was acquired by Detroit industrialist Charles Lang Freer, whose interest in Asian art was inspired by his close friendship with the American painter James McNeill Whistler.

Currently 15 galleries are devoted to changing exhibitions of the arts of Asia. An additional three galleries are for American paintings, and one holds the permanent installation of the Peacock Room, originally the dining room of Frederick Leyland, which was designed by Whistler to properly accommodate his painting of "The Princess from the Land of Porcelain" that hangs over the fireplace. The dual legacy—and mutual influence—of Asian art and American art is a unique strength of the collections at the Freer.

At the Freer Gallery of Art, exhibitions are drawn exclusively from its own reserves. These are supplemented by annual evening lecture series, which are free and open to the public, and an active program of publications concerning materials in the collection. Tours by specially trained museum docents are offered several times daily free of charge. In addition there are very popular tours of the Freer's collections and laboratories arranged through Smithsonian Associates' programs.

Perhaps most familiar to the viewing public are the Japanese folding paper screens of the Rimpa school, whose gilded designs with cranes and irises have often been reproduced. In this unique form of Japanese painting, the Freer has works by several masters, especially Sotatsu and Korin, both of whom developed distinctive styles in the seventeenth century. Evolving out of earlier traditions of screen painting in the Muromachi period (1392–1568) and the Momoyama period (1568–1614), artists of the Rimpa school drew upon the familiar literary subjects, genre scenes and seasonal views of nature, but treated these in a more personal manner, with particular attention to form, rhythm and graphic design.

Another well-known area within the collections comprises ancient Chinese bronzes of the Shang and Chou dynasties, which exhibit in their form and decoration the extraordinary ad-

Muhammad Sadiq
Shah Jahan,
Ink/color/gold on paper, 1751 A.D.

vancements in metallurgical techniques during the second millenium B.C. The variety of shapes represents different ritual and ceremonial uses, while the repertory of motifs and their arrangement evince a highly sophisticated sense of aesthetics.

Of later periods among the arts of China, the Freer has a good selection of Chinese painting and calligraphy, including several early surviving examples of paintings on silk attributed to the Sung dynasty (960–1279) which show new styles of brushstroke used to depict landscapes and figural subjects. Works from the Yüan dynasty (1279–1368) are also represented, as well as hanging scrolls, handscrolls and album paintings by artists of the Ming and Ching dynasties.

Buddhist art at the Freer is represented by Indian stone sculpture from Gandhara and Mathura, and later sculpture from Central Asia and China, which is dependent on its Indian antecedents for both style and iconography. Recent acquisitions of sculpture from southeast Asia illustrate the seminal significance of Indian art in the stylistic development of Buddhist art there too. Hindu art also developed from its Indian origins, and images of deities from the Hindu pantheon similarly incorporate an artistic indebtedness, as illustrated by bronze sculpture from India and elsewhere.

Indian book illustrations from the Mughal court and earlier Muslim dynasties show the richness of the miniature tradition, the later paintings reflecting a shared heritage of Indian, Persian and European styles. The

Mughal imperial albums demonstrate a wealth of royal imagery and a concern for dynastic history, along with a strong interest in naturalism in the rendering of botanical and zoological subjects. The extraordinary collection of manuscripts and miniatures produced on the Indian subcontinent also includes several major works from the Rajput school, which was prolific in the eighteenth century.

The Freer's collection of Islamic art is considered to be one of the finest in North America. In addition to paintings from the Mughal court and other artistic centers in India, there is an excellent selection of Persian literary and historical works opulently illustrated with miniature paintings of the highest quality. Drawings and paintings from the Ottoman court in Istanbul are also represented. Other categories of Islamic art which merit international distinction include enameled and gilded glass vessels of the Mamluk period in the thirteenth and fourteenth centuries, and a series of brasses inlaid with silver intricately decorated with complex figural scenes. Surprisingly, one of these depicts scenes from the life of Christ; it was probably produced for a Christian patron.

The exquisite design, layout and arrangement of the magnificent collections of Asian art at the Freer remain unsurpassed. And masterpieces among the collections provide an insight into the patterns of collecting in nineteenth century America, in which Charles Lang Freer played such a paramount role. It is within his collections and their subsequent development as a national museum that one has the rare chance to observe the interdependence of eastern and western artistic traditions that affected American art at that time, as well as the growth of art museums and Asian art collections in America.

ISABELLA STEWART GARDNER MUSEUM

280 THE FENWAY, BOSTON, MA 02115. Tel: (617) 566-1401.
Hours: Tues 12–9 pm (July–August 12–5 pm), Wed–Sun 12–5 pm, closed Mon and national holidays.
Admission: Suggested contribution $2.
Publications:
 Oriental and Islamic Art in the Isabella Stewart Gardner Museum. 1975, np.
Reproductions: Posters, prints, postcards and slides of the collection.
Research: Reference library for staff use.

Oriental art at the Isabella Stewart Gardner Museum comprises only a portion of the highly eclectic collection exhibited in what was once Mrs. Gardner's residence at Fenway Court. Art provides the extraordinary interior decor that reflects the very personal style and taste of Mrs. Gardner, who through the display of her collection sought to engage her visitors directly in an aesthetic experience. The erratic arrangement of works of art of diverse origins and different periods in a seemingly haphazard way illustrates Mrs. Gardner's theory that objects may often be better appreciated out of their original historical context.

Although this method at times precludes a careful examination of the narrative scenes on Japanese painted paper screens or observations of the carved details of Chinese relief sculpture, the presence of so many fine works of art crowded together indeed conveys a sense of wonder and demands appreciation on many levels.

The Gardners began collecting art on their trip around the world in 1883–84 and later continued to make purchases on the advice of friends. Nearly all major periods of Chinese art are represented in the collection, including a *ku* ritual wine vessel of the Shang Dynasty, a limestone votive stele dated 543 A.D. and giving the names of its donors, a Kuan-Yin sculpture of the twelfth century, and several examples of early Ming painting. The arts of Japan are highlighted by narrative illustrations from the *Tale of Genji* on screens and doors of the Momoyama and early Tokugawa periods, and the arts of Islam include several miniature paintings, ceramics, metalwork and fragments of architectural decoration.

Unknown, Chinese.
Votive Stele,
Stone, Wei Dynasty 543 A.D.

KIMBELL ART MUSEUM

3333 CAMP BOWIE BOULEVARD, FORT WORTH, TX 76107.
Tel: (817) 332-8451

Hours: Tues–Sat 10 am–5 pm, Sun 1–5 pm, closed Mon, Thanksgiving, Christmas, New Year's, July 4th.
Admission: Free.
Publications:

> *Arts of the Islamic Books: The Collection of Prince Sadruddin Aga Khan.* 1982, $24.95.
> Richard F. Brown, *Kimbell Art Museum Catalogue of the Collection.* 1972, $25.
> *Great Age of Japanese Buddhist Sculpture:* A.D. *600–1300.* 1982, $24.95.
> David M. Robb, Jr., *Kimbell Art Museum: Handbook of the Collection.* 1981, $9.75.
> *Ways to Shiva.* 1980, $4.95.

Reproductions: Posters, prints, postcards and slides from the collection and special exhibitions.
Research: Reference library open to teachers and scholars by appointment.

The Kimbell Art Museum in Fort Worth is one of the newest additions to the list of museums with major importance for the enjoyment of Asian art. In

Unknown, Indian.
Head of a Jina,
Sandstone, 11th century A.D.

spite of its youth (the tenth anniversary of its foundation was celebrated in 1982), the Kimbell has established a high profile in the field, having organized and hosted a major international traveling exhibition of Japanese Buddhist sculpture, much of it on loan from Japanese temples. The new curator of East Asian art is to be complimented for her international pursuits and for offering such a rewarding opportunity to the public.

The museum has established an active schedule with regular involvement and participation in loan exhibitions. Along with other art museums in the state of Texas (the Houston Museum of Fine Arts and the Dallas Museum of Fine Arts), it is progressively improving its holdings in the arts of Asia. It already has a noteworthy collection acquired in a relatively short period of time, including Gandharan Buddhist sculpture, a standing female deity from Rajasthan in the tenth to eleventh centuries, and Jain religious sculpture as well as pottery, prints and painting from Japan. Of particular interest is a pair of six-fold screens *(namban byōbu)* from the turn of the seventeenth century depicting the arrival of Europeans in Japan.

LOS ANGELES COUNTY MUSEUM OF ART

5905 WILSHIRE BOULEVARD, LOS ANGELES, CA 90036.
Tel: (213) 937-2590
Hours: Tues–Fri 10 am–5 pm, Sat–Sun 10 am–6 pm, closed Mon, Thanksgiving, Christmas, New Year's.
Admission: $1.50 adults, $.75 students, senior citizens, children 5–17; free on second Tuesday each month.
Publications:
  Bizarre Imagery of Yoshitoshi. 1980, $12.50.
  Elephants and Ivories in South Asia. 1981, $10.
  Far Eastern Lacquer. 1982, $15.95.
  Islamic Art from the Nasli and Alice Heeramaneck Collection. 1973, $7.50.
Reproductions: Selection of slides and photographic posters of objects in the collection.
Research: Reference library available for scholarly research; open by appointment.

Asian art at the Los Angeles County Museum of Art is particularly strong in Indian sculpture, much of it from the collection of Nasli and Alice Heeramaneck purchased for the museum by Joan Palevsky. Early Buddhist art is represented by several stone sculptures from Sanchi, Mathura and the Gandharan regions. An excellent collection of carved architectural reliefs from Gandhara exhibits a synthesis of Indian Buddhist and Greco-Roman traditions that were introduced into India first with the conquests of Alexander the Great. Stone and bronze sculpture link these early arts to those of later periods, preserving stylized images of deities throughout the ages. Shiva and the dancing lord Krishna are depicted among the works of north and south India, and from Rajasthan in the eleventh century. Later Mughal and Rajput paintings portray royal images and literary and historical texts, which blend Indian art with neighboring artistic developments. Brightly patterned textiles and costumes add color and the glitter of gold, while iconic images, mandalas and tankas offer their somber presence. The arts of Tibet and Nepal are well represented, as are those of Khmer and Java, which reveal a debt to the classic Guptan art of India.

Bichitr. (attribution)
Shah Shuja with Gaj Singh,
Opaque watercolor on paper, 1633

A fragmentary knotted pile carpet, the gift of J. Paul Getty, is a counterpart to the world-famous "Ardebil" carpet in the Victoria & Albert Museum in London. Beautiful examples of Islamic calligraphy and ceramics also derive from the Heeramaneck collection, which includes art of the ancient Near East as well.

The arts of China in the collections of the Los Angeles County Museum span over 3,000 years of a continuous artistic tradition. A large stone Kuan-Yin of the late fifth century from the Northern Wei Dynasty cave temples of Yun-kang and later sculptures of Buddhas and Bodhisattvas of the Tang Dynasty reflect the influence of Indian Buddhist art. The Buddhist art of China and the brushwork of Chinese calligraphy and painting affected the development of Japanese styles of sculpture and painting seen here.

JACQUES MARCHAIS CENTER FOR TIBETAN ART

338 LIGHTHOUSE AVENUE, STATEN ISLAND, NY 10036
Tel: (212) 987-3478
Hours: April 1–Nov. 30: Sat–Sun 1–5 pm, check for Fri hours during June–Aug; closed Dec 1–Mar 31.
Admission: $1 adults, $.50 children.
Publications: Free fact sheet.
Reproductions: None.
Research: Extensive reference library open to public on Saturday. Includes many rare books on Oriental art, especially Tibetan.

Situated on a hill in Staten Island and overlooking terraced gardens and a lotus pond above lower New York Bay, the Tibetan Museum simulates in reduced scale the Potala in Lhasa, a monastery in Tibet that served as the residence of the Dalai Lamas. Inside one of the two stone buildings, displays of Tibetan Buddhist art immerse the visitor in a ceremonial ambience. Although the collection is of uneven quality, the overall effect is mesmerizing, transcending the normal museum experience of viewing art separate from its original context. Here, the visitor senses a spiritual aura like that which must have accompanied the ritual use of the objects forming this very special collection.

Assembled by Madame Jacques Marchais, several of the objects were associated with the late Panchan Lama of North Tibet and may have been used in religious ceremonies performed by him in China. In addition, there are bronze images from shrines and temples and many brightly colored paintings of Tibetan Buddhism. The religious arts of such neighboring regions as Nepal, China, India, and Southeast Asia are also on view.

THE METROPOLITAN MUSEUM OF ART
FIFTH AVENUE AT 82ND STREET, NEW YORK, NY 10028.
Tel: (212) 535-7710
Hours: Tues 10 am–8:45 pm, Wed–Sat 10 am–4:45 pm, Sun and holidays 11 am–4:45 pm, closed Mon, Thanksgiving, Christmas, New Year's.
Admission: Suggested contribution $4 adults, $2 children and senior citizens, free to children under 12.
Publications:
 Wen Fong, *Summer Mountains: The Timeless Landscape.* 1979, $38.
 Momoyama: Japanese Art in the Age of Grandeur. 1975, $6.95.
 Alan Priest, *Chinese Sculpture in The Metropolitan Museum of Art.* 1944, $33.
Reproductions: Extensive selection of posters, prints, postcards, slides and reproductions of sculptures and other works from the collection.
Research: Library open to staff of the museum and other qualified researchers and graduate students with identification. Most comprehensive art and archaeology collection in Western Hemisphere, including 210,000 books and 1200 periodicals subscriptions. It covers all areas in which museum has holdings.

Founded in 1870, The Metropolitan Museum of Art was well on its way to greatness when it became actively involved in acquiring arts of Asia, during the early years of this century. It has long had an extensive collection of the arts of China and Japan, and very recently has been making admirable efforts to improve its holdings of Indian and southeast Asian art. As for southwestern Asia, its collections of arts of the Ancient Near East and Islamic lands are already among the finest in the world. To supplement its excellent permanent collections, the Met organizes and hosts major international loan and traveling exhibitions and has managed to attract considerable corporate support for its shimmering installations of several "blockbuster" exhibitions.

The Far Eastern galleries are imaginatively designed, presenting art within its cultural context. A map by the elevator indicates the plan and layout of the stunning and superbly arranged Astor Chinese Garden Court and the Douglas Dillon Galleries of Chinese painting. Situated around the central court, the galleries are arranged chronologically to show the development of Chinese painting and allied arts. Starting with the hall of Buddhist sculpture, one may walk clockwise around the central court through galleries with moody landscapes of the Sung dynasty (960–1279), to see the literati works of great masters of the Yüan dynasty (1279–1368), for whom the alliance of calligraphy, poetry and painting was paramount, then into the scholar's room with its finely crafted furniture and furnishings of the Ming dynasty (1368–1644), and finally through galleries featuring paintings of the Ching dynasty (1644–1911) on view with contemporary jades and eighteenth-century robes.

The paintings in the galleries surrounding the garden include some of the finest in the world. Handscrolls—hand-painted with brush, ink and colors—were meant for the few to see. The individual viewer would unroll it before him, one section at a time, exploring languorously the careful rendering of a landscape or story. The collection also has fine examples of larger hanging scrolls, mounted on silk, and of smaller fans and album paintings, all produced to beautify the court's daily environment as well as to promote philosophical and aesthetic ideals. The so-called "literati" painters of the Yüan dynasty were recognized and respected in their own time, and remembered as masters by succeeding generations. Later observers often admired these works, adding praise with a few calligraphic strokes of the brush or by stamping a seal of ownership directly on the work. The subdued lighting in the galleries enhances the natural colors, materials, fibers and textures, all of which must have delighted the original owners as they do today.

From the adjacent scholar's room with its wooden posts and beams, fretwork and doorways, one sees vistas of court and garden. In the nearby case with scholar's table are shown the tools and equipment of the scholar-painter: seals and sealing stones, pastes and inks, brushes and brush-rests, water jars and ornamental rocks on elaborately carved wooden bases, which provided inspiration for the scholar in his studio.

The Chinese garden court was built on the model of a garden in Suzhou, dating back to the Ming dynasty. Here, it was constructed by twenty workmen sent from the People's Republic of China as one of the first cooperative endeavors with an American cultural institution. They brought their own tools and materials, constructing the garden with its pavilions and irregularly shaped, pedigreed rocks according to traditional methods. The roof tiles and grey bricks laid in the pavement were fired locally in kilns near Suzhou. The garden itself serves as a metaphor of nature in harmony with the cosmos.

Elsewhere in the museum, in the Arthur M. Sackler Gallery of Chinese Sculpture, monumental works are displayed dating from the fifth and sixth centuries A.D. A fourteenth-century wall painting of Yüan dynasty shows a haloed Buddha seated cross-legged and flanked by Bodhisattvas along with divine and semi-divine beings, musicians, and attendant figures. In spite of its grand size, the carefully drawn lines define the facial expressions, drapery of the garments, and the flow of ribbons, as well as the exquisite jewelry and elaborately decorated crowns.

Clear on the other side of the museum, at its southern end, the arts of Islam are arranged chronologically and geographically. Works of the early periods are displayed in cases subtly designed to convey the strong geometric sense of composition and mathematical precision so prevalent in Islamic art. More than ten galleries are devoted to the arts of Islam, making this one of the largest permanent installations of Islamic art in the world, and one of the finest in quality. An introductory gallery presents masterpieces produced in many centers of the Islamic world, and a map introduces the visitor to key points in the origins and early history of Islam. Immediately to the left of the introductory gallery is the Nur al-Din room, an architectural gem from residential Damascus. Built at the beginning of the 18th century, its richly ornamented interior incorporates in its decor poetic inscriptions painted and gilded on wood in addition to floral arabesques on textiles and tiles. Two additional galleries present archaeological materials excavated in the 1930's of the medieval city of Nishapur in northeastern Iran.

In the other galleries of Islamic art, objects of glass, metalwork, ceramics, textiles, wood, stone and ivory are arranged sequentially following the political history of several dynasties from the time of the early conquests in the seventh century A.D. to the Umayyads, Abbasids, Fatimids, Seljuks, Mongols, Ayyubids and Mamluks. A carved and painted ceiling from Muslim Spain covers the gallery of arts of the Mamluk and Nasrid periods; at the far end of this gallery there is an alabaster arcade closely resembling those in the Alhambra. In an adjacent room, religious aspects of Islamic art are on view, with a ceramic tile *mihrab*, or prayer niche, providing a focus of attention. In other galleries Islamic miniature paintings of the highest quality are displayed in long desk-like cases with chairs thoughtfully provided so you can really appreciate the carefully painted and gilded detail of narrative scenes which served to illustrate literary and historical works.

Further along, arts of the great empires are exhibited in succeeding galleries. These include the most famous Oriental carpets, and illuminated manuscripts with miniatures from the greatest periods of court patronage and artistic development. Here the sumptuous court arts of Safavid Iran, Ottoman Turkey and Mughal India are arranged so that one gains a sense of historical continuity as well as geographic diversity within the unity of the Islamic world.

Taken together these arts of western Asia, the Indian subcontinent, and the Far East comprise one of the most comprehensive collections of Asian art in the entire world. Japanese, Korean, Indian and Southeast Asian galleries are closed for renovation in 1983, but will offer equally spectacular treasures when they reopen.

THE MINNEAPOLIS INSTITUTE OF ARTS
2400 THIRD AVENUE SOUTH, MINNEAPOLIS, MN 55404.
Tel: (612) 870-3046
Hours: Tues–Wed, Fri–Sat 10 am–5 pm, Thurs 10 am–9 pm, Sun 12–5 pm, closed

Mon and some holidays.

Admission: $2 adults, $1 students, free to senior citizens and children under 12; free Thurs 5–9 pm.

Publications:

David Gredzens, *Visions from the Top of the World: The Art of Tibet and the Himalayas.* 1983, $5.

J. Hiller, *A Catalogue of the Japanese Paintings and Prints in the Collection of Mr. & Mrs. Richard P. Gale.* 2 Vols. 1970, $50.

Robert D. Jacobsen, *The Asian Galleries.* 1982, $5.

Dr. Na Chih-liang, *Chinese Jades: Archaic and Modern.* 1977, $25.

Reproductions: Posters, prints, postcards from the collection and special exhibitions.

Research: Reference library open to public.

A city renowned for its support of the arts, Minneapolis has a long-established tradition of presenting the arts of other cultures in an educational environment. Asian art from Japan, China, Cambodia, Thailand and India is arranged to encourage the visitor to view it both aesthetically and culturally. The well-lighted galleries are laid out in a series of alcoves that permit the pursuit of more than just visual interests. Resource areas and study areas are located off to the side, and curatorial asistance is readily available for those seeking additional guidance in understanding the art. Audiovisual presentations provide introductory orientation to the materials on exhibition.

Thai and Cambodian sculpture, as well as Chinese bronzes and jades and a range of ceramics from different periods, are represented in the Pillsbury Collection. The bronzes exhibit intricate designs that awaken an appreciation of advanced technologies developed in a preindustrial age; many of them appear on ritual vessels made during the Shang Dynasty, in the late second millenium B.C.

The Richard P. Gale Collection, also housed in the museum, contains Japanese art of the Ukiyo-e School, with prints and paintings executed in muted colors and forceful lines that depict both pleasure and street life.

MUSEUM OF FINE ARTS

465 HUNTINGTON AVENUE, BOSTON, MA 02115. Tel: (617) 267-9300

Hours: Tues, Thurs–Sun 10 am–5 pm, Wed 10 am–10 pm, closed Mon, Thanksgiving, Christmas eve and day, New Year's. July 4th. West Wing only: Thurs–Fri 5–10 pm.

Admission: $3.50 adults, $2.50 adults Thurs–Fri 5–10 pm, $2.50 senior citizens, free to children under 17 and members, free Sat 10 am–12 pm.

Publications: Gallery guides, plus:

Jan Fontein, *Asiatic Art in the Museum of Fine Arts, Boston.* 1982, $18.50.

Wu Tang, *Painting in China since the Opium Wars.* 1980, $5.

Hsein-Ch'i Tseng, Robert Paul Dart, *The Charles B. Hoyt Collection in the Museum of Fine Arts, Boston:*

Volume I: Chinese Art: Neolithic Period through the T'ang Dynasty and Sino-Siberian Bronzes. 1964, $22.

Volume II: Five Dynasties, Liao Sung Yuan. 1972, $38.50.

Reproductions: Large selection of posters, postcards, prints, slides from the collection and special exhibitions.

Japanese Screen Room
Museum of Fine Arts, Boston

Research: Main library open to public; reference libraries of specific departments available to students and scholars by appointment.

Pioneered by individual connoisseurs from America and the Far East, the collections of the Boston Museum of Fine Arts have grown to comprise what has been described as the largest collection of Asian art under one roof. Twenty-six new galleries house a comprehensive array of the arts of China, Japan and Korea, the arts of the Indian subcontinent and the arts of Islam. The greatest strength lies in the area of Japanese art, for which the museum achieved early international recognition. The quality and breadth of these holdings, acquired long before most other museums had developed a strong interest in Japanese art, are still among the finest outside Japan.

The collections of Asian art in general and the care with which they are displayed evince respect and recognition on the part of the museum's sensitive directors to the original religious intent of many of these works of art. The view from the Japanese screen room, for example, to the hall of Buddhist sculptures, provides the effect of peering into a Buddhist shrine. Design and structure of the upstairs galleries allude to original architectural contexts, which impart at least an understated religious aspect for the works on view. The fiber optics lighting in the temple room is perhaps too dramatic, with carved images of Buddhas from different periods each displayed and individually illuminated in darkness. But the intent of conveying a sense of iconic significance is nonetheless achieved.

Carved Buddhist images in bronze, clay, wood and lacquer or painted on cotton or silk reveal artistic traditions as well as the development of a religion still active and alive. In Japan today, the majority of Buddhist sculpture remains in temples where they are preserved as religious icons and worshiped. The Japanese Buddhist sculptures on view here evoke their Indian origins and the incorporation of Chinese influences.

Respect for this heritage is preserved throughout the museum's Asian displays. Indian sculpture includes carved architectural elements with figural subjects that come from the important Indian sites of Amaravati, Sarnath, Bharhut, Mathura and the region of Gandhara. Together, these represent major developments in art and religion of the Buddhist and Hindu traditions, which served to influence so much of the arts across Asia, reaching northward through Nepal and Tibet into China eastward and south to Sri Lanka, Java, Burma, Thailand and Cambodia, all of which may be documented in these rich collections.

Of a secular nature from private residences are magnificent Japanese screens from the Momoyama and Muromachi periods decorated with landscapes that carry the eye across the surfaces of the folding panels. Drawn and painted delicately in ink with colors and gold on paper, the panels are framed in silk on wood and are ingeniously designed with paper hinges to fold in either direction. They are mounted on tatami mats, exhibited behind glass on a platform so they may be viewed at eye level.

An important Islamic work of art is a miniature painting illustrating a scene from the Iranian national epic, the *Shahnama.* Dating from the midfourteenth century, the painting shows Alexander the Great, according to Iranian legend, in combat with a horned monster. The style of the painting and that of other miniatures from this manuscript (now dispersed), strongly reflect Chinese influences in the rendition of landscape.

The museum's collections of Islamic and Indian painting are particularly strong; additional holdings in the fields of Chinese painting and the ancient arts of China are also noteworthy. The span and extent of the entire Asian collection is truly vast, with materials dating from the dawn of civilization excavated in the 1930s by a museum expedition to the Indus Valley to contemporary works of living craftsmen who represent the ongoing development of these artistic traditions.

THE NELSON-ATKINS MUSEUM OF ART

4525 OAK STREET, KANSAS CITY, MO 64111. Tel: (816) 561-4000

Hours: Tues–Sat 10 am–5 pm, Sun 2–6 pm, closed Mon and Nov 25th.

Admission: $1.50 adults, $.75 children 6–12, free to members, students, children under 6; free on Sundays.

Publications:

> Ross E. Taggart et al, *The Nelson Gallery of Art and Atkins Museum, Kansas City, Vol. II:* 1973, $7.50.

Reproductions: Posters, prints, postcards from the collection and special exhibitions.

Research: Reference library and reading room open to public; reference services available in person or by telephone. Emphasis of collection on Asian and Western arts: painting, sculpture, decorative.

Spanning the ancient arts of China from the neolithic period to the present, as well as the arts of Japan, Korea, Indonesia, India and southeast Asia, Iran and the ancient Near East, the Nelson-Atkins Museum has attained an excellent reputation for its collections of Asian art. Nearly half of the galleries on the second floor are devoted to exhibition of the permanent holdings in these areas. The museum shows particular strength in Chinese painting, with all major periods represented by the works of great masters. These are supplemented by materials in other media contemporary in date. The collection of Indian sculpture is also of world renown. Plans have been announced to improve holdings of Japanese art, and the museum has recently received through bequest excellent collections of Japanese painting, primarily of the seventeenth and eighteenth centuries, and Japanese ceramics from the seventeenth century to the present. Persian arts of the book are also well-represented, including exquisite miniature paintings by recognized masters including Musawwir and Muhammadi.

Islamic miniature paintings and delicate drawings from northern India and the Punjab hills, may be compared with the richly decorated, more brightly colored book illustrations painted in the southern and central regions from the fifteenth-eighteenth centuries. Several very fine paintings are folios from imperial Mughal albums.

Stone and bronze sculpture of Hindu and Buddhist images illustrate the artistic and spiritual developments of each tradition. The museum is especially strong in its collection of Hindu bronzes from south India. Early works in stone and stucco from Afghanistan and ancient Gandhara reveal artistic influences from the Graeco-Roman world which penetrated these regions after their conquest by Alexander the Great. Other sculpture shows the contrast in style between the physical sensuousness of voluptuous figures from Mathura and the Deccan, and the more highly restrained figures of the Gupta period, which came to be considered the classical style of Indian sculpture.

Unusually fine examples of Buddhist art as it developed eastwards may be seen in the stone and bronze sculpture from Java and Indonesia, which date from the eighth to ninth centuries. One head of Buddha is executed in a style similar to that of the sculpted Buddha images adorning the great temple of Borobudur. The selection of stone sculpture from Thailand and Cambodia also come mainly from religious contexts, where narrative scenes carved in reliefs formed part of the architecture of shrines and temples. One finely carved standing image of Buddha is thought to date from the beginning of the Dvaravati kingdom, which ruled in Thailand from the seventh to the eleventh centuries, before the Khmers came to power. Its elegantly carved form owes many stylistic features to the southeast Asian heritage of Classical Indian sculpture of the Gupta period. Khmer sculptures from the Cambodia of the tenth and eleventh centuries show later stylistic refinements in southeast Asian art.

Hsu Tao-ning
Yu-fu (Fishermen),
Ink/color on silk, c. 1040-1050

The museum is strongest in its Chinese collection. For Chinese painting, it is the largest collection in the United States and one of the finest in the world outside of China. In the hall of Chinese paintings, works are skillfully arranged and lighted so as to permit careful observation of the extraordinary detail and subtle effects achieved through the accomplished brushwork of Chinese masters and literati. The evolution of Chinese painting was intimately connected with philosophical concerns, poetry and social development. The height of landscape painting was reached in the Northern Sung period (960–1127). Philosophical discourse and the expression of metaphysical ideas took hold among highly educated scholar-painters, who explored the nature of the world to put man's social place in perspective. The results of their intellectual endeavors produced a class of literati painters, whose works became the classic models for succeeding generations. Among the holdings of the Nelson-Atkins Museum are works of many of the great masters of early landscape painting from the eleventh–thirteenth centuries, as well as celebrated masterpieces of later periods.

In the Chinese temple room, off the main gallery of Chinese art, a monumental wall painting (50 feet wide by 25 feet high), illustrates the Buddhist theme of Tejaprabha Buddha accompanied by the deified sun, moon and planets, with guardians and attendants. Executed around 1300 A.D., the wall painting with its subdued earth colors derives from the Kuang-sheng Ssu, in Chao-ch'eng Hsien, Shansi province. In sharp contrast to the two dimensionality of the painting, before it are placed several later Buddhist images sculpted in wood. Included among these is one monumental image of the Bodhisattva Kuan-Yin, polychromed and gilded, more directly appealing due to its bright color and languid corporeality. There are also several rare Buddhist sculptures dating from the Yüan dynasty (thirteenth–fourteenth century), which visually represent the last important phase of Buddhism in China.

Among the arts of Japan, one of the finest monuments is the colorful painting on silk of Benzai-Ten, goddess of language, music and eloquence. She is shown seated on the bank of a stream, strumming the *biwa,* a short-necked stringed instrument like the lute. Other important works include woodblock prints by recognized masters of the Edo period (1615–1867) such as Utamaro and Hokusai, as well as by lesser known printmakers and painters. Pairs of six-fold screens from the Momoyama period (1568–1614) show traditional scenes of seasonal landscapes in ink washes. The conceptual continuity of each pair is reinforced by the subtle tonalities and the layout and placement of design, which carries the eye across the entire surface. Buddhist art of the Heian (794–1185) and Kamakura (1185–1392) periods provide Japanese versions of themes and images whose earlier origins may be traced in the arts of India and China.

THE NEWARK MUSEUM
49 WASHINGTON STREET, NEWARK, NJ 07101. Tel: (201) 733-6600
Hours: Sun–Sat 12–5 pm, closed Thanksgiving, Christmas, New Year's and July 4th.
Admission: Free.
Publications: a quarterly magazine, plus:
> *Art Called Amlash: An Art of Ancient Iran as seen in its Ceramics.* 1968–69, $.25.
> *Catalogue of the Tibetan Collection and other Lamaist Articles in The Newark Museum:*
>> Vol II: *Prayer and Objects Associated with Prayer—Music and Musical Instruments—Ritualistic Objects.* 1950, 1973, $7.50.
>> Vol IV: *Textiles—Rugs—Needlework—Costumes—Jewelry.* 1961, $7.50.

Reproductions: Postcards.
Research: Reference library open to public; Strong in areas covered by the collection, especially decorative arts.

The Newark Museum maintains permanent collections of Asian art representing the development of the major civilizations. Of particular importance is the Collection of Tibetan Art and Ethnography, one of the most distinguished in the world. It was originally gathered by Dr. Albert Shelton, a missionary who lived and traveled in Tibet from 1905 to 1920.

While the museum has since acquired art from China, Japan and Korea and from India and the Near East, it has consciously sought to enrich its unusual Tibetan collections. Representing both secular and Tibetan Buddhist traditions, this rich assemblage includes ritual and ceremonial objects from monasteries and temples, as well as functionally aesthetic clothing and domestic arts of the nomads of eastern Tibet and richly ornamental costumes and jewelry of nobility from the capital at Lhasa.

Arts of the Himalayan regions exhibited in Newark reflect the art and ways of life of past centuries, which survived in these out-of-the-way places until the present day. With the advent of modern means of transport, air traffic has reduced the inaccessibility of these areas and prompted more rapid change only in the past few decades.

Other strengths of the museum's Asian holdings are Chinese, Japanese and Korean ceramics, Japanese wood block prints and netsuke, and ancient glass, much of which is Near Eastern.

PHILADELPHIA MUSEUM OF ART
BENJAMIN FRANKLIN PARKWAY, PHILADELPHIA, PA 19101.
Tel: (215) 763-8100
Hours: Wed–Sun 10 am–5 pm, closed Mon, Tues and legal holidays.
Admission: $2 adults, $1 children under 18, students, senior citizens.
Publications:
　Mary Baskett, *Footprints of the Buddha*. 1980, $8.95.
　Roger Keyes, Keiko Mizushima, *Theatrical World of Osaka Prints*. 1973, $12.95.
　Stella Kramrisch, *Manifestations of Shiva*. 1981, $16.95.
Reproductions: Large selection of posters, prints and postcards.
Research: Library, print and study collections open to those with professional interest by appointment.

The Philadelphia Museum of Art is most famous for its architectural installations that provide authentic settings for viewing the collections. The arts of Asia are displayed amid a Chinese palace replete with furnishings

Chinese Scholar Study
Philadelphia Museum of Art

and a Buddhist shrine with altar. Architectural sculpture is incorporated into the structure of an Indian temple, and a Japanese tea house and temple are set in a garden to re-create the sense of landscape and aesthetic physical context that once surrounded such artwork. In addition, there is a Chinese scholar's study and a Persian domed room with an antechamber and an intricately vaulted ceiling. The relationship between furniture and decoration in each display further indicates the functions of art and provides a sense of time and place.

Particularly strong in its collection of Buddhist and Hindu sculpture from India, the Philadelphia Museum of Art has been instrumental in organizing major traveling exhibitions that draw on loans from other great collections of Asian art throughout the world.

SEATTLE ART MUSEUM

VOLUNTEER PARK, SEATTLE, WA 98112. Tel: (206) 447-4710

Hours: Tues–Wed, Fri–Sat 10 am–5 pm; Thurs 10 am–9 pm; Sun 12–5 pm; closed Mon, Christmas, New Year's.

Admission: $2 adults, $1 senior citizens, students, free to members and children under 6, free on Thursdays.

Publications:

> Henry Trubner, *Asian Art in the Seattle Art Museum: Fifty Years of Collecting.* 1983, np.

Reproductions: Posters, postcards, prints and reproductions of artifacts and works from the collection and special exhibitions.

Research: Reference library open to public Tues–Fri; slide library open by appointment.

Guardian animals from imperial Chinese tombs flank the entrance to the Seattle Art Museum, welcoming the visitor to a wealth of Asian art that befits the history of this Pacific port city. Mrs. Eugene Fuller and her son, Richard E. Fuller, the founders of the museum, had particular interests in

Tawaraya Sotatsu
Handscroll of Deer and Poems,
Ink/gold/silver on paper, 17th c. A.D.

the arts of Asia and established the direction the museum would take with the donation of their own fine collection.

The collection of Japanese art is one of the best outside of Japan. It consists of traditional pairs of six-fold paper screens, paintings on silk, wood block prints, ceramics, as well as objects in other materials. Galleries of Chinese and Japanese art display changing exhibitions, but the Buddhist, Jain and Hindu sculpture of India is on permanent view.

The museum has also been instrumental in organizing major international loan exhibitions and exchanges with Far Eastern collections.

THE WALTERS ART GALLERY
600 NORTH CHARLES STREET, BALTIMORE, MD 21201.
Tel: (301) 547-9000
Hours: Tues–Sun 11 am–5 pm, closed Mon, Thanksgiving, Christmas eve and day, New Year's, July 4th.
Admission: $2 adults, $1 senior citizens and students, free to children under 18 and members; free on Wednesdays.
Publications:
>Martha Boyer, *Catalogue of Japanese Lacquers in The Walters Art Gallery.* 1970, $30.

Reproductions: Prints, posters, postcards and reproductions from the collection.
Research: Reference library open to public by appointment.

Based upon the original collection of William Walters, who favored Chinese porcelains and Japanese lacquers, the Walters Art Gallery has continued to expand its holdings in several fields of Asian art. Although Walters's son Henry, also a collector, chose to acquire in other areas, more recent gifts and purchases have strengthened the collections of Indian and Chinese sculpture, Chinese painting, and Islamic art.

Galleries of Asian art on the fourth floor of the new wing are arranged

Unknown, Japanese.
Cherry Trees,
color on gold paper, 17th c. A.D.

geographically, with three areas devoted to the arts of China, and other spaces is given over to the display of Indian sculpture and Japanese art. The latter includes an excellent selection of lacquerware and a very fine pair of six-panel folding screens of the Momoyana period (1515–1615) with a traditional seasonal landscape painted against a gold ground.

Islamic art is exhibited on the third floor. Relatively unknown, it comprises one of the finest collections of Islamic art in the United States. Though not comprehensive, it includes superior examples of inlaid metalwork and carved ivories, as well as an excellent collection of illustrated Persian and Mughal Indian manuscripts.

One lovely feature of viewing art at the Walters is the thoughtful placement of catalogues and other reference works alongside benches in most galleries.

YALE UNIVERSITY ART GALLERY

BOX 2006, YALE STATION, NEW HAVEN, CT 06520. Tel: (203) 436-0547
Hours: Tues–Sat 10 am–5 pm, Sun 2–5 pm; Thurs 6–9 pm Sept 15–May 15 only; closed Mon, Thanksgiving, Christmas, New Year's, July 4th.
Admission: Free.
Publications:
> George J. Lee, *Selected Far Eastern Art in the Yale University Art Gallery.* 1970, $5.
> Mary Gardner Neill, *The Communion of Scholars: Chinese Art at Yale.* 1982, $15.
> Barbara Tai Okada, Mary Gardner Neill, *Real and Imaginary Beings: the Netsuke Collection of Joseph and Edith Kurstin.* 1980, $22.

Reproductions: Posters, prints and postcards of selected works in the collection.
Research: Gallery does not maintain reference library. Special arrangements may be made to use reference material of a specific curatorial department.

Founded in 1832, the Yale University Art Gallery is one of the oldest university art museums in the United States. It has maintained distinction in the Oriental field particularly in its Chinese collections, which derive from the generous donations of Yale alumni and their families. The Hobart and Edward Small Moore Memorial Collection, given by Mrs. William H. Moore in memory of her two sons who attended Yale, consists of Chinese bronzes, jades, ceramics, paintings and textiles. It was gathered by Mrs. Moore in the United States and on several jaunts in the 1920s to the Far East, accompanied by her maid. The Chinese collection at Yale has since then steadily grown, most recently with the addition of a gift of scholars' equipment, pertinent to the art of calligraphy that was so highly respected in China.

In recognition of its role as a teaching collection utilized by the Department of Fine Arts, the curator of Oriental Art, Mary Gardiner Neill, has drawn on the expertise of Chinese art historians who taught at Yale or were trained there to organize an exhibition, "Communion of Scholars," that brings together the art of the painter and calligrapher with the tools of their trade. Circulated to museums throughout the United States, this exhibition has now returned to Yale, where it will reside. Other aspects of the collection are shown from time to time in special exhibitions.

CHAPTER FOUR

EUROPEAN ART

by
PETER FRANK

THE ART INSTITUTE OF CHICAGO
MICHIGAN AVENUE AT ADAMS STREET, CHICAGO, IL 60603.
Tel: (312) 443-3600
Hours: Mon–Wed 10:30 am–4:30 pm, Thurs 10:30 am–8 pm, Fri 10:30 am–4:30
pm, Sat 10:30 am–5 pm, Sun and holidays 12–5 pm, closed Christmas.
Admission: Discretionary. Suggested contribution $4 adults, $2 children, senior
citizens, students; free to children under 6; free Thursday.
Publications:
> *Selected Works of 18th Century French Art in the Collections of The Art Institute
> of Chicago.* 1976, $12.50.
> *The Art Institute of Chicago: One Hundred Masterpieces.* 1978, $35.
> *The Golden Age of Naples: Art and Civilization Under the Bourbons, 1734–1805.*
> 1981, $45.
> Susan Wise, *European Portraits 1600–1900.* 1978, $10.

Reproductions: Selection of posters, prints, postcards and slides from collec-
tion and special exhibitions.
Research: Library open to museum affiliates, visiting scholars and curators.
Collection strong in history of art and architecture.

The Art Institute, housed in a grand Beaux Arts structure inherited from
the 1893 Columbia Exposition, is best known as one of the world's great
repositories of early modern art. It cannot claim such renown for its earlier
painting and sculpture, as its collection of Renaissance-to-Second Empire
works is far less focused and far less studded with art historical landmarks.
The institute is strong in several areas, however and does own quite a few
outstanding old-master and pre-modern pieces—several masterworks.

The institute's strongest suit is Spanish art, from the late fourteenth
century *Ayala Altarpiece* to several electrifying Goyas *(The Hanged Monk,
The Capture of Maragavo by Fray Pedro)*. In between are El Greco's
overwhelming, deservedly world-famous *Assumption of the Virgin;* Velázquez in various moods, including religious *(St. John in the Wilderness)*, royal
(Isabella of Spain) and domestic *(The Servant)*; the stark and haunting
Zurbarán *St. Roman;* and a crisp yet luscious still life of hanging vegetables,
fruit and fowl by Juan Sanchez Cotán.

El Greco
The Assumption of the Virgin
Oil on canvas, 1577

Other regions' representations are less consistent, but none is without its highlights. Among the early Italian works of note at the institute are a Giovanni di Paolo panel, *St. John the Baptist in Prison;* a static but still graceful Botticelli *Madonna and Child with Angels;* an odd and pleasingly architectonic *Flight into Egypt* by Bernardino Butinone; and a *Baptism of Christ* that Perugino arrayed hieratically in a panoramic landscape. Later Renaissance works from Italy include Correggio's stylized yet sensuous *Virgin and Child with St. John the Baptist;* a Bronzino portrait (presumed to be Francesco de'Medici); and the vigorous Mannerist *Mystical Vision of St. Jerome* of Giorgio Vasari (better known for his book, *Lives of the Painters,* than for his own painting). Notable among the later Italian paintings are a few choice Tiepolos.

The Northern representation is still less consistent, but its more select items are especially impressive. Hans Memling and Gerard David provide important religious works. A Quentin Massys portrait, *Man with a Pink,* prefigures seventeenth-century portraiture, which is itself displayed in Frans Moreelse's precise and opulent *Portrait of a Lady* and early and middle-period Rembrandt figures, the early one presumed to be his father and the latter a *Young Girl at an Open Half-Door.* A major Rubens, the *Holy Family with St. Elizabeth and St. John the Baptist,* is the prime work among Flemish Baroque art here.

The English pieces of remark include colorful full-length female figures by Sir Joshua Reynolds (*Lady Sarah Bunbury Sacrificing to the Graces,* if you would) and Sir Thomas Lawrence (*Mrs. Jens Wolff*) and landscapes of some breadth and tone by Constable (*Stoke-by-Nayland*) and Turner (the wild *Valley of Aosta—Snowstorm, Avalanche, and Thunderstorm*).

The French holdings barely touch on the Baroque, most particularly with Poussin's lovely classical *St. John on Patmos.* The eighteenth-century selection yields more pictures of remark, including a Hubert Robert view of the Villa Medici in Rome and a Chardin still life in which the table and especially the cloth are the predominating aspects of the image. Two relatively intimate J.-L. David Portraits—the mottled, perhaps unfinished *Mme. Pastoret and Her Son* and the earlier (pre-Revolutionary) *Portrait of Mme. Buron*—prefigure Gerôme's own oddly angular *Portrait of a Lady,* while

Ingres's portrayal of the Marquis de Pastoret harks back to the more formal male subjects of Bronzino. The seated female figures rendered by Corot *(Interrupted Reading)* and Courbet *(Mère Gregoire)*, however, build on the informal and actively brushed nature of *Mme. Buron*. The emphasis throughout the collection is not on landscape (the Barbizon scapes here are few and far between) but on the figure.

BOSTON-AREA MUSEUMS
MUSEUM OF FINE ARTS
465 HUNTINGTON AVENUE, BOSTON, MA 02115. Tel: (617) 267-9300

Hours: Tues, Thurs–Sun 10 am–5 pm, Wed 10 am–10 pm, Closed Mon, Thanksgiving, Christmas eve and day, New Year's, July 4th. West Wing only: Thurs–Fri 5–10 pm.

Admission: $3.50 adults, $2.50 adults Thurs–Fri 5–10 pm, $2.50 senior citizens, free to children under 17 and members; free Sat 10 am–12 pm.

Publications:
> Anne Poulet, *Corot to Braque: French Paintings from the Museum of Fine Arts, Boston.* 1979, $13.95.
>
> Perry T. Rathbone, *The Forsyth Wickes Collection.* 1968, $2.50.

Reproductions: Large selection of posters, prints, postcards, slides from the collection and special exhibitions.

Research: Main library open to public; reference libraries of specific departments available to students and scholars by appointment.

ISABELLA STEWART GARDNER MUSEUM
280 THE FENWAY, BOSTON, MA 02115. Tel: (617) 566-1401

Hours: Tues 12–9 pm (July–Aug 12–5 pm), Wed–Sun 12–5 pm, closed Mon and national holidays.

Admission: Suggested donation $1.

Publications:
> *Guide to the Collection.* 1976, $3.
>
> Philip Hendy, *European and American Paintings in the Isabella Stewart Gardner Museum.* 1974, $25.
>
> Cornelius C. Vermeule, III, et al., *Sculpture in the Isabella Stewart Gardner Museum.* 1977, $12.

Reproductions: Posters, prints, postcards and slides of the collection.

Research: Reference library for staff use.

WILLIAM HAYES FOGG ART MUSEUM, HARVARD UNIVERSITY
32 QUINCY STREET, CAMBRIDGE, MA 02138. Tel: (617) 495-2387

Hours: Mon–Fri 9 am–5 pm, Sat 10 am–5 pm, Sun. 2–5 pm; closed weekends July 1–Labor Day; closed holidays.

Admission: Free; suggested contribution for special exhibitions.

Publications:
> Marjorie B. Cohn, *Wash and Gouache: A study of the Development of the Materials of Watercolor.* 1977, $9.95.
>
> Denys Sutton, *The Fogg Art Museum: Highlights from the Collection.* 1978, $10.

Reproductions: Large slide selection from the collection; posters, prints and postcards from the collection and special exhibitions.

Research: Library open to Harvard affiliates; others may apply for permission.

Any one of the three institutions which comprise Boston's constellation of fine art museums could qualify for citation in a roster of the country's outstanding museums. Taken together they make an awesome group.

The largest of them is, of course, the city's Museum of Fine Arts. It was the first museum of art incorporated in the United States, in 1870. It has been housed in its present structure on the edge of the Fenway since 1909. In the area of old-master to pre-modern art, the museum's strengths are in Italian and French art (its French moderns outstripping its holdings in earlier Gallic work). The arrangement tends to segregate sculpture and the decorative arts from painting. Among the especially important sculpture that is displayed with the functional objects on the first floor is a bronze figure of *St. Christopher*, notable for its modeling all the way around and probably one of the earliest Renaissance sculptures to feature this veristic treatment. The piece, from the very beginning of the fifteenth century, is believed to be the work of Brunellesco and Nanni di Banco. Other sculptures of note include a painted porcelain relief. *Madonna of the Lilies*, by Luca della Robbia; Donatello's *Madonna of the Clouds*, a very low relief in marble that is the only major work of this master in the United States; a *Bust of Cleopatra* by Pier Jacopo Alari Bonacolsi whose reliance on the stylizations and subjects of ancient Greece and Rome gained him the nickname "Antico"; and the charming allegorical bust, *Le Printemps*, by Jean-Baptiste Carpeaux.

Upstairs, the Italian paintings, especially from the thirteenth to fifteenth centuries, make a tremendous impression. Sienese and early Florentine developments are exemplified by Duccio's spare, rhythmic *Crucifixion: St. Nicholas and St. Gregory;* the similarly stylized and hieratic but vivid *Marriage of St. Catherine* of Barna di Siena; a flora-filled *Madonna of Humility* by Giovanni di Paolo; *Presentation of the Virgin in the Temple,* an early and forceful essay in perspective by the anonymous Master of the Barberini Panels (of which this panel is one); and Fra Angelico's calm and engrossing *Virgin and Child with Angels, Saints and Donor.*

Spanish and Northern work receives equal attention. An especially striking early *retable,* Martín de Soria's *Life of St. Peter,* introduces the visual and spiritual complexity of Spanish art, continued in El Greco's haunting portrait of *Fray Felix Hortensio Paravicino,* sensed as a hidden element in Velázquez's portraits of the poet *Luis de Góngora* and of *Don Balthasar Carlos and His Dwarf;* and once again made manifest in Goya's mysterious *Allegory: Spain, Time and History.* A similar level of intensity, given very different form, is experienced in the Northern works by Cranach (a glowing and expressive *Lamentation*) and Rogier van der Weyden, whose meticulous *St. Luke Painting the Virgin* looks directly out a window onto a distant landscape. A beautifully symmetrical *Crucifixion* by Joos van Cleve; a rare painting, *Moses After Striking the Rock,* by Lucas van Leyden; and superb seventeenth-century works by Rubens (*Head of Cyrus Brought to Queen Tomyris*), Hals (a portrait of an older man), Jacob van Ruisdael and Rembrandt bring the survey to a climax.

A few fine paintings are prominent in the English holdings, including George Romney's *Anne, Lady de la Pole* and characteristic landscapes by Constable *(Stour Valley and Dedham Church)* and Turner (a wild marine work, *The Slave Ship*). Notable among the pre-Impressionist French pictures are characteristic figure-in-landscape compositions by Claude Lorrain (the light-filled *Parnassus*) and Nicolas Poussin (a *Mars and Venus* unusual in its emphasis on the figures); one of Watteau's characteristic *fêtes galantes, La Perspective,* and an especially robust Boucher, *Halt at the Spring;* a very simple Chardin, *The Teapot;* Millet's famous and influential *The Sower;* a viscerally affecting *Entombment* by Delacroix; pictures by Corot (early and late); and Courbet's *The Quarry.*

Behind the Museum of Fine Arts on the Fenway stands the Isabella Stewart Gardner Museum, a Venetian-Moorish palazzo built in 1902 as Fenway Court. Although it was the residence of the widowed Mrs.

John Constable.
Stour Valley and Dedham Church,
(detail) Oil on canvas, 1815

Gardner, it was meant from the first to serve as the museum she and her husband had been planning ever since they began collecting art in the 1880s. It became that museum after her death in 1924. Fenway Court is built around an elegant and commodious courtyard, where Mrs. Gardner, a patron of music as well as art, held chamber concerts. Some artworks are on display downstairs, but the bulk of the collection is on the two upper floors. Especially on these floors there is some arrangement according to period and nationality, but the whim of the owner is still reflected in the situation of many works. A description of the collection, therefore, would best follow the floor plan rather than the flow of art history.

Impressionist and post-Impressionist works are mixed in with the Old Masters in many places, especially on the ground floor. Notable among the latter in the Yellow Room here are two nineteenth-century English paintings, Turner's *The Roman Tower, Andernach* and a characteristic pre-Raphaelite picture, *Love's Greeting* by Dante Gabriel Rossetti. Upstairs, the Early Italian Room begins a more concerted presentation, displaying a substantial selection of exemplary work under this rubric. Andrea Mantegna's *Sacra Conversazione,* grouping the Madonna and Child with several saints in a landscape—supposedly in "sacred conversation"—is one of the earliest (perhaps the earliest) Italian painting to follow this Northern format. Also notable in the Early Italian Room is Masaccio's *A Young Man in a Scarlet Turban;* a fresco depicting *Hercules* by Piero della Francesca, originally in his house; a Simone Martini polyptych *Madonna and Child with Four Saints;* Fra Angelico's glorious and curious *Dormition and Assumption of the Virgin*, a reliquary tabernacle done for Santa Maria Novella in Florence, in which Byzantine and Medieval methods of depicting the Virgin's death are conjoined; *The Madonna and Child with a Goldfinch* by Bernardo Daddi; and Giovanni di Paolo's *The Child Jesus Disputing in the Temple*.

Later Renaissance painting hangs in the Raphael Room, including Botticelli's *Tragedy of Lucretia*, a narratively and perspectively dramatic picture. The Little Salon features only Francois Boucher's exuberant *Car of Venus*, while the Dutch Room features Spanish work—particularly Zurbarán's portrait of *A Doctor of Law*—as well as Northern paintings. By German painters are *A Man in a Fur Coat*, rendered by Albrecht Dürer, and a pair of portraits of English nobility, *Sir William and Lady Butts*, by Holbein. Artwork from the Low Countries includes van Dyck's *Lady with a Rose; Thomas Howard, Earl of Arundel* decked out in the family armor for his portrait by Rubens; and a *Lesson on the Theorbo* in which ter Borch sweetly portrays an intimate musical encounter.

On the third floor, the Gothic Room affords a look at the dawn of the Italian Renaissance, most especially in a *Madonna and Child* by Lippo Memmi and *Presentation of the Infant Jesus in the Temple*, one of the few Giottos in America. Tintoretto's *Lady in Black* hangs in the North Stair Hall leading to the Veronese Room. The room is named after *The Coronation of Hebe*, but as it turns out, this portrayal of the daughter of Jupiter and Juno, cupbearer to the gods, was painted by one of Veronese's more able assistants. *The Wedding of Barbarossa* is a true Tiepolo, however, and the room also features a *Story of David and Bathsheba* by the infrequently seen sixteenth-century Netherlandish painter Herri met de Bles, as well as two Venetian scenes by Guardi. The Titian Room is dominated by what is probably the Gardner Museum's best known artwork, the Venetian master's large and voluptuously active *Rape of Europa*, distinguished among other things for an unusual panoramic landscape view in the distance. The Titian Room is also graced by the presence of Paris Bordone's *The Child Jesus Disputing in the Temple*, a Velázquez full-length portrait of King Philip IV (who was owner of the Titian masterpiece), and *Bindo Altoviti*, one of only two surviving portrait busts by the sixteenth-century Florentine Benvenuto Cellini. The Long Gallery's northern section is distinguished by paintings of Botticelli—his *Madonna and Child of the Eucharist*, better known as the *Chigi Madonna*—and a head, *A Young Lady of Fashion*, by Paolo Uccello, a master infrequently seen in American collections. The middle section is notable for the largest altarpiece of the Sienese school, Giulano da Rimini's 1307 *Madonna and Child with SS. Francis and Clare and Other Saints*.

Harvard boasts several museums of outstanding importance, and the Fogg—with its neighbor, the Busch-Reisinger Museum of Germanic Art—is its contribution to fine art. The Fogg is currently undergoing an extensive

J. A. D. Ingres.
Odalisque with the Slave,
Oil on canvas, 1840

renovation and expansion program; its physical plant has long been far too small to display adequately its formidable collection. The Busch-Reisinger—which specializes in modern Germanic art, although it does have a few Old Master items of remark (such as Joos van Cleve's version of *St. Jerome in His Study,* taken from Dürer)—is in more comfortable circumstances.

The Fogg's primary importance to Harvard is as a training museum; its museological programs are among the most respected in the country. The collection itself, a result of donations and acquisitions by its astute faculty-staff, is especially strong—like other Boston institutions—in Italian art. At the Fogg are Taddeo Gaddi's *Stigmatization of St. Francis,* a dramatic depiction once believed the work of Giotto rather than his pupil; a spare *Tabernacle: Crucifixion, Agony in the Garden and Six Saints* by Bernardo Daddi; a *Christ on the Cross* by Simone Martini and a somewhat more detailed *Crucifixion,* including a Dominican cardinal as donor figure, by Fra Angelico; a high-keyed and rhythmic depiction of the *Construction of the Temple of Jerusalem* by Francesco Pesellino; an especially straightforward and affecting Lorenzo Lotto, *Portrait of a Dominican Friar as St. Peter Martyr;* Tintoretto's *Allegory of Fidelity* (originally owned by John Ruskin—as a Veronese); Dosso Dossi's *Condottiere,* a handsome and dramatically-lit portrait; and a luminous *Madonna with the Sleeping Christ Child* of Orazio Gentileschi. The Fogg also boasts a holding of some fifteen terracotta *bozzetti* (sketches) by Bernini, one of the largest study collections of work by that Baroque master in the world.

The Fogg also has concentrated collections of work by Rembrandt and Ingres, mostly drawings but including three Rembrandt heads in oil: *Portrait of a Man, Portrait of an Old Man* and *Head of Christ*. The centerpiece of the Ingres items is the opulent *Odalisque with a Slave,* one of his most intensely colored oils. Other French artists of the nineteenth century are also well represented: *The Bull Market* is the most notable of several Gericaults, and is augmented by Delacroix's *Giaour and Pasha,* while the Ingres holding is accented by Jacques-Louis David's portrait of *Emmanuel Sieyes, Aged 69.* Peter Paul Rubens' oil sketch, *Commanding the Waters* provides another look at Baroque art from the Low Countries, and, from the same period in France, the Fogg owns two Poussins, *The Infant Bacchus Entrusted to the Nymphs* and the less lighthearted but every bit as beguiling *Holy Family in a Landscape.* From seventeenth-century Spain are Murillo's sober *Holy Family* and the moving portrayal of a penitent *St. Jerome* by Ribera. Finally, the Fogg is a repository for some noteworthy English nineteenth-century paintings, including Dante Gabriel Rossetti's high-dudgeon Pre-Raphaelite *Blessed Damozel.*

THE CLEVELAND MUSEUM OF ART
11150 BOULEVARD AT UNIVERSITY CIRCLE,
CLEVELAND, OH 44160. Tel: (216) 421-7340
Hours: Tues, Thurs, Fri, 10 am–6 pm, Wed 10 am–10 pm, Sat 9 am–5 pm, Sun 1–6 pm; closed Mon, Thanksgiving, Christmas, New Year's, July 4th.
Admission: Free.
Publications:
   Sherman E. Lee, Edmund P. Pillsbury, *Florence and the Arts.* 1971, $1.
   Edward Oiszewski, *The Draftsmans Eye: Late Italian Renaissance Schools and Styles.* 1981, $10.
   Andrew Wilton, *Turner's Watercolors.* 1977–78, $5.95.
   William D. Wixom, *Gothic Art.* 1963, $1.
Reproductions: Posters, prints, postcards and slides from the collection and special exhibitions.
Research: Reference library open to members, visiting curators, faculty and graduate students with identification.

The Cleveland Museum's preeminence is in non-Western art but it boasts as well a leading collection of Medieval artwork, one whose excellence spills over into subsequent European art. The growth of the building has resulted in several discrete wings that cohere perfectly with the 1916 original. The museum has a consistently graceful and airy environment in which diverse artworks can be displayed in the diverse ways they require. The curators of the European collections have taken advantage of this flexibility by arranging the installations in a manner accentuating the nature of each era by conjoining fine art and decorative artifacts. This conjunction is far more extensive than is typical in American museums, but the craft objects are invariably shown in dignified juxtaposition to the less supposedly utilitarian pieces. Following the Gothic emphasis of the Cleveland's Medieval holdings, the European collection shows a bias toward Northern Renaissance and Baroque art.

The Cleveland's magnificent Northern holdings run from the late Medieval period right through the English eighteenth century. The German Renaissance is represented by a few choice pieces, including Hans Baldung Grien's *Mass of St. Gregory* and a Cranach landscape, *Stag Hunt.* The period in the Low Countries is similarly spare but select, the outstanding pieces here being a Robert Campin *St. John the Baptist,* a Gerard David *Nativity,* and panels by Aelbrecht and Dieric (or Dirck) Bouts, the former an annunciation scene, the later a *grisaille* depiction of a statue of St. John the Baptist. Various figures sculpted from wood and stone also figure in the Northern Renaissance, including

Caravaggio.
The Crucifiction of St. Andrew,
Oil on canvas, ca. 1607

some rather transfixing examples by Veit Stoss, Claus Sluter and Tilman Riemenschneider.

Like many other American museums, the Cleveland shines in its selection of seventeenth-century Dutch art and in its eighteenth-century English. Unlike many other American museums, the Cleveland moves into seventeenth-century Northern art with several prescient sixteenth-century works: Three landscapes from the later 1500s—*Landscape with St. John the Baptist Preaching* by Henri Met de Bles, Gilles van Coninxloo's *Landscape with Venus and Adonis,* and *Diane and Actaeon* by Joachim Uytewael. In the seventeenth century itself, it was Peter Uytewael who joined with Gerrit Honthorst in practicing Caravaggist chiaroscuro in the North, as seen in the Cleveland's melodramatic Uytewael, *The Denial of St. Peter,* and their Honthorst rendition of *Samson and Delilah.* But this, too, seems a prefiguration, considering the drama of form and light that plays in work of such diverse Northerners as Hendrik Terbrugghen (the touching *Weeping Heraclitus*), Jacob Jordaens *(The Betrayal of Christ)* and, of course, Rembrandt (whose *Old Man Praying* is the finest of the four Rembrandt portraits at the museum). A couple of significant Rubens pictures, including the boisterous *Diana and Her Nymphs Departing for the Chase* and lesser (but still good) pieces by van Dyck and Teniers are among the Flemish highlights. The Dutch, on the other hand, are copiously represented. Particular among their work is a beautiful panoramic *View of Emmerich Across the Rhine,* a later work of Jan van Goyen's; a similarly broad *View of Orleans on the Loire* by the lesser-known Lambert Doomer; a wonderfully atmospheric Amsterdam church interior by Emanuel de Witte; an early Jacob van

Ruisdael landscape with a windmill, plus later, more dramatic views *(Landscape with a Dead Tree, Wooded and Hilly Landscape)*; other panoramas by Salomon van Ruysdael *(River Landscape with Castle)* and Meindert Hobbema; Jan Wijnants' Amsterdam cityscape; a handsome *Portrait of a Lady* by ter Borch; Jan Steen's depiction of the Jewish story of Purim *(Esther, Ahasuerus and Haman)*; and Pieter de Hooch's restrained *Music Party*, a group in a well-appointed interior.

The eighteenth-century English grouping is rich in full-length portraiture, including major examples by Reynolds *(The Ladies Annabel and Mary Jemima Yorke)*, Gainsborough *(George Pitt, First Lord Rivers)*, Raeburn *(General Duncan Campbell)* and Lawrence *(Lady Louisa Manners, later Countess of Dysart, as Juno, The Daughters of Colonel Thomas Carteret Hardy)*. Two lovely Constable views of Hampstead Heath, a Biblical scene, *Eve of the Deluge* by John Linnel Sr., and a Turner *Burning of the Houses of Parliament* sample English landscape painting of this time. German works from the eighteenth century are primarily decorative at the museum, but an appealing Anton Raphael Mengs self-portrait is among them.

The Cleveland collection returns primacy to the Latin countries in the eighteenth and nineteenth centuries. The room full of Italian Rococo pieces argues for Canaletto's Venetian views, for Guardi as a Biblical painter with his stunning *Abraham* cycle and as an interior painter with his depiction of *Pope Pius VI's Visit to Venice,* and for that odd Bolognese-Genoese painter Alessandro Magnasco, who trains his nervous brush here on a subject more "exotic" than his usual monks, *The Synagogue.* French painting of this period is also quite well represented, although the selection concentrates less on the *fêtes galantes* of Fragonard, Boucher and other narrative painters and more on portraitists such as Hyacinthe Rigaud *(Portrait of Cardinal Dubois)* and Nicholas de Largilliere—and Fragonard himself, with a study of a boy that may be his son. Calm, detailed compositions by Chardin *(Kitchen Utensils, Still Life with Herrings)* and Jean-Baptiste Oudry *(Hare and Leg of Lamb)* also put still life in a good light. Architectural themes are rendered by Hubert Robert in two oval pictures, and Jean Pillement *(Landscape with Shepherds)* and Henri de Valenciennes *(View of Rome)* provide samplings of the Rococo landscape.

Early and late Corots grace the French nineteenth-century representation, as do other Barbizon(esque) works such as a George Michel landscape and Francois Daubigny's relatively large panorama, *Coast near Villerville.* Figuration of the pre-Impressionist era is more broadly represented, by Barbizonists like Millet *(Return from the Fields)* and by more academically oriented painters: David's luscious soft-core portrayal of *Cupid and Psyche* is here along with narrative works by Charles Gleyre *(The Roman Bandits)*, Ary Scheffer *(The Shades of Francesca and Paolo Appear to Dante and Vergil)* and Baron Antoine-Jean Gros *(General Kleber* and *Native Family,* lateral panels for his *grande machine,* the *Bataille des Pyramides)*. French sculpture from the eighteenth and nineteenth centuries is quite prominent, in fact, with excellent examples by Barye, Carpeaux, Carrier-Belleuse, Jules Dalou and, naturally, Rodin. With Rodin, figures and landscapes by Courbet

(Mme. Laure Boneau, Grand Panorama of the Alps with the Dents du Midi), Fantin-Latour *(Mme. Henry Lerolle)* and Manet, the Cleveland Museum moves into modernism.

THE FRICK COLLECTION
ONE EAST 70TH STREET, NEW YORK, NY 10021. Tel: (212) 288-0700
Hours: Sept–May: Tues–Sat 10 am–6 pm, Sun 1–6 pm, closed Mon, Thanksgiving, Christmas eve and day, New Year's. June–Aug. Wed–Sat 10 am–6 pm, Sun 1–6 pm, closed Mon, Tues, July 4th.
Admission: Tues–Sat $1 adults, $.50 senior citizens, students; Sun $2. Children 10–16 must be with adult, under 10 not admitted.
Publications:
  The Frick Collection: An Illustrated Catalogue.
    Vols I & II: Paintings, nd, $50.
    Vols III & IV: Sculpture: nd, $50.
Joseph Focarino, *Handbook of Paintings.* 1971, $5.
Edgar Munhall, *Guide to the Galleries.* 1978, $4.
Reproductions: Postcards, prints, slides and photographs of collection available.
Research: Reference library open to any adult with serious interest; undergraduate students permitted under special circumstances. Strong in European and American art from the 4th–19th centuries.

More so than most private collections turned over to public view, the Frick Collection retains much of its original private setting and former arrangement. This gives the collection its "lived-in" look, only possible in palatial surroundings like these. Artworks are not arranged in chronological or geographical order; they hang pretty much where Mr. and Mrs. Frick (or their decorators) thought they ought to hang. Some works have been acquired since Mrs. Frick's death in 1931; most of these hang in one of the two galleries in the far wings of the building. Even here, though, the hanging is based on keen aesthetic discretion, not on historical continuity.

Given this, it would be best to conduct a verbal tour of the collection, not just a citation of works present from each country or century. The liberal presence of *objets d'art,* arranged in manners complementary to the paintings and larger sculpture, enhances the visual qualities of the works on view. The two Vermeers in the South Hall—entitled *Officer and Laughing Girl* and *Girl Interrupted at Her Music*—catch the artist in a lighthearted genre mood, but not without his exquisite purlescent colors and silky touch. Paolo Veneziano's *Coronation of the Virgin,* realized with his son Giovanni Paolo in the mid-fourteenth century, lends an antique majesty to the room, one only partly offset by the first of many Francois Bouchers in the collection, a genial portrait of his wife, reclining. A Corot painting, *The Boatman of Montefontaine,* is more subtly effervescent.

Imposing in its own right in the Octagon Room is Fra Filippo Lippi's *Annunciation.* Its company is another scene from the Nativity cycle, a less radical Renaissance rendition of the *Adoration of the Magi,* by Lazzaro Bastiani. The Boucher Room—preceded by an anteroom where sits the late-fifteenth-century marble *Bust of a Lady* by Francesco Laurana—is occupied

Hans Holbein the Younger.
Sir Thomas More,
Oil on canvas, 1527

by an eight-panel cycle, *The Arts and Sciences,* in which Boucher personifies the various disciplines as children. The cycle was originally created for Madame de Pompadour in the mid-eighteenth century. The dining room features English portraiture from the eighteenth and early nineteenth centuries, including Hogarth's *Miss Mary Edwards,* George Romney's *Henrietta, Countess of Warwick, and Her Children,* John Hoppner's *The Ladies Sarah and Catherine Bligh,* a portrait of General John Burgoyne by Sir Joshua Reynolds and two portraits by Gainsborough—who is also responsible for the single non-portrait in the room, the Watteauesque *Mall in St. James Park.* Another Boucher cycle, *The Four Seasons,* hangs in the West Vestibule leading to the Fragonard Room, with its cycle of fourteen pictures concerning *The Progress of Love.* Here Fragonard presents a comedy of manners and errors in paint.

Prominent in the Living Hall is Giovanni Bellini's *St. Francis in Ectsasy,* easily the most significant (and glorious) Bellini in the Western Hemisphere. It is also the most important painting in this room, but it gets stiff competition from the two august Titian portraits flanking it and from two Holbein portraits interesting for their subjects—Sir Thomas More and his archenemy in King Henry VIII's court, Thomas Cromwell—as well as their characteristically virtuosic and sensitive rendering. El Greco's glorious *St. Jerome* also commands attention with its massive, transcendent dignity. The sculptures, mostly mythological figures, are less imposing.

More English portraiture and landscapes hold court in the Library. It is intriguing to see how sitters similar in their class and cultural outlook are rendered so differently by painters like Sir Thomas Lawrence, Sir Joshua Reynolds, Thomas Gainsborough and George Romney. The best known of the portraits here is the latter's *Lady Hamilton as 'Nature,'* but to modern tastes it probably takes a back seat to Turner's proto-impressionist *Mortlake Terrace: Early Summer Morning,* his homage to a predecessor called *Antwerp: van Goyen Looking Out for a Subject,* and Constable's less fanciful but no less engaging view of *Salisbury Cathedral from Bishop's Garden.*

For a change of pace, the North Hall features mostly French work, eighteenth- and nineteenth-century pictures of a relatively simple nature, but the West Gallery is the central showcase of the Frick Collection and is in fact characteristic of turn-of-the-century mansions; such profound displays of conspicuous wealth were a conceit adopted from European royalty. Frick's gallery is indeed regal. Rembrandt's *Polish Rider* and a late self-portrait; one of the better-known Velázquez portraits of Philip IV; Turner's *Harbor of Dieppe* (plus his *Cologne: Arrival of the Packet-Boat: Evening*); four Hals portraits of varying but unflagging personality; George la Tour's *Education of the Virgin* by candlelight and a religious scene, the *Deposition*, by Gerard David; van Dyck's portraits of his compeer Frans Snyders and his wife Margareta; exemplary landscapes by Hobbema, Constable, Corot, and Jacob van Ruisdael; sixteenth-century Italianate portraiture, Bronzino's of *Lodovico Capponi* and El Greco's of *Vincenzo Anastagi;* Vermeer's intimate *Mistress and Maid;* Goya's rough-hewn, even violent *The Forge;* and typically glowing allegories of *Virtue and Vice* and *Wisdom and Strength* by Veronese: all commingle to provide an awesome visual experience.

The adjoining Enamel Room is a little less unrelenting, but its attractions are substantial, too, even beyond the charm of the enamel miniatures: Gentile da Fabriano's *Virgin and Child with Sts. Lawrence and Julian,* Piero della Francesca's *St. Simon the Apostle,* Jan van Eyck's *Virgin and Child with Saints and Donor,* the unusual grisaille *Three Soldiers* of Peter Breughel (the Elder), a Hans Memling *Portrait of a Man,* and scenes from the life of Christ by Duccio (a *Temptation*) and Barna da Siena.

The Oval Room following is devoted mostly to James A. M. Whistler's painting, enhanced by a Houdon full figure, the graceful *Huntress*. Beyond that, the East Gallery once again pulls the visitor into a virtual vortex of masterworks. Some of the best Gainsborough, Goya and van Dyck portraits in the U.S. are right here, accompanied by Jacques-Louis David's *Comtesse Dary;* a sweet genre piece, *The Wool Winder,* by Jean-Baptiste Greuze; religous subjects by El Greco (the emphatic *Purification of the Temple*) and Claude Lorrain (a *Sermon on the Mount*); and various landscapes. After this second massive immersion in masterpieces one can only catch one's breath in the Garden Court, where bronze figures by lesser but still accomplished sculptors make the transition to the real world somewhat less abrupt.

LOS ANGELES-AREA MUSEUMS

LOS ANGELES COUNTY MUSEUM OF ART

5905 WILSHIRE BOULEVARD, LOS ANGELES, CA 90036.
Tel: (213) 937-2590
Hours: Tues–Fri 10 am–5 pm, Sat–Sun 10 am–6 pm, closed Mon, Thanksgiving, Christmas, New Year's.
Admission: $1.50 adults, $.75 students, senior citizens, children 5–17; free on second Tuesday each month.
Publications: None
Reproductions: Selection of slides and photographic posters of objects in the collection.
Research: Reference library available for scholarly research; by appointment.

THE NORTON SIMON MUSEUM OF ART AT PASADENA

COLORADO BOULEVARD AT ORANGE GROVE BOULEVARD, PASADENA, CA 91105. Tel: (213) 449-3730

Hours: Tues–Sun 12–6 pm, closed Mon.
Admission: Tues–Sat $2 adults, $.75 senior citizens, students; Sun $3 general; always free to members and children under 12.
Publications:
 Degas In Motion. 1982, $5.95
 Frank Hermann, *Selected Paintings at The Norton Simon Museum*. 1981, $12.95.
Reproductions: Posters, prints, postcards and slides of the collection and special exhibitions.
Research: Research library open to inquiries by letter.

THE J. PAUL GETTY MUSEUM
17985 PACIFIC COAST HIGHWAY, MALIBU, CA 90265.
Tel: (213) 459-2306
Hours: Sept 15–June 15: Tues–Sun 10 am–5 pm, closed Mon. June 15–Sept 15: Mon–Fri 10 am–5 pm, closed Sat–Sun. No admission after 4:30 pm.
Admission: Free. Reservations are required for those arriving by car; pedestrians not admitted, must use taxi, bicycle, public bus.
Publications:
 Burton B. Fredericksen, *Masterpieces of Painting in the J. Paul Getty Museum*. 1980, $16.
Reproductions: Large selection of posters, slides, postcards from the collection and special exhibitions.
Research: New research center being created with a focus on art history to be used by scholars in the humanities engaged in interdisciplinary research. International information retrieval systems. Open to interested persons with defined goals by arrangement.

HENRY E. HUNTINGTON LIBRARY AND ART GALLERY
1151 OXFORD ROAD, SAN MARINO, CA 91108. Tel: (213) 792-6141
Hours: Tues–Sat 1–4:30 pm, closed Mon and major holidays.
Admission: Free.
Publications:
 C. H. Collins Baker, *Catalogue of William Blake's Drawings and Paintings in the Huntington Library*. nd, $7.50.
 Robert R. Wark, *The Huntington Art Collection*. 1970, $3.
Reproductions: Reproductions, facsimiles and slides of the collection.
Research: Reference library open to qualified students. Excellent for British art.

The persistent image of Southern California as a cultural wasteland has been inapplicable since the middle 1960s, and with the appearance of two formidable museums devoted in great part to the old masters in the last decade, the Los Angeles area in particular has become one of the best places in America to see not just modern and contemporary art, but the work of past masters—east and west—in serious, well-documented and well-displayed collections.

The Los Angeles County Museum of Art has recently completed the first expansion of the building on the edge of the La Brea Tar Pits into which it moved in 1965. This expansion allows the museum to put much more of its collection on view—including the trove of gems donated by Armand Hammer. Old-master highlights of the new Hammer bequest include female figures by Rembrandt *(Juno)* and Rubens *(Young Woman with Curly Hair);* Goya's *El Pelele;* and French works from the eighteenth and nineteenth centuries, among which are Fragonard's *Education of the Virgin* and Chardin's fairly complex *Attributes of Painting.* Also new is a large gallery devoted to British art, housing works such as Gainsborough's *Peasant Smoking at a Cottage Door* (his last landscape); *St. Cecilia* as painted by Sir Joshua Reynolds; Sir Thomas Lawrence's endearing *Portrait of Arthur Atherly as an Etonian;* Henry Fuseli's illustration to Milton's *Paradise Lost;* Turner's *Lake Geneva from Montreux;* and another Genevan scene

Georges de La Tour.
Magdalen with the Smoking Flame,
Oil on canvas, ca. 1630-1635

which combines the talents of animal painter Sir Edwin Landseer and architectural painter David Roberts.

The viewable collection of the museum proper is less concentrated, featuring a few good works by artists exemplary of most historical periods. Standing out among the Renaissance Italian pieces is Bartolo di Fredi's Sienese-style *Virgin of the Annunciation.* (Later Italian painting is briefly but well served by a Canaletto *Capriccio: Piazza San Marco looking South and West.*) El Greco's head of the apostle Andrew is the greatest Spanish item here, but Alonso Cano's depiction of *Christ in Limbo,* with its perhaps jarring juxtaposition of the figure of Christ with fleshy, almost pulchritudinous nudes, is quite interesting as well. Northern painting highlights include an altarpiece, *Donor with His Patron, St. Peter Martyr; Madonna and Child with Angels; St. Jerome and His Lion,* by The Master of the St. Lucy Legend; an intriguing *Portrait of Hans Jacob Fugger* by Christoph Amberger which combines Holbeinian and Bronzino-style portraiture; a cartoon, *Israelites Gathering Manna in the Desert,* for the Eucharist tapestries by Rubens; and two striking Rembrandts, *Raising of Lazarus* and *Portrait of Marten Looten.* French art of remark in the main collection includes de la Tour's haunting *Magdalen with the Smoking Candle;* a merry depiction of *Winter* as children playing on the ice, by Fragonard; a Houdon *Bust of George Washington,* free of adornment; the famous Chardin picture of a boy at a window blowing *Soap Bubbles;* and works from the nineteenth century by Corot *(Seine and Old Bridge at Limay)* and Millet *(Norman Milkmaid).*

Pasadena's Norton Simon Museum, by contrast, brims with old-master and pre-modern work, much of it exemplary and even magnificent. The

Frans Hals.
Portrait of a Painter,
Oil on canvas, 1650-1655

collection is proportionately lighter in the Renaissance than in later eras, but everywhere there are remarkable works to behold. An enthroned *Madonna and Child* by Paolo Veneziano, a colorful Giovanni di Paolo *Baptism of Christ*, Guariento de Arpo's imposing polyptych, *Coronation of the Virgin*, a beautiful *Virgin Annunciate* by Lorenzo Monaco, and the *Beauregard Madonna*, an exquisite marble relief by Desiderio da Settignano, all stand out among the early Renaissance holdings, while later developments in Italy are seen in Botticelli's gorgeous *Madonna and Child with Adoring Angel; SS. Benedict and Apollonia* and *SS. Paul and Frediano* rendered glowingly by Filippino Lippi; seven panels from Bernardino Luini's complex *Torriani Altarpiece;* Raphael's *Madonna and Child with Book;* and *Venus and Cupid in a Landscape* by the early Venetian School painter Palma Vecchio. Pre-Baroque Spanish paintings are crowned with an especially engaging El Greco *Portrait of an Old Man with Fur.* Northern Renaissance highlights include a Gerard David *Coronation of the Virgin*, Hans Memling's intimate *Blessing Christ, Adam* and *Eve* by Cranach, and unusual works by the lesser-known Jan Metsys—a fey but superbly rendered *Susannah and the Elders*—and George Pencz.

Baroque and Rococo art, abundantly represented in the Norton Simon collection, is especially well surveyed for the North. The Northern Baroque holdings are glorious. Especially good floral images by Jan Brueghel, Jan de Heem and Ambrosius Bosschaert, and a splendid *Still Life with Fruits and Vegetables* of Frans Snyders—a "still life" that includes a seated figure—set the table, as it were, for the bounty. In among the treasures are Rubens pictures including *David Slaying Goliath* and the *Holy Women at the Sepulchre.* The Dutch masters here include Gabriel Metsu, with a *Woman at Her Toilette;* Jan van der Heyden, whose *Library Interior with Still Life* is a diversion from his usual townscapes; Nicolaes Maes and Thomas de Keyser, with figure groups; Rembrandt, with *Self Portrait, Portrait of the Artist's Son Titus* and *Young Girl Leaning on a Windowsill;* the infrequently seen Matthias Stomer, whose *Mocking of Christ* takes place in Caravaggesque chiaroscuro; Jan Steen, responsible for bumptious genre scenes like *Wine is a Mocker* and the *Wedding Feast at Cana;* Aert van der Neer, demonstrating his specialty, skakers on a pond or river; and landscapists ranging from Roelant Savery *(Landscape with Animals and Birds)* to Jan Lievens *(Panoramic Landscape)*, from Salomon van Ruysdael *(Landscape with a Sandy*

Road, Halt in Front of an Inn) and Jan van Goyen *(River Landscape with a View of Dordrecht)* to Nicolas Berchem *(A Pastoral Scene)* and Aelbert Cuyp (a luminous *Evening in the Meadows*), and culminating with Jacob van Ruisdael and his heroic view of the landscape *(Three Old Beech Trees, Landscape with a Pool and Figures).*

Heralded by a *St. Jerome* of the pre-Romantic Spanish painter Francisco Goya, the nineteenth century is represented at the Norton Simon, not surprisingly, as predominantly French. Notable works preceding (and pre-figuring) the Impressionists include Delacroix's dramatic and exotic *Abd Er Rahman, Sultan of Morocco, Reviewing His Guard;* Daumier's dark and sinister *Mountebanks Resting;* and Barbizon and quasi-Barbizon landscapes by Narcise Diaz de la Pena *(The Approaching Storm),* Paul Guigou *(Landscape in Martiques),* Henri-Joseph Harpignies (a placid *Farmhouse*), and Charles-Francois Daubigny (a broad *Hamlet on the Seine Near Vernon*). J.-B. C. Corot and Gustave Courbet are represented by several excellent pictures including Corot's *View of Venice, the Piazzetta, Seen from the Riva degli Schiavoni* (a sharp-focused scene obviously influenced by Canaletto), *Site in Italy with the Church at Ariccia,* and the early figure composition, *Rebecca at the Well,* and Courbet's *Cliffs at Etretat, la Porte d'Aval* along with a flat, dramatically empty *Marine.*

In the few years the palatial J. Paul Getty Museum has been open, its collection—ranging from antiquity to the early twentieth century—has grown in all directions. Beginning with a very respectable collection of old-master and pre-modern works, it has expanded this holding significantly, and continues to do so. With the exception—at this writing—of Spanish art, the major centers and periods of recent Western art are exemplified by small constellations of major works. The Sienese Simone Martini's early-fourteenth-century *St. Luke the Evangelist,* a dramatic yet charming depiction by Bernardo Daddi of *The Arrival of St. Ursula in Cologne,* and a slightly later pair of panels—a *Coronation of the Virgin* and a *Nativity*—by Gentile da Fabriano sample the early Renaissance in Italy, while the fifteenth century is seen through several beautiful items, including Masaccio's noble *St. Andrew,* the polyptych *Madonna and Child with Christ and Various Saints* by Bartolomeo Vivarini with its highly-modelled figures, and the spacious, marvellously described *Hunting on the Lagoon* by Vittore Carpaccio. Two paintings, a *Bust Portrait of a Man* with a landscape behind him and a *Holy Family,* are attributed to Raphael, ushering in the sixteenth century. That period is illustrated with Bacchiacca's sedate, carefully drawn *Portrait of a Lady with a Book of Music;* the gentle, vividly colored *Madonna and Child with Donors* of Lorenzo Lotto; and two Veroneses, the *Full-length Portrait of a Man* and the momentous *Baptism of Christ.* The Italian Baroque is portrayed with an odd but impressive selection that includes works by Salvator Rosa (his golden-hued *Allegory of Fortune*), heroic—and heroically-rendered—subjects by Giovanni Lanfranco *(Moses and the Messengers from Canaan);* Giovanni Benedetto Castiglione *(Shepherds in Arcadia);* and Ludovico Carracci *(St. Sebastian Thrown By Soldiers into the Cloaca Maxima).* A Marco Ricci *Landscape with Ruins and Figures* introduces the architec-

Carpaccio.
Hunting on the Lagoon,
Oil on panel, 1490–1496

tural emphasis of eighteenth-century art, which Canaletto's *Arch of Constantine* continues—as, in their own way, do Alessandro Magnasco's classical revels, *Bacchanale* and *Triumph of Venus.*

Northern Painting fares similarly at the Getty, represented not encyclopedically but with an engaging group of very fine pictures. The pre-Baroque works of particular stature include a handsome *Dream of St. Sergius,* attributed to Rogier van der Weyden, and Bernaert van Orley's fantasy-enveloped *Holy Family.* Otherwise, the Netherlandish Golden Age of painting takes center stage. *Diana and Her Nymphs* by Rubens and Anthony van Dyck's *Portrait of Agostino Pallavicini*—plus an oil sketch, *Four Studies of a Negro's Head* by either van Dyck or Rubens—sample the era in Flanders, while Holland boasts a relative wealth of pictures: Gerrit Honthorst's *Musicians on a Balcony,* the earliest known illusionistic ceiling painting to be done outside Italy; still lifes by Pieter Claesz (a Vanitas setting), Willem Kalf, and two floral pictures by Jan van Huysum; characteristic landscape subjects and treatments by Nicolas Berchem, Salomon van Ruysdael and Salomon's nephew Jacob van Ruisdael; Old Testament scenes by Jan Lievensz *(Eli Instructing Samuel)* and Aert de Gelder (the more robust *Banquet of Ahasuerus)* and a folk fantasy, *The Peasant and the Satyr,* by Jan Steen; and moving portraiture by Rembrandt—*Portrait of an Old Man* and a rendition of *St. Bartholomew.* Michael Sweerts' lesser-known *Head of an Old Woman* is notable as an astonishingly realistic and sympathetic portrayal.

Two Poussins dominate the French holdings at the Getty: *St. John Baptizing the People* and a *Holy Family with Putti.* George de la Tour's well-loved *Beggar's Brawl* holds its own, however, as does the mythological subject depicted by Simon Vouet, *Venus and Adonis.* Later French accomplishments are touched upon with Boucher's seductively lighthearted and gorgeous *Fountain of Love* and a more directly lascivious Bouguereau, *Young Girl Defending Herself against Eros.* A single Gainsborough double portrait, *The Earl of Essex and Thomas Clutterbuck,* represents the English eighteenth-century, while the nineteenth century is spoken for by two academic works, Everett Millais' narrative *The Reunion* and the Alma-Tadema fancy, *Spring.*

English art fares better across town at the Huntington Library and Art Gallery, near Pasadena. The library is an Anglophilic collection, and the art gallery displays the same tendency. A far more private, "genteel" institution than the opulent but no-nonsense Norton Simon and Getty museums, the Huntington Library was assembled by a magnate of an earlier era. The

English portrait painters are the heroes here, with Gainsborough's *Blue Boy,* Thomas Lawrence's *Pinky,* Reynolds' *Sarah Siddons as the Tragic Muse,* Raeburn's *Master William Blair* and other pictures. Other portraits and still other subjects by British painters like Hogarth, Romney, Constable and Turner also stand out here.

THE METROPOLITAN MUSEUM OF ART
FIFTH AVENUE AT 82ND STREET, NEW YORK, NY 10028.
Tel: (212) 535-7710.
Hours: Tues 10 am–8:45 pm, Wed–Sat 10 am–4:45 pm, Sun and holidays 11 am–4:45 pm, closed Mon, Thanksgiving, Christmas, New Year's.
Admission: Suggested contribution $4 adults, $2 children and senior citizens, free to children under 12.
Publications:
> Katharine Baetjer, *European Paintings in The Metropolitan Museum of Art by Artists Born in or Before 1865: A Summary Catalogue.* 1980, $75.
> Charles Sterling, Margaretta Salinger, *A Catalogue of French Paintings: XIX Century.* 1966, $7.50.
> ———, *A Catalogue of French Paintings: XIX and XX Centuries.* 1966, $7.50.
> Federico Zeri, Elizabeth E. Gardner, *Italian Paintings: A Catalogue of the Collection of The Metropolitan Museum of Art.*
> ———, *Florentine School.* 1979, $12.95.
> ———, *Sienese and Central Italian Schools.* 1980, $12.95.
> ———, *Venetian School.* 1973, $12.95.

Reproductions: Extensive selection of posters, prints, postcards, slides and reproductions of sculptures and other works from the collection.
Research: Library open to museum staff and other qualified researchers and graduate students with appropriate identification. Most comprehensive art and archaeology collection in Western Hemisphere, including 210,000 books and 2100 periodicals subscriptions. It covers all areas in which museum has holdings.

To judge from its stupendous array of artifacts—from all periods—certainly not least the old-master and pre-modern eras—the Metropolitan Museum has one of the largest art collections in the world. It leaves no area of any significance neglected in European painting.

The awesome collection of early Italian Renaissance painting includes work by virtually all the major figures of the Sienese and Florentine schools, among them Giotto (an engrossing little *Epiphany*); Lippo Memmi, providing a powerful depiction of *St. Paul,* and Simone Martini, who does the same for *St. Andrew;* Bernardo Daddi, renderer of the *Two Scenes from the Life of St. Reparata* (a patron saint of Florence); Giovanni di Paolo, most particularly with a polyptych, *Madonna and Child with Sts. Monica (?), Augustine, John the Baptist, and Nicolas of Tolentino,* as well as a cunning depiction of *Paradise;* Sassetta, who provides a gem-like *Adoration of the Magi;* and Lorenzo Monaco, whose polyptych showing the Patriarchs is seen in the panels bearing Noah, David, Moses and Abraham. From the High Renaissance are two Fra Filippo Lippis, a *Portrait of a Man and a Woman at a Casement* and *Madonna and Child Enthroned with Two Angels;* Domenico Ghirlandaio's tender portrait of *Francesco Sassetti and His Son Teodoro;*

Rembrandt van Rijn.
Aristotle with a Bust of Homer,
Oil on canvas, 1653

profound religious works by Carpaccio, Vivarini, Botticelli (including his *Last Communion of St. Jerome*), and Luca Signorelli; a typically austere and dignified Bronzino, *Portrait of a Young Man;* Andrea del Sarto's *Holy Family with the Infant St. John;* and the *pièce de resistance* in the High Renaissance selection, Raphael's large altarpiece, *Madonna and Child Enthroned with the Young Baptist and Sts. Peter, Catherine, Lucy and Paul.*

Sixteenth century Venetian painting is substantially represented, with several Titians (most notably his luxurious *Venus and Lute Player*), Tintorettos (of which the largest and most dramatic is The *Miracle of the Loaves and Fishes,* but which is rivalled by *The Finding of Moses*), and Veroneses (a *Mars and Venus United by Love* which is as odd as it is forceful in its roles and positions). The Baroque era is somewhat abbreviated in its representation, but the museum does boast a magnificent Caravaggio, *Sts. Peter, Martha, Mary Magdalene and Leonard.* A broader representation is afforded the eighteenth century, with three large *Fantastic Landscapes* by Guardi, several pictures by Canaletto including one from his stay in England, an excellent Bernardo Bellotto scene, *Vaprio d'Adda,* fine works by Pannini and Pompeo Batoni, and most noticeably, a cycle of huge Tiepolo wall paintings depicting historic battles (e.g. *The Battle of Vercellae, The Triumph of Marius, The Capture of Carthage*).

Even more impressive than the Met's Italian holdings are the collections it maintains of Northern painting, collections which feature works by every major figure in each period of the Netherlandish Renaissance (by which is also meant the seventeenth century). From the fifteenth century are two powerful panels by Jan van Eyck, a *Crucifixion* and a *Last Judgment;* an *Annunciation* by van Eyck's outstanding pupil, Petrus Christus; the imposing and yet touching *Christ Appearing to His Mother* by Rogier van der Weyden; two by Dieric Bouts, a *Virgin and Child* and a *Portrait of a Man;* two as well by the infrequently seen Hugo van der Goes, an earlier *Portrait of a Man* and a later *Portrait of a Monk;* and two by Gerard David, a *Nativity* and a *Rest on the Flight into Egypt.* The collection also includes important Hans Memlings, *Thomas Portmann* and *Maria Maddalena Baroncelli* (actually two separate but paired pictures) and a *Mystic Marriage of St. Catherine.* From the sixteenth century are Dürer's intimate, realistic *Virgin and Child with St. Anne;* pictures by Cranach including a *Judgment of Paris* and *John, Duke of Saxony;* Pieter Breughel's justly famous *Harvesters,* with its comical figures working (and not working) amidst a stylized but vivid landscape; and portrait and religious images by Hans Holbein.

The seventeenth century holdings are dominated by something like a dozen Rembrandts, most of them portraits (including self portraits) and figures. These masterpieces and near-masterpieces include *Man with a Magnifying Glass, Lady with a Pink (Carnation), Flora, Man in an Oriental Costume, Hendrickje Stoffels, Toilet of Bathsheba* and of course *Aristotle Contemplating the Bust of Homer.* Other painters from the Dutch Golden Age fare well, too. Several Vermeers, including *Girl Asleep* and *Young Woman with a Water Jug* are complemented by similar subjects treated by less well-known painters like de Hooch *(Interior with Young Couple),* ter Borch *(Curiosity)* and the more low-life-oriented Jan Steen *(Merry Company on a Terrace).* Frans Hals is represented by one of the most important collections of his work in the world, including *Young Man and Woman at an Inn*—a.k.a. *Yonker Ramp and His Sweetheart*—*Merrymakers at Shrovetide* and other paintings.

Spanish works are in relative abundance. El Greco is represented by his most remarkable landscape, the *View of Toledo* and by several striking, elongated portraits. Diego Velázquez is responsible for one of the Met's best known paintings, *Juan de Pareja,* but his *Supper at Emmaus* and to a lesser extent, portrait of *Pope Innocent X* are also impressive examples of his mastery. Likewise, several oils by Francisco Goya attest to his pre-eminence in world as well as Spanish art; several portraits, both formal *(Infante Maria Luisa)* and informal *(Don Tiburcio Perez),* accompany the well known *Majas on a Balcony* here. An even larger English representation allows a good look at the late eighteenth century portraitists, in such works as Gainsborough's *Charles Rousseau Burney*, Reynolds's *George Greville*, and the early Hogarth depiction of the *Wedding of Stephen Peckingham and Mary Cox*. Other subjects of interest to the English in the late eighteenth and early nineteenth century include landscapes and urban scenes as rendered by Constable (*Tottenham Church* and *Salisbury Cathedral*) and bucolic genre scenes (such as Gainsborough's *Wood Gatherers*). A Turner depiction of the *Grand Canal, Venice* and Dante Gabriel Rossetti's Pre-Raphaelite portrait of *Mrs. William Morris* help represent the nineteenth century in England.

The nineteenth-century galleries in the Metropolitan are heavily given over to the French accomplishment, with good reason. The seventeenth- and eighteenth-century predecessors to these are substantially sampled, too. From the Baroque era came George de la Tour's *Penitent Magdalen* and the earlier, lighter, more jovial genre scene, *The Fortune Teller*; portraits by Philippe de Champaigne and, from near the eighteenth century, Nicolas de Largilliere; an *Allegory of Music* by the classicist Laurent de la Hire; and landscapes and figures by the leaders of French seventeenth-century classicism, Claude Gellee le Lorrain *(Sunrise)* and Nicholas Poussin (*Sts. Peter and John Healing a Lame Man, Blind Orion Searching for the Rising Sun*, and one of his best known works, *The Rape of the Sabine Women*). The eighteenth century yields some of the best extant examples of the not insubstantial confections for which Fragonard, Boucher, and others made their reputations. *Love Letter* is one of a number of exuberant scenes by Fragonard here, while *Interrupted Sleep* stands out among the Bouchers. One of Watteau's most charming and most loved images, the *Mezzetin* musician, hangs at the Met, along with similarly endearing works by Greuze (*Broken Eggs*) and Chardin (*Boy Blowing Bubbles*). A sympathetic portrait by Vigee-Lebrun *(Mme. de la Chatre)* and an especially impressive Hubert Robert architectural space, *Return of the Cattle*, also stand out as unusually fine works by these Rococo masters.

The mass of nineteenth-century items in the Met's collection can be dealt with here only from a bird's-eye view. Jacques-Louis David's *Death of Socrates* is here, with its architectonic composition and restrained drama. The prominence of Ingres slightly later in the century is also affirmed with portrait paintings including the entrancing *Mme. Leblanc*. The emergence of the realist attitude in mid-century is exemplified not just with Courbet's direct, relatively unsentimental pictures (e.g. *Young Ladies from a Village, Woman with a Parrot*), but with the active depictions of horses and other animals of Rosa Bonheur. The glimmerings of Symbolism are sensed in Gustave Moreau's treatment of *Oedipus and the Sphinx*.

NATIONAL GALLERY OF ART
4th STREET AND CONSTITUTION AVENUE, NW,
WASHINGTON DC 20565. Tel: (202) 737-4215.
Hours: Winter: Mon–Sat 10 am–5 pm, Sun 12–9 pm. Summer: 10 am–9 pm, Sun 12–9 pm.
Admission: Free.

Publications:
European Paintings: An Illustrated Summary Catalogue. 1975, $6.50.
H. Diane Russell, Claude Lorraine: 1600–1682. 1982, $15.
John Walker, The National Gallery of Art. 1978, $60.
Reproductions: Selection of posters, postcards, and slides from the collection and special exhibitions.
Research: Reference and circulating library open to graduate students, visiting scholars, and other researchers by special permission. Circulation desk open Mon–Fri 9 am–5 pm; stack open all week.

One expects the official fine art repository of the world's richest nation to brim with artwork of great importance and beauty. What is surprising is that the National Gallery's collection consists entirely of gifts to the nation from a few wealthy and generous citizens.

There isn't a major period or center of art that isn't represented by substantial, even major examples at the National Gallery. The galleries, arranged to both sides of the immense central corridor, are arranged geographically and, within that, chronologically. The order of the geographic areas is, traditionally and logically, determined by the earliest prominent periods. Italian art, not surprisingly, comes first. The collection begins with thirteenth-century Florentine works, including a striking depiction, still showing Byzantine influence, of Christ Between St. Peter and St. James Major attributed to Cimabue; two Paolo Venezianos, a Coronation of the Virgin and a Crucifixion; a late Giotto Madonna and Child, and a small Bernardo Daddi, Madonna and Child with Saints and Angels. Sienese traditionalism—surveyed in the National Gallery as in few other museums in the world—begins with a smashing altarpiece, Nativity with the Prophets Isaiah and Ezekiel, by Duccio (di Buoninsegna), initiator of the Sienese tradition. The tradition continues in panels by Simone Martini, a Madonna and Child with Donor by Lippo Memmi, and splendid late-Sienese works by Giovanni di Paolo (the wonderfully colored Annunciation and Adoration of the Magi), Sassetta (most especially several panels—evidently painted with an assistant—devoted to the life of St. Anthony), and the Umbrian Gentile da Fabriano, whose Madonna and Child is here accompanied by A Miracle of St. Nicholas.

Masaccio's introduction of quasi-veristic principles in the early fifteenth century distanced Florentine painting from the Gothic model still followed in Siena; the National Gallery features only his Portrait Profile of a Young Man, but Masaccio's inheritors are well represented. Four works by Domenico Veneziano stand out, most notably the enchanting, rose-bedecked Madonna and Child. Fra Filippo Lippi is represented by a Nativity, a Madonna and Child, and a narrative panel, St. Benedict Orders St. Maurus to the Rescue of St. Placidus. A remarkable Adoration of the Magi tondo, or round painting, is believed to be a collaboration between Fra Filippo and Fra Angelico, and the latter master also provides a Madonna of Humility and The Healing of Palladia by Sts. Cosmos and Damian. High Renaissance painting in Florence is cogently illustrated with a roomful of vivid portraits by Andrea del Castagno, Lorenzo di Credi (a self portrait), Filippino Lippi,

Nicolas Poussin.
Holy Family on the Steps,
Oil on canvas, 1648

Sandro Botticelli and, most importantly, Leonardo da Vinci. *Ginevra de'*
Benci, an early Leonardo depicting a woman at the time of her marriage, is
one of the few extant paintings by the master—and the only one housed on
this side of the Atlantic. Florentine glory is also reflected in religious subject
matter, including Botticelli's *Adoration of the Magi,* Perugino's *Crucifixion*
and the famed *Alba Madonna* of Raphael. (These three paintings were
among the 21 masterpieces bought by Mellon from the Hermitage Museum,
a purchase that formed the core of his collection.)

The later Renaissance, notably its flowering in Venice, is broadly represented. Giovanni Bellini's *Feast of the Gods,* a depiction of an Ovidian revel, is
one of this elusive master's more ambitious and exciting pictures. Representative oils by Veronese and Tintoretto are on view, as is a rare *Adoration of*
the Magi by Giorgione. Another work, *Portrait of a Venetian Gentleman,* was
begun by Giorgione but finished by Titian. Works entirely by Titian dominate the Venetian galleries, in number and in impact. Among the Titian
masterworks are an imposing portrait of *Doge Andrea Gritti;* a more
engaging portrait of the artist's gifted friend *Cardinal Pietro Bembo;* a
steeply skyward view of *St. John the Evangelist on Patmos,* the heavens
opening to command the saint to write the Book of Revelations; and several
mythological pictures concerning Venus, most notably *Venus and Adonis,*
showing the goddess failing to dissuade her mortal love from going off on
his fatal boar hunt.

The Mannerist era in other parts of Italy is evidenced in work by Piera de
Cosimo, Luca Signorelli, Jacopo Pontormo, Andrea Mantegna, Bernardino

Luini, Vittore Carpaccio and a host of others leading to the seventeenth century. The outstanding items from the Baroque era include paintings by the brothers Carracci, Annibale's vivid *Landscape* and classically organized *Venus Adorned by the Graces* and Ludovico's *Dream of St. Catherine of Alexandria*, in which the saint's reverie concerning her mystic marriage to Christ is as "real" as the dreaming figure herself. Among the eighteenth century works, the lively *Portrait of a Man* by Vittore Ghislandi stands out against the more predictably impressive works by Tiepolo, Magnasco and the Venetian architectural painters, especially Canaletto.

German painting is exemplified by some monumental works, among them several Cranachs, especially his spare, almost surreal *Crucifixion with the Converted Centurion;* Hans Holbein's portrait of *Edward VI as a Child,* well known for the vivacious aspect given the prince; the wrenching crucifixion scene by Grunewald known as the *Small Crucifixion* to distinguish it from the similar "large crucifixion," Colmar's Isenheim Altarpiece; and, incredibly, two paintings by Albrecht Dürer, a *Portrait of a Clergyman* and a *Madonna and Child* with a depiction of *Lot and His Daughters* verso. Similarly, most of the high points of Spanish paintings are touched with stunning works. Two El Grecos lead the way to less stylistically and subjectively exalted, but no less magnificent, seventeenth-century works by Velázquez—his head of *Pope Innocent X* and the intimate *Needlewoman;* Bartolomé Estéban Murillo's charming, strikingly composed *Girls and Her Duenna* (plus a *Return of the Prodigal Son*); Zurbarán's *Santa Lucia* and a convincing depiction of St. Jerome preaching to his disciples Sts. Paula and Eustochium; a stunning little still life by the Hispano-Flemish Juan van der Hamen y León; and a whole separate roomful of Goyas, nearly all of them portraits, among which stand out the early *Condesa de Chicón, Don Bartolomé Suereda,* and the transfixingly beautiful *Señora Sebasa García.*

Netherlandish art enjoys a large, quite thorough representation at the National Gallery, especially that from the fifteenth and sixteenth centuries. Netherlandish painters for the Spanish court make a particularly strong showing with the intricate *Mary, Queen of Heaven* by the Master of the St. Lucy Legend, and several panels for a *retable* (Spanish polyptych) by Juan de Flandes depicting the life of Christ. More locally oriented artists—many patronized by the Burgundian court—are abundant: Jan van Eyck is represented by his spectacular little *Annunciation;* Rogier van der Weyden's *St. George and the Dragon* and perhaps his best known portrait, *Portrait of a Lady;* Petrus Christus' *Nativity;* a *Madonna and Child with Saints in the Enclosed Garden* by Robert Campin (a.k.a. the Master of Flemalle) and his assistants; and three Memlings, including an unusually light and playful *Madonna and Child with Angels.* Religious items by Gerard David, Adriaen Isenbrant, and Bernaert van Orley join portraits by Joos van Cleve and Jan Gossert and, outstandingly, parable illustrations by master caricaturists Hieronymous Bosch *(Death and the Miser)* and Quentin Massys *(Ill-Matched Lovers)* in providing a well-rounded idea of sixteenth-century art in the Low Countries. As could be expected, a host of seventeenth-century works, Flemish and Dutch, follow: Rubens' *Daniel in the Lions' Den* and his sympathetic portrait of *Deborah Kip, Wife of Sir Balthasar Gerbier, and Her Children;* van Dyck portraits, most especially the slightly disconcerting *Queen Henrietta with Her Dwarf:* Rembrandt, Hals and Gerrit Dou portraiture; landscape subjects rendered masterfully by van Goyen, Pynacker, Cuyp, Jacob van Ruisdael and Hobbema; interior scenes by de Hooch and particularly Vermeer; genre scenes by David Teniers, Adriaen van Ostade, Gerard ter Borch and Gabriel Metsu; and a still life by Willem Kalf.

The French representation is more than a smattering, too. Four Poussins— including the early, almost hallucinatory *Assumption of the Virgin* and the later, classical *Holy Family on the Steps*—join three peopled landscapes by Claude Lorrain (including *Landscape with Merchants* and *Judgment of Paris*); figures by Sebastian Bourdon and Simon Vouet; and de la Tour's moving essay in chiaroscuro, *Penitent Magdalene,* all demonstrating the increasingly elegant restraint of the French Baroque. Two Chardin still lifes; typical pictures by Watteau *(Ceres)*; Boucher's *Madame Bergret, Allegory of Painting* and *Venus Consoling Love;* Houdon busts of Diana and of Voltaire; and other exemplary eighteenth-century works support a very large assembly of Fragonard paintings, among which are the charming *Visit to the Nursery, Young Girl Reading, Blindman's Buff* and *The Swing.*

Substantial works by David, Ingres and Gericault—the latter's *Trumpeters of Napoleon's Imperial Guard*—herald the nineteenth century. That divisive period's academic achievements are shown in, among other works, the charming bourgeois realism of Alfred Stevens *(Young Woman in White Holding a Bouquet)* and James Tissot (his *Hide and Seek,* with its meticulously rendered Victorian sentiment). The more painterly images of the classicist Pierre Puvis de Chavannes and, of course, the landscapes of Corot *(A View Near Volterra),* Daubigny and other Barbizon and Barbizon-related painters lead into the National Gallery's trove of Impressionists—as do the independent gestures of Adolphe Monticelli (a delicate portrait of *Madame Cahen),* Eugene Boudin *(Return of the Torre-Neuvier,* one of his small beach scenes), Henri Fantin-Latour (several portraits and still lifes of formal exactitude and limpid light), and the versatile Gustave Courbet.

The highpoints of English painting are evinced, covering the later eighteenth century and the first third of the nineteenth, and relying on the portraits and landscapes that made this period one of English artistic splendor. The "three Rs" of British portraiture are here, each with several pieces: *Lady Caroline Howard* stands out among the Joshua Reynoldses; Sir Henry Raeburn's *David Anderson* engages for its sympathetic frankness; and *Miss Willoughby* by George Romney is a charming child picture. Portraits by John Hoppner, Sir Thomas Lawrence (notably *Lady Robinson)* and Thomas Gainsborough (the fresh *Miss Catherine Tatton* prominent among several) are also displayed—as are Gainsborough's landscapes and those of Constable (particularly a *View of Salisbury Cathedral),* Turner *(Keelman Heaving in Coals by Moonlight* the most entrancing among several excellent proto-Impressionist images), and John Crome (his lovely *Moonlight on the Yore).* An odd-man-in is Henry Fuseli, with a stylized pre-Blakian Greek classic subject, *Oedipus Curses his Son, Polynices.*

THE NELSON-ATKINS MUSEUM OF ART
4525 OAK STREET, KANSAS CITY, MO 64111. Tel: (816) 561-4000.
Hours: Tues–Sat 10 am–5 pm, Sun 2–6 pm, closed Mon and Nov 25th.
Admission: $1.50 adults, $.75 children 6–12, free to members, students, children under 6; free on Sundays.
Publications:
> Ross E. Taggart, George L. McKenna, *The Nelson Gallery of Art and Atkins Museum, Kansas City, Vol I.* 1973, $7.50.

Reproductions: Posters, prints, postcards from the collection and special exhibitions.
Research: Reference library and reading room open to public; reference services available in person or by telephone. Emphasis of collection on Asian and Western arts: painting, sculpture, decorative.

The Nelson-Atkins boasts a fine, well-rounded collection. If it falters anywhere, it is in Italian work from the Baroque and Rococo periods—and, with masterpieces like Caravaggio's portrayal of *St. John the Baptist,* a Bernini bronze head and Canaletto's rendition of the clocktower in Venice's Piazza San Marco, this "faltering" is entirely a matter of breadth, not quality.

Earlier Italian art is far from lacking. The fourteenth-century Florentine "primitives" are especially impressive, with two panels by Bernardo Daddi (*St. John the Evangelist* and *Madonna and Child Enthroned with Saints and Angels*); *The Presentation in the Temple* by Jacopo del Casentino with its almost lacy architectural superstructure; and a *Madonna of Humility* (i.e., Madonna seated on a cushion rather than enthroned) by Lorenzo Monaco.

Later Florentine art is also well represented, by the *Madonna and Child with the Infant St. John* of Leonardo-follower Bernardo di Credi and Bronzino's typically clear and wistful *Portrait of a Young Man.* Venetian painting is superbly outlined with Giovanni Bellini's *Madonna and Child,* Veronese's breathtaking *Christ and the Centurion,* and Titian's *Portrait of Antoine Perrenot de Granvella.*

Northern painting—and sculpture—is similarly well served, beginning with a *Mourning Virgin* in wood from a Crucifixion group by the early-sixteenth-century German sculptor Tilman Riemenschneider. Other Germanic works include an oddly moving depiction of *St. John the Evangelist on Patmos* by Albrecht Altdorfer's brother Erhard, and three important works by Lucas Cranach the Elder, *The Three Graces, Portrait of a Bearded Man* and a small, Bosch-influenced *Last Judgment.*

The Nelson-Atkins also does well by Low Countries Renaissance art, featuring a *Virgin and Child in a Gothic Interior* by Petrus Christus (van Eyck's most illustrious pupil), a more regal *Virgin and Child Enthroned* by Hans Memling (from early in his career, as indicated by the gold-leaf sky), Bernaert van Orley's *St. Martin Knighted by the Emperor Constantine,* and the *Portrait of Jean de Carondelet (Archbishop of Palermo)* by Jan Gossaert, a.k.a. Mabuse, who may also have been the author of the museum's strange and alluring *Temptation of St. Anthony,* with its circular archway opening up the drama in the foreground onto a dangerously rocky but inviting landscape.

Peter Paul Rubens.
The Sacrifice of Abraham,
Oil on canvas, 1613

Sixteenth-century Flemish art is exemplified by a splendid *Landscape with St. Jerome* by Joachim Patinir and a rendition of *Summer* by Pieter Breughel the Younger, suggesive of his father's cycle of seasons.

Flemish painting in the next century is yet better served by a van Dyck *Portrait of a Man* and two of the most affecting Rubens works in captivity, the operatic *Sacrifice of Abraham* and a *Portrait of an Old Man,* almost Rembrandtian in its pathos. Rembrandt himself is represented by *Portrait of a Youth with Black Cap.*

The high points of Spanish, English and French paintings are profiled substantially in the Nelson-Atkins holdings. Three El Grecos—including a moving *Penitent Magdalene* and an ethereal *Crucifix,* as well as the more earthbound *Portrait of a Trinitarian Monk*—a Ribera *Good Samaritan,* a stunning *Entombment* of St. Catherine by Zurbarán, and a major Goya portrait (of *Don Ignacio Omulryan y Rourera*) do Spain justice. While virtuosic landscapes by Constable, Bonington and Turner (especially the latter's *Fish Market at Hastings Beach*), animals in a landscape (called *Repose*) by Gainsborough, portraits by Raeburn and Wright of Derby and figures by Hogarth (an oil sketch for one of his *Rake's Progress* scenes) and Burne-Jones (a study for a stained glass window, *Musical Angel*) survey England's best.

The growing preeminence of French painting from Baroque times to the nineteenth century is demonstrated with a *Triumph of Bacchus* by Poussin, two wonderfully lambent Claude Lorrain landscapes and a stark and moving *Crucifixion* by Philippe de Champaigne; François Boucher in two moods, the bucolic (a French scene with an Italian backdrop) and the sensuous (*Jupiter in the Guise of Diana and the Nymph Callisto*); Etienne Aubry's moralizing genre scene, *The First Lesson of Fraternal Friendship;* portrait sculptures by Joseph Rosset (a full-length marble of Voltaire) and Houdon (a marble bust of Benjamin Franklin, draped classically); and, from the nineteenth century, a remarkably informal portrait of the sculptor Paul Lemoyne by Ingres, landscapes by Corot, Daubigny and Courbet (the latter's view of the sea at low tide), an informal Courbet portrait of Whistler's mistress Jo Heffernan, and Millet's affecting genre picture, *L'Attente.*

PHILADELPHIA MUSEUM OF ART
BENJAMIN FRANKLIN PARKWAY, PHILADELPHIA, PA 19101.
Tel: (215) 763-8100.

Hours: Wed–Sun 10 am–5 pm, closed Mon, Tues and legal holidays.
Admission: $2 adults, $1 children under 18, students, senior citizens.
Publications:
Alan Shestack, *Master E.S.: 500th Anniversary Exhibition*. nd, $2.50.
Barbara Sweeny, *The John G. Johnson Collection: Flemish and Dutch Paintings*. 1965, $11.
———, *The John G. Johnson Collection: Italian Paintings*. 1965, $7.95.
Reproductions: Large selection of posters, prints, and postcards.
Research: Library, print and study collections open to those with professional interest by appointment.

The old-master and pre-modern collection at the Philadelphia Museum is actually two collections. The one upstairs is a quite passable assortment of European works, with a decided bias toward nineteenth-century France and, to some extent, late-eighteenth- and early-nineteenth-century England. Italy and especially the North seem oddly neglected. A visit to the John G. Johnson collection downstairs sets the balance aright: along with fine examples of Italian Renaissance works, the Johnson Collection boasts what must be the most exciting assembly of Northern European painting in America. Its seventeenth-century paintings are impressive enough, but its fifteenth- and sixteenth-century works are what give the collection its *éclat*.

As noted, the upstairs display is fairly spotty before the eighteenth century, although it does feature charming depictions of the Virgin and Child in low relief by Desiderio da Settignano (in marble) and Luca della Robbia (in painted terra cotta, with fructo-floral trim by his nephew Andrea) and Peter Paul Rubens's wrenching and magnificent *Prometheus Bound*, depicting the poor god's daily disembowelment by an eagle.

The English works of remark are mostly landscapes, although a Lawrence portrait of Lady Fraser and an Alma-Tadema "Victorians in togas" picture, *Reading from Homer*, have their appeal. There is also an attractive *Nativity* by William Blake. The landscapes include a Gainsborough *River Landscape, Figures in a Boat*, a *View on the Thames—Westminster Bridge* by Richard Wilson and a similar view under very different circumstances and commanding very different techniques, Turner's *Burning of the Houses of Parliament*. The French eighteenth-century paintings also emphasize the landscape, with accent on architectural details, an emphasis which continues into the nineteenth century in one of Corot's least typical pictures, the *House and Factory of M. Henry at Soissons*, a virtual throwback to Dutch town paintings of the late seventeenth century. The other French pre-modern works upstairs are more characteristic in their subjects and treatments: genre images, landscape and figure paintings and a pair of allegorical compositions.

The Johnson Collection adds to this brief survey of nineteenth-century France with its own Corot, Courbet and Theodore Rousseau landscapes and genre scenes by the lesser-known François Bonvin *(Woman Ironing)* and the Belgian Baron Leys *(Interior of an Inn)*. As mentioned, it also amplifies the museum's general Italian holdings into a serious, if incomplete, collection, offering such impressive items as Pietro Lorenzetti's post-Giottoesque *Virgin*

Roger van der Weyden.
Christ on the Cross,
Oil on panel, c. 1445-1455

and *Child Enthroned,* Giovanni di Paolo's intimate *Miracle of St. Nicolas of Tolentino,* endearing in its stylizations, a Carlo Crivelli *Pietà,* Titian's dignified portrait *Filippo Archinto* and Tiepolo's treatment of a mythological theme, *Venus and Vulcan.* But the *raison d'être* for the Johnson Collection— and, indeed, what legitimizes keeping it intact and separate within the precincts of the Museum—is its Northern art.

The Johnson Collection may be the only large holding of Northern art in America where the pre-seventeenth-century masterworks equal or even outstrip the Baroque-era works in number. A roster of these earlier works would have to begin with Jan van Eyck's awesome *St. Francis Receiving the Stigmata,* with its wealth of surface and distant detail, and especially with the two-panel *Crucifixion with the Virgin and St. John,* Rogier van der Weyden's vertiginously stark, restrained symbolic portrayal of Christ on the cross and the reaction of his mother. This is one of those monumental, almost cinematic paintings that evoke irresistible empathy for the pathos of the event, irrespective of one's beliefs. Among the collection's slightly lesser Northern Renaissance lights are works by anonymous masters such as the Master of the St. Lucy Legend (a depiction of *St. Catherine*), the Master of the Magdalene Legends (*Mary Magdalene Preaching*) and the Master of the Morrison Triptych (an *Adoration of the Magi*); Dirck Bouts (*Moses and the Burning Bush*), Jan Mostaert (a *Crucifixion*) and Gerard David (a *Pietà*); two works by Joos van Cleve the Elder (a *Portrait of a Young Man* and a portrait of Francis I of France) and a prescient genre picture, *Peasant Woman Holding a Beer Mug*, by Joos's nephew Marten; Quentin Massys' *Mary Magdalene and Mary of Egypt*; a slyly witty *Venus and Cupid in a Picture Gallery* by Jan Bruegel the Younger; and two panels by Hieronymus Bosch, a mild *Adoration of the Magi* and a *Mockery of Christ* in which the macabre Bosch we know and love is given freer rein.

If it is overshadowed by the glory of the earlier paintings, the assembly of seventeenth-century Dutch and Flemish works in the Johnson Collection is still magnificent in its own right. It features some unusual but important items: a depiction of the interior of *St. Bavokerk* by Pieter Saenraedam, the exacting refiner of the church interior genre who is not often found in American museums; a Biblical subject by Jan Steen, *Moses Striking the Rock*, in which the genre painter rises to a more solemn and dramatic occasion; and a *Study for an Old Jew*, its Rembrandtian subject and technique limned by the short-lived Carel Fabritius, perhaps Rembrandt's outstanding pupil. Also notable here are the *Portrait of a Couple* by Frans Meiris the Elder; genre paintings of great charm by David Teniers the Younger, Willem Duyster, and Gerard ter Borch; an especially good Pieter Claesz still life; and important landscapes by Jan van Goyen (*Utrecht Cathedral*), Jacob van Ruisdael (*View of Dunes*) and the lesser but still gifted Adriaen van de Velde.

THE JOHN AND MABLE RINGLING MUSEUM OF ART

5401 BAYSHORE ROAD, SARASOTA, FL 33580. Tel: (813) 355-5101.
Hours: 9 am–7 pm, Sat 9 am–5 pm, Sun 11 am–6 pm.
Admission: $4.50 adults, $1.75 children 6–12.
Publications:
> Denys Sutton, *Masterworks from The John and Mable Ringling Musuem of Art.* 1981, $8.
> Peter Tomory, *The Italian Paintings before 1800.* 1976, $19.50.
> Bill Wilson, *Dutch 17th Century Portraiture—The Golden Age.* 1980. $10.
> Bill Wilson, Frank Robertson, *The Flemish and Dutch Paintings: 1400–1900.* 1980, $25.

Reproductions: Posters, prints, postcards from the collection and special exhibitions.
Research: Research library open to public Mon–Fri 9–4:30.

This museum, founded and built with money made from the successful management of the country's largest circus (and including on its grounds another museum entirely devoted *to* the circus), was designated Florida's state art museum in 1980 and benefits from state munificence. Still, its collection—including what is considered one of the finest Baroque selections in the country—is built around a nucleus amassed by a single couple.

The Museum's Italian collection brims with lesser-known and even obscure names, but these—even the copies, imitations and unidentified follower pieces—are frequently of unusually high quality. Painting and sculpture from all periods and centers of Italian art are present, at least from the sixteenth century on. From the beginning of that century are High Renaissance works by Francesco Gianacci (his *Madonna della Cintola*), Piero di Cosimo (the world-famous essay in perspective, *Building of a Palace*) and a *Holy Family with Donors* by Gaudenzio Ferrari characterized by glowing colors and natural treatment of figures and landscape elements. The Veronese *Rest on the Flight into Egypt*, as well as his *Portrait of Francesco Franceschini*, plus works by Tintoretto and especially the sons of Jacopo Bassano (primarily Francesco, who is responsible for the *Allegories* of fire and water and a striking proto-Caravaggesque *Christ in the Garden of Olives*) provide a good taste of sixteenth-century Venetian painting. The dawn of the seventeenth century is represented by Agostino Carracci's version of *Susannah and the Elders* and Sassoferrato's bright *Portrait of Cardinal Paolo Emilio Rondonini*. Slightly later highlights of the Italian Baroque include Bernardino Luini's elegant *Madonna and Child With Saints Sebastian and Roche*, the handsome and moving *Act of Mercy: Giving Drink to the Thirsty* by Bernardo Strozzi, a captivating version of *Judith with the Head of Holofernes*, a subtle psychological portrait of Judith by the little-known Francesco del Cairo, and two mountainous panoramas by Salvator Rosa. *Kneeling Angel*, a Bernini *bozzetto*, or study in terra cotta, is the outstanding Baroque sculpture here.

From the eighteenth century are Tiepolo's curious *Allegory: The Glory and Magnanimity of Princes*, several Luca Giordanos including a depiction of the *Adoration of the Shepherds* as an extended procession, architectural motifs by Luca Carlevaris (the presumed inventor of Venetian view painting), Giovanni Paolo Panini and, of course, Canaletto, and the cycle *The Disguises of Harlequin* by Giovanni Domenico Ferretti, appropriate to a collection assembled by a circus man.

The Ringling's holdings in Northern art are not as extensive as those in Italian, but special items abound here, too. Most of these are from the seventeenth century. Prominent are the various Rubens paintings, including his portrayal of Archduke Ferdinand, Biblical and mythological scenes *(The Departure of Lot and His Family from Sodom, Achilles Dipped into the River Styx)*, and the cycle of four huge cartoons for a series of tapestries depicting the triumph of the Eucharist. The Biblical images here are simple, yet vigorous and muscular in treatment, and the colors very bright. A depiction by Anthony van Dyck of his name saint dates from the artist's apprenticeship in Rubens's studio. In Dutch painting, most of the genres are represented by at least one or two excellent works: Willem van Aelst and Jan de Heem are responsible for lush, opulent still lifes (van Aelst's replete with dead game birds, de Heem's with a live parrot!); Jan Steen weighs in with a *Rape of the Sabine Women* that is obviously a masque acted out by his usual genre folk; Karel Dujardin's *Hagar and Ishmael in the Wilderness* is an especially good example of Dutch Biblical painting; landscapes in several formats by Salomon van Ruysdael, Frans Post (a view of rural Brazil), Paulus Potter (his cows prominent in the foreground), and a brilliant Italianate *Landscape with Hunters* by Adam Pynacker; and important and affecting portraits by Rembrandt (a late *Portrait of a Lady*), Frans Hals (his full-length *Portrait of Pieter Jacobszoon Olycan*), and two female sitters by Nicolas Maes.

Adam Pynacker.
Landscape with a Silver Birch,
Oil on canvas, 17th century A.D.

The Ringling's Northern collection is notable in a lesser way for several post-seventeenth-century works of high quality, including Jan ten Compe's early-eighteenth-century view of Haarlem and nineteenth-century works by the Belgian Baron Jan A.F. Leys (a Vermeer-influenced but more tonal interior scene), a bit of Dutch history rendered as human tragedy by proto-Impressionist Isaac Israels, and a Barbizon-influenced landscape by Hague School painter Anton Mauve. Also notable are several German works, by Lucas Cranach the Elder (an oddly distorted rendition of *Cardinal Albrecht of Brandenburg as St. Jerome*) and by the eighteenth-century painter Anton Raphael Mengs *(The Dream of Joseph)*. More significant are representations from other countries, spottier than from Italy and the North but hardly bereft of superb works. Spanish paintings include a full-length Velázquez portrait of King Philip IV and an El Greco *Crucifixion,* as well as Angelo Cano's pair of *Visions of St. John the Evangelist.* Among French items are a handsome Poussin *Holy Family with the Infant St. John,* Sebastian Bourdon's cycle *The Seven Acts of Mercy,* Simon Vouet's imposing yet intimate *Venus, Mars, Cupid and Chronos* and the immensely attractive *Lovers' Pilgrimage* by Pierre Gaudreau, an early-eighteenth-century painter who worked in Mannheim. Standing out among the Ringling's English paintings are portraits by Lawrence, Romney and Reynolds and Thomas Gainsborough's largest painting, the equestrian *General Philip Honeywood.* Throughout, the museum mixes high quality and interesting taste.

THE TOLEDO MUSEUM OF ART
2445 MONROE STREET AT SCOTTWOOD AVENUE,
TOLEDO, OH 43697. Tel: (419) 255-8000.
Hours: Tues–Sat 9 am–5 pm, Sun 1–5 pm, closed Mon and national holidays.
Admission: Free.

Publications:
"Holland in the Eighteenth Century", *Museum News.* 1975, $1.
Otto Wittman: *Guide to the Collection.* 1976, $3.95.
————, *Toledo Museum of Art: European Paintings.* 1976, $12.95.
Reproductions: Prints, posters, postcards and slides of the collection and special exhibitions.
Research: Glass Study Room, Print Room, Art Reference library open to public; museum affiliates and visiting scholars may borrow.

Anywhere in the world, but especially in America, it is unusual to find a museum of the breadth and quality of the Toledo Museum in a town the size of Toledo. The origins of this institution are in the enlightened collecting habits of Edward Drummond Libbey, who moved his glass-manufacturing factory to Toledo in 1880. (This is also reflected, as it were, in the museum's famed glass collection.) Libbey's collection of Golden Age Dutch and Flemish paintings was the core of the museum's outstanding holdings in Northern art. Extensions and renovations, the last completed in 1982, have given the museum the space to exhibit many of its strong examples by lesser-known artists.

The museum's fortes are Low Countries and French painting, but it boasts some excellent Italian, Spanish and English works as well. Many of these it displays to maximum advantage in its Great Hall, a huge, naturally lighted core space where large works from the late Medieval, Renaissance and Baroque eras are to be found. Beginning with Lorenzo Monaco's *Madonna and Child,* all periods of Italian painting between Giotto and Canaletto are represented with fine, often exquisite pieces. The Toledo's Spanish and English holdings are relatively abbreviated but are studded with impressive works. Two famed El Grecos, *Agony in the Garden* and *The Annunciation,* are here, as are scenes from the life of Christ by Zurbarán *(The Return from Egypt)* and Murillo *(Adoration of the Magi),* simple portraits by Ribera and Velázquez (the latter, *Man with a Wine Glass,* an attribution of appealing, almost Halsian robustness) and sweet but not at all sentimental depictions of children by Juan Baptista del Mazo *(A Child in an Ecclesiastical Dress)* and Francisco Goya *(Children with a Cart).* Standing out among English works are engrossing portraits by Reynolds, Hoppner, Raeburn and Lawrence, figures in meadows by Gainsborough and landscapes bucolic (Constable's *Arundel Mill and Castle*), spacious (Turner's view of the Campo Santo at Venice) and frightening (John Martin's horrific *Destruction of Tyre*).

The French and Northern collections are magnificent to behold, and beyond the Great Hall, the galleries are arranged so that their breadth and detail can be comprehended. Gems by well-known masters hang by contemporaneous pieces of near-equal quality by lesser-known figures, often arguing for reevaluation of those latter, more obscure artists. As a result, one can gaze upon works by Hans Holbein the Younger *and* the Elder (both fine portraits, although in his *Lady of the Cromwell Family,* son does outshine father), by Lucas Cranach the Elder *and* the Younger and a pair of portraits, breathtaking in their detail simplicity and sensitivity, by Hans Muelich—a name hardly on every museum goer's tongue.

Isaak Ouwater.
The Prinsengracht,
Oil on canvas, 1782

The above-mentioned are all German painters, a comparatively rare breed. Their Dutch and Flemish cousins are all over the Toledo Museum, representing periods of glory and obscurity alike. Three sequences stand out among the Northern Renaissance works: the *Morrison Triptych*—a work of such splendor that its anonymous creator is known as the Master of the Morrison Triptych—Gerard David's *Three Miracles of St. Anthony of Padua* and the wings of the *Salamanca Triptych,* with their holy figures depicted as ensconced in ornate niches, by Jan Gossaert (a.k.a. Mabuse). Among the highlights of the sixteenth century are landscapes by Pieter Brueghel's two sons, Jan the Elder (a *Landscape with a Fishing Village*) and Pieter the Younger (a *Winter Landscape with Bird Trap),* that prefigure the landscape preoccupations of the next century and a clever *Artist with a Portrait of His Wife* in which Jacob van Oostsaanen shows himself seated at a completed painting of his wife, effecting a double portrait.

The seventeenth century yields a cornucopia of delicacies. There are landscapes by Jan van Goyen, Salomon van Ruysdael, Jacob van Ruisdael (a *Landscape with Waterfall),* Nicolas Berchem and Aelbert Cuyp, the latter two rendering figures prominently in their scapes and giving their bucolic genre scenes emphasis with marvelous light. Cuyp's glorious *Riding Lesson,* especially, basks in lambent late afternoon sunlight. More specialized land-scape subjects are demonstrated by Jan van de Cappelle's marine scene, a cityscape, *The Garden of the Old Palace, Brussels,* by Jan van der Heyden, and even Hendrik van Streek's Amsterdam church interior. Portraiture by Rembrandt, Bart van der Helst, Anthony van Dyck, Nicolas Maes, Willem Moreelse, and Thomas de Keyser; a *Crowning of St. Catherine* loosely and richly painted by Rubens; genre scenes by Avercamp (one of his skating scenes), Jan Miense Molenaer (the droll *Allegory of Vanity*), Adriaen and Isaak van Ostade, Nicolas Maes, Jan Steen, Gerard ter Borch; and two lively domestic scenes by Pieter de Hooch, among his best in America, provide a range of figurative subjects. Still life motifs include florals by Daniel Seghers and Rachel Ruysch, a still life with game and a live animal scene by Nicolas d'Hondecoeter, and lavish groaning-board settings by Abraham van Beyeren, Pieter Claesz and especially Jan Davidszoon de Heem (his *Still Life with a View of the Sea* provides two genres for the price of one).

Interestingly, one sees those genres continued into work of the following centuries, work that should come as a revelation to most American museum visitors. The eighteenth-century Isaak Ouwater, for instance, is responsible for an irresistible sharp-edged rendition of *The Prinsengracht, Amsterdam,* while Barbizon and even impressionist painterliness inflects Johan Barthold Jongkind's harbor scene, the tender and sometimes sentimental genre scenes of Jozef Israels and Johannes Bosboom's interior *In Trier Cathedral.*

The influence on these latter Dutch painters is as much French as Dutch, and the Toledo's collection allows an ample overview of art in France as well as Holland. The post-Renaissance flowering of French art is embodied by the majesty of Poussin's *The Holy Family with St. John* and the *Landscape with Nymph and Satyr Dancing* of Claude Lorrain, one of his most inviting scapes. It is also bespoken in the stiff elegance of Eustache le Sueur's *Annunciation* and Laurent de la Hyre's *Allegory of Geometry* and in the romantic vigor and pathos of Jean Jouvenet's *Deposition* and Jacques Blanchard's *Allegory of Charity*—as well as in the crisp, forthright, almost Dutch simplicity of *The Family Dinner* by Mathieu le Nain and the classical modeling of Michel Anguier's limestone figure, *Amphitrite.* The fluffier preoccupations of the Rococo era are introduced by Watteau's *Conversation* and brought to fruition by Fragonard's coy *Blind Man's Buff.* Francois Boucher, however, offers a picturesque landscape, *The Mill at Charenton,* and Claude-Joseph Vernet's *Evening* surveys a port, harking back to seventeenth-century interests, while *Lady Folding a Letter* and particularly the portrait of *Isabella Teotochi Marini* by Louise-Elisabeth Vigée-Le Brun usher in the nineteenth century with their sympathetic vivacity. Classicism is introduced into the nineteenth-century dialectic in Jacques-Louis David's famed *Oath of the Horatii* (a reduced version of the picture in the Louvre). Works in various genres by Delacroix, Courbet, Daumier, Millet, Daubigny, Rousseau, Troyon, Corot and Narcisse-Virgile Diaz hurtle French art toward the modern era—but not before the bourgeois reportorial academicism of James-Jacques-Joseph Tissot, learned in France and transported to London, produces a curiously convincing image like *London Visitors.*

CHAPTER FIVE

MODERN/ POST-MODERN ART

by
SARAH MCFADDEN

THE ALBRIGHT-KNOX ART GALLERY

1285 ELMWOOD AVENUE, BUFFALO, NY 14222. Tel: (716) 882-8700.
Hours: Tues–Sat 11 am–5 pm, Sun 12-5 pm, closed Mon, Thanksgiving, Christmas and New Year's.
Admission: $1 suggested contribution.
Publications:

> Katherine Kuh, *Clyfford Still: Thirty-three Paintings in the Albright-Knox Art Gallery.* 1966, $12.95.
>
> Steven A. Nash, *Albright-Knox Art Gallery. Paintings and Sculpture from Antiquity to 1942.* 1979, $17.50.
>
> ———, *Contemporary Art, 1942–72: Collection of the Albright-Knox Art Gallery.* 1972, $12.50.

Reproductions: Posters and postcards of works exhibited, and of modern works of interest.
Research: Reference library open to members, qualified scholars and research students. It is strong in its collection of contemporary American and European art books, and has a special collection of artists' books.

New York Times art critic John Russell has writen, "Inch for inch and painting for painting, no museum in this country can better the Albright Knox Art Gallery in Buffalo when it comes to the art of the second half of this century." And for the first half, as well, one would be hard pressed to find a superior collection, other than that of the Museum of Modern Art in New York City.

There are no serious gaps but plenty of masterpieces in the gallery's modern holdings. Many individual artists and art movements, although not covered in depth, are represented by irreplaceable works. Such is the case with Gauguin, whose *Yellow Christ* (1889), in the light of much of today's painting, seems nearly a century ahead of its time. A smattering of the choice early works includes Picasso's Rose Period *La Toilette* (1906) and transitional Cubist *Nude Figure* (1909–10), Balla's Futurist *Dynamism of a Dog on a Leash* (1912), de Chirico's metaphysical painting *The Anguish of Departure* (1914), Franz Marc's *The Wolves (Balkan War)* (1913), O'Keeffe's early abstract *Black Spot No. 3* (1919), Miró's Surrealist *Carnival of Harlequin* (1924–25), Soutine's *Carcass of Beef* (1925), Arthur Dove's *Fields of Grain as Seen from Train* (1931), Pollock's *Cotton Pickers* (ca. 1935), one of his earliest surviving oils, Henry Moore's wood *Reclining Figure* (1935–36), the first Moore acquired by a U.S. museum, Ben Nicholson's Constructivist *White Relief* (1937–38), Stuart Davis's *New York Waterfront* (1938), Matisse's *La Musique* (1930) and Mondrian's *Composition London* (1940–42).

Among the gallery's hallmarks of Abstract Expressionism are Gorky's *The Liver Is the Cock's Comb* (1944), Pollock's *Convergence* (1952), a late, high-key, allover drip painting, Motherwell's *Elegy to the Spanish Republic #34* (1953–54), de Kooning's *Gotham News* (1955) and thirty-three paintings by Clyfford Still, who donated thirty-one of his works (1937–63) in 1964. Gottlieb, Baziotes, Sam Francis, Hofmann, Philip Guston, Kline, Joan Mitchell, Rothko, Reinhardt, Twombly . . . all are here, along with the movement's second generation practitioners and Color Field painters.

There is a (disputed) claim that the gallery's *Painting with the Letter S* (1957) was the first Rauschenberg to enter a U.S. museum collection. Stella's *Jill,* a black painting from 1959, seems a herald of both Minimalism and Conceptualism, which the Albright-Knox has in abundance. It is also replete with Pop art, one of the wittiest and most charming examples being Jim Dine's *Child's Blue Wall* (1962).

Although there is no Photo-realism, fanciers of optical tricks and illusions (according to attendance figures, these aficionados are legion) can visit Lucas Samaras's *Mirrored Room* (1966), a cubic installation twelve feet on a side guaranteed to disorient the senses. The collection continues with fine pieces from the 1970s (Bartlett, Graves, Pfaff, Winsor, Ger van Elk) up to the current wave of photo-derived work by such young Americans as Charles Clough, Robert Longo and Cindy Sherman, all of whom made their professional debuts at Buffalo's well-known alternative space, Hallwalls. The museum is not yet the place to see Italy's trans-avant garde or Germany's Neo-Expressionists; however, it does offer substantial rewards for those interested in English art since the 1940s.

THE ART INSTITUTE OF CHICAGO
MICHIGAN AVENUE AT ADAMS STREET, CHICAGO, IL 60603.
Tel: (312) 443-3600.
Hours: Mon–Wed 10:30 am–4:30 pm, Thurs 10:30 am–8 pm, Fri 10:30 am–4:30 pm, Sat 10:30 am–5 pm, Sun and holidays 12–5 pm, closed Christmas.
Admission: Discretionary. Suggested contribution $4 adults, $2 children, students, senior citizens, free to children under 6; free Thurs.
Publications:
John Maxon, *The Art Institute of Chicago.* 1970, 1977, $6.95.
Reproductions: Selection of posters, postcards and slides.
Research: Library open to museum members, museum staff, students and

faculty of the School of the Art Institute, visiting scholars and curators. Collection is strong in history of art and architecture.

The Art Institute is an ideal place to go for a crash course in what might be called Masterpieces of Modernism and its Antecedents. Except for Futurism and Constructivism, all major movements in the history of twentieth-century art up to the present are embodied here in what are essentially classics of their kind. And Modernism's roots, too, are elaborated. There may not be an equal in the U.S. to the Institute's collection of French Impressionism, of which thirty-five Monet water lily paintings spanning the artist's career (the largest such grouping outside France) serve as the cornerstone. Monuments of form and expression—Seurat's *Sunday Afternoon on the Island of La Grande Jatte* (1884–86), van Gogh's *The Bedroom at Arles* (1888)—are seen in the context of other first-rate, contemporary works.

A lineup of eleven Picassos (1901–10), along with works by Braque and Gris, provides an unforgettable lesson in the development of Cubism. Picasso's *The Old Guitarist* (1903), his Cubist portrait of art dealer Henri Kahnweiler (1910) and his *Head of a Woman* (1909) in both bronze and oil stand as benchmarks along the way. Four landscapes of houses among trees demonstrate what the Fauves (Matisse, Braque, Derain, Vlaminck) were up to between 1903 and 1908. Kandinsky's shift to Abstraction is evidenced by four canvases (two of them from the artist's "Improvisations" series), 1911 to 1913. German Expressionism is well documented in works by Kirchner, Schmidt-Rottluff, Kokoschka, Beckmann and Corinth, and Surrealism in stunning paintings by Miró (*The Kerosene Lamp*, 1924, and *Personnages with Star*, 1933).

The reinstallation of the twentieth-century European galleries (currently under way) may alter the choice and arrangement of works on view. Until now, many of these have involved didactic juxtapositions of paintings and sculpture of the female figure. Matisse's huge *Bathers by a River* (1916–17), an experimental, Cubist-influenced canvas, faced, on the opposite wall, Picasso's large-scale *Nude Under a Pine Tree* (1959), a parodic treatment of the nude-in-a-landscape convention. Five smaller Picasso women (1921–54) were hung near sculptural works: Henry Moore's bronze *Reclining Figure*, 1957 (which echoed the pose in the 1921 Picasso painting *Maternity*, behind it), Brancusi's marble *Leda* (1923), Matisse's bronze *Seated Nude* (1925) and Giacometti's bronze *Spoon Woman* (1926). Comparisons of materials, styles and expression quite literally leaped out at the viewer. Nearby were disparate treatments of the human head by Dubuffet (1947), Francis Bacon (1954) and Giacometti (1966); a group of still lifes (1928–39) by Picasso, Braque, Léger and Matisse; and abstract works by Mondrian, Hélion and Ben Nicholson.

The American collection ranges from early Modern to Post Minimal, with particularly exemplary works from mid-century and a strong concentration of Chicago artists. Early Modernists Hartley, Dove and O'Keeffe; Surrealists Peter Blume, Leonid and Eugene Berman; Regionalists Grant Wood (represented here by his famous *American Gothic*, 1930), John Steuart Curry and

Reginald Marsh; Realist Edward Hopper (*Nighthawks*, 1942, a key work) and the obsessive Ivan Albright are some of the principal pre-1950s artists.

The high point of the American collection is in the splendid group of Abstract Expressionist works: Gorky's surrealistic *The Plough and the Song II* (1946), de Kooning's *Excavation* (1950), Pollock's *Grayed Rainbow* (1953), Clyfford Still's massive, black *Painting 1952*, two Rothkos (1949 and 1953–54) and six Hofmanns.

As far as U.S. art is concerned, contemporary trends from Pop to the present are covered fairly comprehensively, but recent European art is spotty at best. This may be in part because the institute purchases many of its contemporary works from its American Biennial exhibitions, which, obviously, do not include European works. But, for the same reason, the institute has perhaps the broadest holdings of recent American art of any general museum in the country. And many of the selections are superb: Warhol's towering *Mao*, an impeccable stainless steel and plexiglass box by Donald Judd, Johns's *Target* (1961) and *Corpse and Mirror* (1974), David Smith's *Cubi VIII* (1963), two modular floor pieces by LeWitt, four early Stellas, paintings and sculpture by Ellsworth Kelly, Robert Morris and Carl Andre, two Bruce Naumans (1965 and 1981) and, most recently, an installation on the main staircase by French Conceptualist Daniel Buren.

THE BARNES FOUNDATION

BOX 128, MERION STATION, PA 19066. Tel: (215) 667-0290.

Hours: Fri and Sat 9:30 am–4:30 pm, Sun 1–4:30 pm, closed holidays. 100 people with reservations and 100 people without reservations admitted Fri and Sat; 50 people with reservations and 50 people without, admitted Sun. Reservations made by telephone.

Admission: $1 each.

Publications:

   Albert C. Barnes, *The Art in Painting*. 1976, no price listed.

Reproductions: None.

Research: Apply to Board of Directors, who review requests on an individual basis.

The general impression that the social history of this magnificent, idiosyncratic collection generates more literature than the art it contains may well be justified. What is said to be one of the world's greatest assemblages of Impressionist and Post-Impressionist (and beyond) work remains, to the irritation and inconvenience of many, unpublished, and therefore more than a bit inscrutable.

Dr. Albert Barnes, the collection's principal hero and culprit, was initially exposed to modern art by a former classmate, the Ash Can School painter Arthur Glackens, whom he sent to Europe on an art-buying expedition in the 1910s. Barnes was won over by Glackens's choices, learned from them and thenceforth relied on his own judgment as he continued to buy art. In 1923, his growing collection was exhibited at the Pennsylvania Academy of the Fine Arts, where it was roundly ridiculed by local critics and connoisseurs. Deeply offended, Barnes refused all further access to "his" art to anyone but his students (he had established an art school) and friends and categorically denied requests for loans and photographs. After his death in 1951, legal suits succeeded in easing these restrictions. The public is now admitted to the collection on a limited basis, and black and white photographs are furnished at the discretion of the foundation's current director, Barnes's erstwhile co-author, Violetta de Mazia.

Every room in the otherwise unfurnished two-story mansion is installed as Barnes directed and, following his wishes, cannot be rearranged. Many works are hung high on the walls, grouped according to size or color, and shown alongside examples of decorative metalwork, Latin American and New Mexican *santos* figures and African carvings. The resulting aura is a mixture of homely clutter and sheer genius.

The imposing, two-story-high entrance gallery is dominated by Matisse's forty-seven-foot-long mural *The Dance* (1932–33), which was executed by the artist in situ on his only visit to the U.S. Beneath and to one side of it is one of his immense Moroccan figures, composed of broad, flat expanses of brilliant green and pink. Across the room are incomparable, large-scale Renoirs and Cézannes and Seurat's pointillist *Les Poseuses.* The constellation is literally dazzling.

A staircase landing is the unprepossessing location of Matisse's sparkling *Joy of Life* (1905–06), which would surely be a focal point in any other museum. The principal second-floor gallery contains more large-scale Matisses—still lifes, portraits, figure groups, as well as the psychologically (and otherwise) complex *Music Lesson* of 1917.

Whether or not Barnes's claim of having "discovered" Soutine and Modigliani is accurate, he indisputably did buy many of their highly prized works. Nor did he neglect Picasso, whose blue, pink and Cubist periods are admirably represented. A few Picasso works on paper are among the collection's revelations. Barnes's appetite for Renoir seems to have been insatiable, and his taste for Courbet, a touch prurient. The foundation's explicitly sexual Courbet from 1864 dispels any doubts as to why this Realist painter was regarded as the radical of his day.

This is just the tip of the iceberg: there are early Cubist still lifes by Braque; enchanting Henri Rousseaus, Monets, Degas, Gauguins, weird and rather degenerate de Chiricos (except for his conventional portrait drawing of Barnes) and a profusion of Lipchitz sculptures, some of which adorn niches on the museum's facade.

A trip to the Barnes offers countless pleasures and considerable frustration, stemming from the absence of informative wall captions (or *any* captions, for that matter). Nor is there so much as a published checklist of the collection.

THE DES MOINES ART CENTER

GREENWOOD PARK, DES MOINES, IA 50312. Tel: (515) 277-4405
Hours: Tues–Sat 11 am–5 pm, Sun 12–5 pm. Check hours on holidays. Closed Mon.
Admission: Free.
Publications: None.

Reproductions: Prints of selected works.
Research: Reference library open to the community at large.

In 1948, the Des Moines Art Center opened in a building designed by Eero Saarinen. It expanded into an I. M. Pei—designed wing in 1968 and is anticipating the completion of a new, three-level addition by Richard Meier in the fall of 1984. The small museum's architectural distinction reflects its dedication to contemporary art while belying the mom-and-pop nature of its operational structure. Still not departmentalized, at this writing the center is preparing to hire its first curator. Until now, the director (since 1969, James Demetrion), along with a small support staff, has attended to every aspect of the museum's functioning.

The majority of the approximately 400 twentieth-century works in the collection are American: American Impressionism, the Eight and Synchronism are represented, as are Grant Wood (an Iowa native) and Joseph Cornell. Edward Hopper's *The Automat* is one of the prides of the museum. The collection picks up again at the mid-1950s with single, strong works by prominent artists: Rothko, Morris Louis, Rauschenberg's 1958 combine painting *Talisman* and Jasper Johns's *Tennyson* from the same year (Des Moines claims to be the first Midwestern museum to buy a Johns), Noland and Stella from 1960, Kelly, Poons, Segal, Lichtenstein, Oldenburg, Estes, Pearlstein and Irwin.

Steering clear of Minimalism, acquisitions in the past decade have leaned heavily toward various other modes of contemporary art. Works by Joseph Beuys, Nancy Graves, Robert Arneson, Ann McCoy, Charles Simonds, Lois Lane, Ellen Lanyon and others have entered the collection during this time. Sculpture, which is installed in the Pei wing, includes pieces by Brancusi, Giacometti, Maillol, Arp, David Smith, Noguchi, Christopher Wilmarth, Jackie Ferrara and Mark di Suvero.

THE SOLOMON R. GUGGENHEIM MUSEUM

1071 FIFTH AVENUE AT 88TH STREET, NEW YORK, NY 10028.
Tel: (212) 860-1313
Hours: Wed–Sun 11 am–5 pm, Tues 11 am–8 pm, closed Mon.
Admission: $2 adults, $1.25 students and senior citizens; free to children under 7; free on Tues eve.
Publications: Volumes, authored by Thomas M. Messer with various co-authors, include the following:

British Art Now. 1979, $8.50.
Expressionism—A German Intuition, 1905–1920. 1980, $17.95.
Handbook: The Guggenheim Museum Collection 1900–1980. 1980, $14.85.
Kandinsky in Munich: 1896–1914. 1982, $19.50.
Paul Klee. 1981, $9.95.
Mark Rothko, 1903–1978: A Retrospective. 1978, $14.85.

Reproductions: Postcards and slides featuring items from the permanent collection and numerous shots of museum itself. Special strengths in Kandinsky, Klee and Miro. Posters from museum exhibitions.
Research: Extensive research library covering history of museum and its collections is open to public by appointment.

Vasily Kandinsky.
Composition 8, No. 260,
Oil on canvas, 1923

The Guggenheim must be one of the only museums in the world whose popular acclaim owes more to its architectural design than to the art it exhibits. Given the excellence of the collection, this state of affairs seems a bit unjust; however, since the architecture itself steadily draws a wide audience, the museum may be under less pressure than other institutions to put on crowd-pleasing shows. The Guggenheim's exhibition program, whatever its shortcomings and notwithstanding active corporate sponsorship, does not stoop to conquer the masses.

The building, designed by Frank Lloyd Wright and completed in 1959, generates controversy to this day, primarily because its open, spiraling interior can seem inhospitable to works of art, especially to flat, rectilinear paintings that are hung on its sloping concave walls. A quarter-mile-long cantilevered ramp winds its way from the ground floor rotunda through what has been described as a chambered nautilus divided into 74 bays toward the skylight dome ninety-two feet above. This physical channeling provides a very powerful kinesthetic experience—too powerful, some feel, to allow for the demands of the art objects one meets along the way.

The person largely responsible for the museum in its early stages was nearly as dogmatic as the architecture has turned out to be. Baroness Hilla Rebay von Ehrenwiesen (a.k.a. Hilla Rebay), a German artist convinced of the supremacy of non-objective (i.e., abstract) painting, became Simon Guggenheim's art adviser in New York in 1929. In 1937, Guggenheim transferred control of his private collection to the Solomon R. Guggenheim Foundation and opened it to the public. It was called The Museum of Non-Objective Painting and was directed by Rebay. There was much superb European abstraction—Kandinsky, Moholy-Nagy, Mondrian, Robert Delaunay, along with less impressive selections of Rebay's and her protegé Rudolf Bauer's own work. In 1948, the year before he died, Guggenheim bought 700 works from the estate of Karl Nierendorf. These included figurative German Expressionist paintings (fifty-four Kirchners and Kokoschkas), eighteen Kandinskys, one hundred ten Klees, six Chagalls, twenty-four Feiningers. Thus, a healthy infusion of non–non-objective art was introduced into the museum.

After Rebay's retirement in 1952, the museum acquired its present name, shed some constraining aesthetic biases and began to operate as a general museum of twentieth-century art. Under the directorship of James Johnson Sweeney (1952–60), the Guggenheim purchased sculpture (eleven Brancusis, three Cubist Archipenkos, seven Calders, Moore, Ernst, Giacometti, Duchamp-Villon, Miró, Maillol) and American art (Abstract Expressionism) and began to accept "outside" bequests, such as that of Katherine Dreier in 1953.

Today, although the museum collects and exhibits contemporary American work, the Guggenheim still possesses a distinctly European air. The strengths of the collection remain Kandinsky, Klee, Miró, Léger, Robert Delaunay, Modigliani, Gleize, Marc, Picasso, Calder and Giacometti. There is little pre–World War II American work, but from the 1950s and 1960s, Morris Louis, Rothko, Krasner and Frankenthaler have been accumulated in some depth.

Two fairly recent gifts have substantially enriched the Guggenheim's holdings. The Justin K. Thannhauser collection, on loan since 1965 and officially bequeathed in 1978, has extended the museum's historical scope to include French Impressionism and Post-Impressionism. Exhibited in its own suite of galleries together with related works from the Guggenheim's holdings (twenty-seven Picassos, for example, dated 1900 to 1960), the Thannhauser collection provides a historical frame of reference for the museum's twentieth-century works. On permanent view are some sixty paintings and sculptures: Pissarro, Manet, Renoir Cézanne, van Gogh, Gauguin, Degas, Vuillard, Braque and Maillol.

The other significant addition was the 1974 bequest of Peggy Guggenheim's Palazzo Venier dei Leoni in Venice, together with her collection of twentieth-century art, consisting of 260 paintings, sculptures and works on paper. The collection, which will remain in Venice but may be drawn upon for special exhibitions in New York and elsewhere, fills many gaps in the Guggenheim's holdings: six Pollocks, Ernsts, Magrittes, Picabia, Gorky and sculpture by the Italian Futurists, Arp, Gonzalez and Cornell.

Most exhibitions organized by the Guggenheim are solo shows, with a fairly even balance of living and dead, American and European artists. The museum gave early attention to Minimalism, with shows of Brice Marden, Robert Ryman, Carl Andre, Robert Mangold and Eva Hesse. Over the past decade, a propensity toward formal, tightly constructed art has been apparent in a constellation of exhibitions: Malevich, "The Art of the Avant Garde in Russia: Selections from the Costakis Collection," "The Planar Dimension: Europe 1912–1932." This tendency toward geometric abstraction is due to curatorial preference, not to policy. During the same period, the museum also organized retrospectives of James Ensor and Joseph Beuys, among others, whose work diverges from Constructivist premises.

Because temporary exhibitions occupy the lion's share of gallery space during most of the year, only a fraction of the permanent collection (approximately 4,000 works) is ever seen. To increase the collection's visibility and as a service to other museums, the Guggenheim loans groups of works to selected institutions that demonstrate specific needs for them.

HIRSHHORN MUSEUM AND SCULPTURE GARDEN
SMITHSONIAN INSTITUTION
INDEPENDENCE AVENUE AT EIGHTH STREET, SW,
WASHINGTON, DC 20560. Tel: (202) 357-1618
Hours: Sun–Sat 10 am–5:30 pm, closed Christmas; extended summer hours determined annually; sculpture Garden open 7:30 am–dusk.
Admission: Free.
Publications:
 Lerner, Abram, et al; *Hirshhorn Museum and Sculpture Garden.* 1974, $50.
 Miranda McClintic, *David Smith: The Hirshhorn Museum and Sculpture Garden Collection.* 1979, $4.95.
 Judith Zilczer, *Joseph Stella: The Hirshhorn Museum and Sculpture Garden Collection.* 1983, $4.95.
Reproductions: 18 posters, 138 postcards, and slides.
Research: Library open to scholars by appointment. It focuses on the collection.

What must be the most massive amount of modern art ever collected by a single individual was presented to the U.S. government by Joseph Hirshhorn in 1966. In 1974, after much squabbling about the provisions of the gift— that it be housed in a government-built and -maintained museum named after the donor and situated on the National Mall—the Hirshhorn Museum officially opened under the auspices of the Smithsonian Institution and the conditions of its benefactor's wishes. Hirshhorn's original donation of 4,000 paintings and drawings and 2,000 sculptures was augmented during his lifetime and further increased by his bequest (he died in 1981) of 6,000 works. The museum now contains some 7,500 paintings and sculptures, two-thirds of which date from this century, and about 900 of which are on view at any one time.

For all its vastness, the collection is a highly personal one and uneven in the extreme. Although he was in fact buying for posterity, Hirshhorn seems to have bought only what he himself liked. Fortunately, his likings encompassed many marvelous things.

Degas, Picassos, Matisses—the bronzes, not the pictures—were avidly collected by Hirshhorn, who assembled one of the world's largest groupings of modern sculpture. It runs from Rodin *(The Burghers of Calais, Balzac)* to Robert Smithson and contains a greater number of Henry Moores (more

Henry Moore
King and Queen,
Bronze, 1952-1953

than sixty) than can be found anywhere else in the U.S. Unlike its paintings, the Hirshhorn's sculpture holdings form a nearly comprehensive historical survey. Besides important, large-scale works and concentrations of Calder and David Smith, among others, there are wonderful rarities, such as two small, blocky Giacometti plasters from the 1930s.

The painting collection, predominantly American, spans the century, just reaching Minimalism. Gems and oddities alike abound, the latter perhaps best exemplified by some 200 Eilshemiuses. Other artists represented in depth are The Eight, Oscar Bluemner, Hartley, Gorky, de Kooning, Cornell and, since a recent gift covering his life's work, Raphael Soyer. There are good Max Webers, O'Keeffes, Hoppers and, generally speaking, Abstract Expressionists and Photo-realists. Uncommon early pieces by Albers (1921 and 1925) and Motherwell (1946) lend valuable historical perspective to those artists' mature periods, and certain works by Miró (*Circus Horse,* 1927), Hartley (*Christ Held by Half-Naked Men,* 1940–41), Pollock, Ben Nicholson (*White Relief,* 1938), Newman (*Covenant,* 1949), Kline (*Delaware Gap,* 1958), Stella (*Arundel Castle,* a black painting from 1959), and Ruscha (*The Los Angeles County Museum on Fire,* 1968) show their authors at or near their best.

The museum's major effort seems to be in presenting, not in expanding or updating, the permanent holdings. The installation is kept in continual flux with changing groupings of works—small "in house" shows based on any number of themes or individual artists. These frequent rotations provide relief from the rigid chronological format adopted by most museums, set up lively relationships among works and make all but obsolete the notion of a storage collection.

MILWAUKEE ART MUSEUM

750 N. LINCOLN MEMORIAL DRIVE, MILWAUKEE, WI 53202.
Tel: (414) 271-9508
Hours: Tues, Wed, Fri, Sat 10 am–5 pm, Sun 1–6 pm, Thurs 12–9 pm, closed Mon, Thanksgiving, Christmas, New Year's.
Admission: $2 adults, $1 students, senior citizens, handicapped, free to children under 12; also free to Milwaukee County residents Wed and Sat 10 am–12 pm, and to members.
Publications:
    Tracy Atkinson, *Personal Selections from the Collection of Mrs. Harry Lynde Bradley.* 1975, $25.
    Russell Bowman, *New Figuration In America.* 1982, $12.

Reproductions: Many posters, postcards and slides of art works in the permanent collection.

Research: Library and print room open by appointment. Holdings include the Prairie Archives, a research-oriented collection associated with the Prairie School and Frank Lloyd Wright Jr.

Perched on Lake Michigan's shorefront, the Milwaukee Art Museum's original 1957 Eero Saarinen building was extended in 1975, quadrupling the facility's exhibition area, which now totals 95,000 square feet. The new wing houses the museum's principal strengths, the bulk of its nineteenth and twentieth-century holdings and temporary exhibitions. Of foremost distinction is the Bradley collection (gift of Mrs. Harry Lynde Bradley, who underwrote a large part of the museum's recent addition) of some 500

Mark Rothko.
Green, Red, Blue,
Oil on canvas, 1955

twentieth-century European and American works. Most notable are representations of early Modernism from Europe, particularly the Fauves, German Expressionists and Blaue Reiter, with concentrations of works by Gabriele Munter, Raoul Dufy, Lyonel Feininger and major pieces by Léger, Braque, Miró, Klee, Soutine, Kirchner; and Americans through Op art, with substantial groups of paintings by Stuart Davis, Avery, O'Keeffe and key works by Rothko, Kelly and Alex Katz. There is sculpture by Lachaise, Giacometti, Moore, Hepworth and David Smith, among others. About eighty percent of the Bradley paintings and sculpture (there are also prints and drawings) are on permanent view in fourteen galleries devoted exclusively to the collection.

Apart from the Bradley holdings, the museum is strong in German Expressionism and boasts fairly thorough coverage of early American Realism (all the members of The Eight are represented by more than one work each, plus Joseph Stella, William Zorach) and Abstraction (Maniere Dawson, Fritz Glarner, Burgoyne Diller) and considerable samplings of Pop (Warhol, Oldenburg), Abstract Expressionism (Reinhardt, Louis), New Realism (Duane Hanson, Al Leslie, Philip Pearlstein), Op and Minimalism (Hesse, Smithson, Robert Morris, Andre, LeWitt, Ryman, Larry Bell).

THE MUSEUM OF MODERN ART

18 WEST 54TH STREET, NEW YORK, NY 10019. Tel: (212) 708-9400
Hours: Daily 11 am–6 pm, Thurs 11 am–9 pm, closed Wed.
Admission: $3 adults, $2 students, $1 children and senior citizens; pay what you wish on Tuesdays.
Publications:

Alfred H. Barr Jr., *Cubism and Abstract Art.* 1974, $7.95.

———, *Painting and Sculpture in the Museum of Modern Art 1929–1967.* 1977, $40.

———, *What is Modern Painting?* 1975, $3.50.

John Elderfield, *Matisse in the Collection of the Museum of Modern Art.* 1978, $12.50.

Robert Goldwater, *What is Modern Sculpture?* 1971, $12.50.

W. S. Lieberman (ed.), *Art of the Twenties.* 1979, $8.95.

Kynaston McShine, *Joseph Cornell.* 1970, $12.50.

William Rubin, *De Chirico.* 1982, $17.50.

———, *Pablo Picasso: A Retrospective.* 1980, $25.

Reproductions: Extensive selection of postcards and slides from the permanent collection; posters from major exhibits.
Research: 80,000-volume library open by appointment. Study center of Department of Painting & Sculpture, open by appointment.

The permanent collection of roughly 100,000 objects is generally acknowledged to be the best survey of international modern art in the world, dating from post-Impressionism to the present. Its classic works are universally known: van Gogh's *Starry Night*, Matisse's *The Dance* and *Red Studio*, Picasso's *Les Demoiselles d'Avignon*, Malevich's *Suprematist Composition: White on White*, Mondrian's *Broadway Boogie-Woogie*, Pollock's *No. 1.* The European holdings from 1905 to 1940 are unexcelled anywhere.

The museum was founded in 1929 by three serious, socially well leveraged New York women concerned with educating the American public in modern art and with raising the cultural standards of the country. They hired Alfred H. Barr, then twenty-seven, as director, and it was he who defined the museum's objectives, steered its course and forged its style.

MoMA was conceived as a multi-departmental museum—its film, photography, architecture and design divisions were the first of their kinds in the U.S. Barr had visited the U.S.S.R. before joining MoMA and led the museum to make maverick acquisitions of Russian Constructivist works. In the 1940s and 1950s, when Barr became interested in American art,

Pablo Picasso.
Les Demoiselles d'Avignon,
Oil on canvas, 1907

MoMA bought and showed new and difficult avant-garde paintings: Pollock's *She Wolf* in 1944, a de Kooning in 1948 and Gorky's *Agony* in 1950. Barr admired the work of Jasper Johns from the start, purchasing for the museum three paintings from the artist's first show and soliciting three more from various collectors. The American holdings were boosted in 1967 by gifts from Philip Johnson (Dine, Flavin, Judd, di Suvero) and Sidney Janis (103 works by Gorky, Kline, Rothko, Pollock, Oldenburg, Warhol, Segal, among others). A combined gift/purchase arrangement with Lee Krasner in 1980 augmented MoMA's Pollock holdings by seven, for a total of seventeen paintings (1936–53) and five works on paper.

MoMA's exhibitions, both historical and contemporary, and their attendant publications, have probably had a more profound impact on artists, and thus on the art of our time, than those of any other single institution. All departments manage to organize their share of major shows. Among the landmarks: "Modern Architecture: International Exhibition" (1932), "Machine Art" (1934), "Fantastic Art, Dada and Surrealism" (1936), the "Useful Objects" series, "Picasso: 40 Years of His Art" (1939), "Jackson Pollock" (1956), "The Photographer's Eye" (1964), "Dada, Surrealism and their Heritage" (1968), "The Machine as Seen at the End of the Mechanical Age" (1968), Frank Stella and "Information" (1970), Barnett Newman (1971), "Cézanne: The Late Work" (1977), Sol LeWitt (1978), "Pablo Picasso: A Retrospective" (1980). A series of small, low-budget, rapidly changing international shows (often solo) of new art, called "Projects," was launched in 1971 as a means of keeping contemporary art constantly on the agenda. In 1974, video was incorporated into the series. "Projects" has fulfilled its mission to mixed reviews: the gallery space set aside for it was cramped and awkward and the shows themselves occasionally resembled the token paliatives that some critics believed they were.

As this guide goes to press, MoMA is nearing the completion of a $41 million expansion and renovation project for increasing exhibition space, enlarging storage and study areas, and improving means for viewers to circulate through the museum. Designed by Cesar Pelli, a new six-story west wing (under a forty-four story luxury apartment tower) will contain 46,500 square feet of additional gallery space. Together, the new structure and the museum's renovated 1964 Philip Johnson building will be twice the size of the former facility while retaining on the interior its generally intimate character. Eight hundred paintings and sculptures from the permanent collection will be on view (compared to 600 previously), arranged in basically chronological order. Sculpture will be interspersed among the paintings, rather than segregated as before. A greater portion of the department's sixty-four Picassos and seventeen Pollocks will be on view, and there will be a full room of de Chiricos. The installation of pre-1940 works will be more or less permanent; more recent pieces will be frequently rotated.

PHILADELPHIA MUSEUM OF ART
BENJAMIN FRANKLIN PARKWAY, PHILADELPHIA, PA 19101.
Tel: (215) 763-8100
Hours: Wed–Sun 10 am–5 pm, closed Mon, Tues and legal holidays.
Admission: $2 adults, $1 children under 18, students, senior citizens.
Publications:
    A. E. Gallatin, *The A. E. Gallatin Collection: Museum of Living Art.* 1954, $5.
    Donald Rosenthal, *The Charlotte Dorrance Wright Collection.* 1978, $4.95.
Reproductions: Large selection of prints, posters and postcards.
Research: Library, print and study collections open to those with professional interest by appointment.

Philadelphia's notorious hostility to Modernism and its exponents notwithstanding, the city's principal museum boasts one of the world's great collections of early-twentieth-century European art. It is *the* place in this country to see Rodin (housed in a separate building nearby), Brancusi and Duchamp, and, in the area of Cubism, its holdings are on a par with those of New York City's Museum of Modern Art. This standing is due mainly to the gifts of Mr. and Mrs. Walter Arensberg and of A. E. Gallatin. The Arensberg Collection, presented to the museum in 1950, contains 216 twentieth-century works, most of which are permanently on view. Kandinskys, Klees, Braques and Picassos, Légers, de Chiricos, the Surrealists, an oustanding group of Mirós, a small gallery of Duchamp-Villon plaster casts and bronzes tracing the formal development of one of his best-known works, *The Horse;* a chapellike room of twenty Brancusis, and the world's largest collection of works by Marcel Duchamp, thirty paintings and objects installed chronologically alongside other of the artists' pieces are owned by the museum. The paintings (1902–12) include *Nude Descending a Staircase,* the *succès de scandale* of the 1913 Armory Show. Readymades (*Bottlerack,* 1961) and assisted readymades (*With Hidden Noise,* 1916, the original *Why Not Sneeze, Rrose Selavy?,* 1921) lead up to the cracked *Large Glass Completed* (1915–65), a diagrammatic narrative that caps Duchamp's early career, and to the artist's last major work, the enigmatic, humorously erotic *Given: 1.*

The Waterfall, 2. The Illuminating Gas (1946–66), a large mixed-medium panorama that defies description within the limits of this guide.

The Gallatin holdings—179 modern works—are particularly rich in abstraction: Cubism, Constructivism, De Stijl. Among the noted Picassos are the 1906 *Self Portrait with Palette;* the 1914 painted bronze *Glass of Absinthe;* and the Synthetic Cubist *Three Musicians* (1921), of which the Museum of Modern Art owns a second version.

There is a wealth of other masterpieces and precursors of Modernism scattered about (Cézanne's late, monumental *Large Bathers* in the Tyson collection, wonderful early Chagalls and Soutines in the Stern collection, for example), but it is best to know what one is looking for in the maze of European galleries, some of which are arranged as units of individual bequests.

The same holds true, although to a lesser degree, for contemporary art,

Marcel Duchamp
Nude Descending a Staircase, No. 2,
Oil on canvas, 1912

which is found in three locations, all on different levels. (This decentralization problem should be greatly reduced—perhaps entirely eliminated—when the museum's interior is remodeled according to plans designed by Robert Venturi. All of the collections are slated to be reinstalled in more coherent fashion.)

Holdings of recent and contemporary art (particularly American) have been augmented substantially over the past ten years, with especially fine examples of Abstract Expressionism. Anne d'Harnoncourt, formerly the curator of twentieth-century art, is now the museum's director and is committed to sustaining Philadelphia's involvement with new art, both through acquisitions (Sol LeWitt's *Wall Drawing No. 348,* 1981, eight white, bold geometric figures over royal-blue ground, has been permanently installed on the vaulted ceiling of a corridor leading to the Arensberg Collection; the piece suggests the marriage of Minimalism and baroque) and exhibitions ("20th Century Design: 1945 to the Present," 1983).

THE PHILLIPS COLLECTION

1600-1612 21ST STREET, NW, WASHINGTON, DC 20009.

Tel: (202) 387-2151

Hours: Tues–Sat 10 am–5 pm, Sun 2–7 pm, closed Mon and some holidays.

Admission: Free.

Publications:

Eleanor Green, *Master Paintings from the Phillips Collection.* 1981, $18.
Sasha Newman, *Arthur Dove and Duncan Phillips: Artist and Patron.* 1981, $18.
Lockland Phillips, Ray Kass, *Morris Graves.* 1983, $20.
Monographs on Braque, Klee, Prendergast, Renoir for $6 each.

Reproductions: Large selection of posters, prints, postcards and slides based on the collection.

Research: Library open to researchers and other interested persons by appointment.

Purported to be the oldest museum of modern art in the U.S., the Phillips Collection opened to the public in 1921 as a "gallery of modern art and its sources" especially committed to the work of living artists. It still occupies its original nineteenth-century building, until 1931 the home of its founder, Duncan Phillips, but has been meticulously restored, technologically equipped and expanded by an annex built in 1960. Phillips felt that an "unpretentious domestic setting" was propitious for experiencing works of art, and this ambience has been faithfully preserved.

Phillips was one of this country's few early collectors of modern art. He began with the American Impressionists and proceeded, according to the dictates of his own eclectic eye, to assemble a diverse, international collection that was to be, in his own words, "unorthodox ... in not segregating periods and nationalities." A few Old Masters (Goya, El Greco) are sprinkled through the galleries; Realism, Expressionism and Abstraction interrelate;

Arthur Dove.
Cows in a Pasture,
Wax emulsion on canvas, 1935

and Europeans and Americans seem to coexist peacefully enough in close proximity. While the gallery continues to add to the more than 2,000 works that currently make up the collection, the volume of contemporary acquisitions has been markedly reduced since the late 1950s (Phillips died in 1966). The last major statement here is that of the Abstract Expressionists.

The European bias, if it can be described as such, comes down in favor of the French. There are seven Daumier oils, six Cézannes (including a superb self-portrait), Renoir's *Luncheon of the Boating Party,* several Picassos (notably, the early *Blue Room*), two Matisses and, commensurate with Phillips's opinion that Braque and Bonnard were the greatest French artists of their period, twelve Braques (1914–58) and sixteen Bonnard oils, the largest group of Bonnards in the U.S. Also in the collection are Kandinskys, Kokoschkas, Soutines, a Schwitters, a Mondrian and thirteen Klees.

Phillips liked to assemble "units" of pictures by artists he admired, in quantities sufficient to fill an entire room or gallery. Among American works he bought are fifty-three Arthur Doves, still more Augustus Vincent Tacks, twenty-one Elshemiuses, John Grahams, John Marins, five O'Keeffes (including *Ranchos Church*), Hartleys, Karl Knaths—a selection that should give some idea of his independent vision. The Phillips acquired works by Noland and a de Kooning in the early 1950s and is thought to be the first museum to add Rothko's work (another "unit") to its holdings. Figurative Diebenkorns entered the collection in the late 1950s, along with paintings by Philip Guston, Joan Mitchell, Sam Francis and Pollock. The prescient acquisitions record is matched by the frequent exhibitions of advanced art that the Phillips organized regularly from the 1930s to the 1960s, and again in the 1980s.

SAN FRANCISCO MUSEUM OF MODERN ART
VAN NESS AT McALLISTER, SAN FRANCISCO, CA 94102.
Tel: (415) 863-8800
Hours: Tues, Wed and Fri 10 am–6 pm, Thurs 10 am–10 pm, Sat–Sun 10 am–5 pm, closed Mon and holidays.
Admission: $3 adults, $1.50 children under 17 and senior citizens, free to children under 5; free Thursdays 6–10 pm.
Publications:
> Thomas Albright, Peter Boswell, *Frank Lobdell: The Paintings and Monotypes.* 1983, $11.95.
> Dave Hickey, Peter Plagens, *The Work of Ed Ruscha.* 1982, $16.50.
> Henry E. Hopkins, Clyfford Still, *Clyfford Still.* 1976, $15.
> ———, Henry E. Hopkins, *Painting and Sculpture in California: The Modern Era.* 1977, $8.95.

Reproductions: Many posters, some prints and slides of art works in the permanent collection and special exhibitions.
Research: Research library open to general public Mon–Wed 1–5 pm. It is mostly concerned with twentieth-century art.

The "Modern" in this museum's name was added as recently as 1975, although the institution has been on its present twentieth-century course officially since 1935, making it one of the oldest exclusively modern

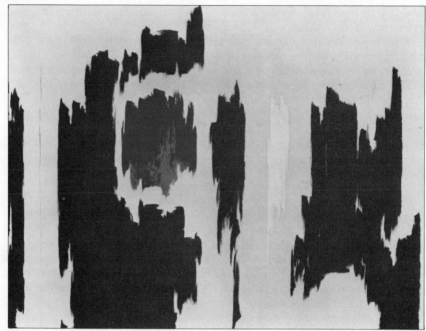

Clyfford Still.
Untitled,
Oil on canvas, 1962

museums in the U.S., and unique on the West Coast. Housed on two floors of the city's War Memorial Building, the museum enjoys handsome but con-straining quarters and is seeking a solution to its needs for greater space. From the painting and sculpture collection of some 2,500 objects, groups of 250 are rotated through the galleries, where they are installed more or less chronologically.

While an international overview of twentieth-century art is the museum's desired goal, certain strengths and shortcomings are apparent. The collec-tion starts with ten early Matisses (most celebrated is *The Girl with Green Eyes*, 1908) and the artist's Fauve colleagues, skips Analytical Cubism and plunges headlong into a wealth of German Expressionism. The Early Abstractionists—Picasso, Braque, Kandinsky—are lacking. De Stijl, Synthetic Cubism, Surrealism, the Mexican muralists and American art from the 1920s to the 1970s (with short shrift for Pop but a healthy sampling of work from the Bay Area) fill out the plan. Not to be missed are the galleries devoted to Clyfford Still and Joseph Albers.

In 1975, Still donated thirty of his paintings (1932–74) to San Francisco MoMA, making it the sole museum to possess a complete survey of his work. About ten of the canvases are on permanent display; the others are stored behind the gallery's movable partitions and are easily accessible for viewing upon special request. The small, skylighted, octagonal gallery where eight of the collection's thirteen Albers paintings are hung is ideally suited to the works' scale and subtle coloration.

Gorky's *Enigmatic Combat* (1936–37), Pollock's *Guardians of the Secret* (1943), Rothko's early *Tentacles of Memory* (1945–46) and Reinhardt's *#12-1955-56* are exceptional works among the fine holdings of Abstract Expressionism and its forerunners. An early Rauschenberg (*Collection,* 1953) and Jasper Johns's *Land's End* (1963) indicate two major directions (assemblage, Conceptualism) that painting would take during the 1960s. Five Stellas (1964–72) point towards the paradoxical end abstraction has reached in the 1980s.

Although there are plenty of abstract Diebenkorns, the museum has not a single example of the artist's earlier figurative painting. Much of Philip Guston's career is summarized in San Francisco MoMA's seven works (1947–77), of which the prize is the 1975 triptych *The Swell, Blue Light, Red Sea.*

There are Minimalist pieces (by Judd, LeWitt, and Bell), a handful of large-scale outdoor works (by Witkin, Tony Smith, Voulkos, and Nauman), David Smith's 1959 *Noon Sun* and, among new works, Bryan Hunt's bronze *Daphne II* (1979) and a signature twig horse (1978) by Deborah Butterfield. Owing largely to economic factors, purchases are made mainly in recent American art, with special, though not overriding, attention to the Bay Area.

UNIVERSITY ART MUSEUM

UNIVERSITY OF CALIFORNIA, 2626 BANCROFT WAY,
BERKELEY, CA 94720. Tel: (415) 642-1209
Hours: Wed–Sun 11 am–5 pm, closed Mon and Tues.
Admission: $2 adult, $1 young adult and senior citizen, free to members and UC students; free Thurs 11 am–12 Noon.
Publications:
Brenda Richardson, *Joan Brown.* 1974, $4.
Mark Rosenthal, *Neil Jenney: Paintings and Sculpture 1967–1980.* 1981, $11.50.
Peter Selz, *Funk.* 1967, $2.
Reproductions: None.
Research: Library reserved for students and faculty of UC. Pacific Film Archives are part of museum.

In terms of area, this is the largest university museum in the country. With 31,000 square feet of exhibition space, it is roughly comparable in size to the Whitney Museum's Marcel Breuer building. Although Berkeley is a general museum with holdings ranging from Asian to Italian baroque, it is esteemed mainly for its collections of Abstract Expressionism (said by some to be the finest west of Chicago) and California art and for its exhibitions of twentieth-century art.

This young museum (it opened in 1970) had auspicious formative years. Charged with getting things started, Peter Selz (formerly a curator at New York's Museum of Modern Art) solicited numerous gifts from artists just prior to a tax-law change that "allowed" artists to deduct from their taxes only the material cost of works donated to nonprofit institutions. In 1963, Hans Hofmann, who had taught summer sessions at Berkeley in 1930 and 1931 and had been given his first U.S. exhibition there, presented the

Helen Frankenthaler.
Before the Caves,
Oil on canvas, 1958

fledgling institution with forty-five of his paintings plus $250,000 toward the construction of the museum's new building.

Twenty-five of the Hofmanns are on continuous view, along with roughly 100 other twentieth-century pieces, which rotate through the museum. Works by Rothko, Reinhardt, Frankenthaler (*Before the Cave,* an exemplary stain painting and winner of the 1958 Paris Biennale), de Kooning (his early *The Marshes*), Clyfford Still, Sam Francis and David Smith (the 1962 *Voltri XIII*) are among the selections typically on view. The outdoor sculpture garden contains large-scale works by Calder, Liberman, Pomodoro and Voulkos; a Flavin *Tatlin Monument* and wooden box by Don Judd are among the Minimalist pieces indoors. Bay area artists—Richard Diebenkorn, Joan Brown, Robert Arneson, Robert Hudson, Jess, Bruce Conner, for instance—are well accounted for at Berkeley, and new works by vanguard practitioners are added to the collection when funds permit (a *Hammering Man* by Jonathan Borofsky is the latest at this writing).

The museum's exhibition record would be impressive even for an institution with double its staff and financial resources. Throughout the years, Berkeley has organized both modern and contemporary exhibitions of major significance. In the early days, Selz produced ambitious shows of great diversity: funk art, kinetic art and a Fernand Hodler retrospective (1972) that traveled to the Guggenheim. Curator Mark Rosenthal perpetuated that tradition with retrospectives of Neil Jenney (1981), Jonathan Borofsky (1983), Franz Marc (1979) and Juan Gris (which opened in 1983 at the National Gallery before its Berkeley showing). Less definitive "Matrix" exhibitions, pioneered by current director James Elliot when he headed Hartford's Wadsworth Atheneum, are a regular feature on the museum's calendar. Here, too, variety is of the essence. Numbering about ten per year, these smaller solo or group shows, most often of work by living artists, run the gamut of styles, nations and generations: offerings in 1983 included California realist Elmer Bischoff and conceptualist Jannis Kounellis.

The museum has also been known to make imaginative use of its extraordinary, reinforced-concrete building, designed by San Francisco architect Mario Ciampi. In a four-part exhibition, "Space and Support," Carl Andre, Daniel Buren, Robert Irwin and Maria Nordman were invited to treat the structure as a site on/in which to make their art.

WALKER ART CENTER
VINELAND PLACE, MINNEAPOLIS, MN 55403. Tel: (612) 375-7600

Hours: Tues–Sat 10 am–5 pm, special exhibitions open until 8 pm, Sun 11 am –5 pm, closed Mon; closing times vary in spring.
Admission: Free. Selected exhibitions: $2 adult, discount for students and senior citizens.
Publications: None.
Reproductions: Posters, postcards and slides of selected special exhibitions.
Research: Library of exhibition catalogues is for the staff, but anyone with bona fide reason welcome.

The *Vogue* writer who not long ago described Walker Art Center as "the best-run, most exciting contemporary art center in America" did not exaggerate. The center maintains the fastidiousness required of an established, historical institution and the zest of an "alternative space"—well, nearly. It has the largest performing arts program, one of the top exhibition agendas and one of the leading post-1960s American art collections of any U.S. museum. And the Walker hasn't peaked: it has just formed a new media department for film and video (which it has collected and shown for some time) and is in the midst of a $3 million expansion project (completion is scheduled for 1984) that will add two large galleries to the facility.

The Walker has good European and American modern holdings, minus Cubism, and boasts some truly great early paintings: Franz Marc's *Blue Horses,* Lyonel Feininger's *Church of the Minorities II* and Edward Hopper's *Office at Night.* In sculpture, there are Raymond Duchamp-Villon's Cubo-Futurist *Large Horse* (1914), David Smith's spikey, skeletal *Royal Bird* (1948), plus works by Nadelman, Giacometti, Lipchitz and so on. But the collection's pivotal years are 1960–65, from which many of its milestone pieces of Pop, assemblage, and Minimal art are derived. Within this period it contains concentrations of work by Noguchi, Nevelson, Oldenburg, Stella and Judd, as well as isolated show-stoppers such as Rauschenberg's *Trophy II* (1962) and di Suvero's *Stuyvesant's Eye.* The pluralist 1970s are manifest in all their motley, except for the deliberate omission of Pattern painting; recently endowed funds for acquisitions of new works by living artists should ensure the center's already proven commitment to the present.

One of the Walker's means of keeping the collection up to date is through its ongoing series of "Viewpoints" exhibitions, solo or group shows that change every eight weeks and focus on recent contemporary art developments. The range is from good-size theme shows (about one a year) to first-time museum exposures for local artists. In between fall one-person shows of artists with national and international profiles. Despite such diversity, the quality of the art featured in "Viewpoints" remains fairly consistent, because the museum regularly buys works from the exhibitions.

The Walker's De Stijl show (1982) was one of the most important international exhibitions of the year (it traveled to Europe), and the museum's retrospectives (most recently, of Chuck Close, William Wiley, Robert Graham bronzes, William Wegman and Jim Dine) and surveys reliably make a national impact. Post-modern music and dance, experimental theater and performance art are staple offerings of the performing arts program; independent film and video artists make frequent personal appearances.

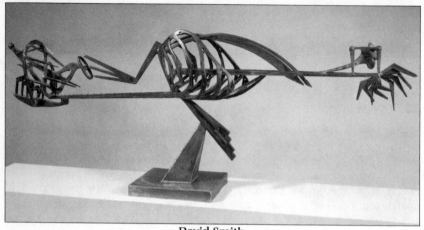

David Smith.
Royal Bird,
Welded stainless steel, 1947-1948

The driving, exacting force behind the Walker is its longtime (twenty-two years, at this writing) director, Martin Friedman, to whom the lion's share of the institution's success is attributed. Among his other achievements, Friedman has trained several generations of curators who began their careers at the Walker. Many of them are now among this country's most prominent museum professionals.

WHITNEY MUSEUM OF AMERICAN ART

945 MADISON AVENUE AT 75TH STREET, NEW YORK, NY 10021.
Tel: (212) 570-3600

Hours: Tues 11 am–8 pm, Wed–Sat 11 am–6 pm, Sun and holidays 12–6 pm, closed Mon.

Admission: $2.50 adults, $1.25 senior citizens, free to members and children, free on Tuesdays.

Publications:

Barbara Haskell, *Marsden Hartley.* 1980, $15.
Gail Levin, *Synchronism and Color Abstraction, 1910–1925.* 1978, $5.
Jean Lipman, *Calder's Universe.* 1976, $10.
Patterson Sims, *Alexander Calder.* 1981, $2.
——, *Georgia O'Keeffe.* 1981, $4.
——, *Ad Reinhardt.* 1980, $2.
——, *Charles Sheeler.* 1980, $2.

Reproductions: Color postcards and slides of many items from the permanent collection, including large groups of Calder and Hopper. Posters from major exhibits, including Hopper, Johns and O'Keeffe.

Research: Archive and library available to advanced students and scholars by appointment.

The origins of this country's foremost museum of twentieth-century American art were both patrician and bohemian. The late heiress and artist

Gertrude Vanderbilt Whitney, who has been aptly characterized as a "one-woman foundation for the arts," amassed a collection of more than 500 works by American artists associated with the Whitney Studio Club in Greenwich Village, an organization she formed in 1914 to exhibit works by her artist peers. (After some years the size of the membership became unwieldy and the club disbanded.) When in 1929 the Metropolitan Museum rejected Gertrude's offer of her collection, she determined to set up her own museum with the principal aim of providing exposure and support for living artists. Thus, her collection—of works by Stuart Davis, John Sloan, Eilshemius, Maurice Prendergast, Charles Sheeler, Oscar Bluemner, Kuniyoshi, Reginald Marsh, Paul Cadmus, George Luks, Joseph Stella, Preston Dickinson and others—became the nucleus of the Whitney Museum of American Art, which opened its doors to the public in 1931.

The Whitney now has a collection of over 10,000 works and has headquarters uptown in a building designed in 1963 by Marcel Breuer and Hamilton Smith. In the past few decades, the museum has been noted primarily for its exhibitions: the Whitney Biennial, a tradition since 1932, is still the preeminent invitational survey of contemporary American art, despite the fact that in recent years it has had some less-than-compelling manifestations. In the record year of 1973–74, the museum organized ten major shows—a variety of historical, contemporary, solo and group exhibitions. The typical mixture is of box-office hits (Edward Hopper, 1980) and more controversial or esoteric work (Richard Tuttle, Myron Stout, Forrest Bess), the latter often relegated to a subsidiary gallery off the main lobby.

In 1970, the film and video department launched its ongoing New American Filmmakers Series, changing exhibitions of independent film and video works. These present a broad, fairly reliable overview of the variety of current concerns among practitioners of these media and the cross-fertilization of ideas that occurs between them and artists working in other fields. This continuing forum for contemporary American film and video is unequaled by any other museum known to this writer. Through it, film and video have gained access to the Whitney's Biennial exhibitions and have qualified for full-blown museum-scale shows of their own (the 1982 Nam June Paik retrospective, for example).

As part of its outreach efforts, the Whitney has established three branch facilities, essentially kunsthalles, where the museum mounts changing exhibitions. The oldest of these, the Whitney Downtown, is in Manhattan's financial district. It provides curatorial experience for participants in the Whitney's Independent Study Program and lunchtime diversion for Wall Street denizens. The newest branch occupies a large pedestrian plaza in Philip Morris's recently opened (April 1983) headquarters on 42nd Street, across from Grand Central Terminal. The 42-foot-high ceiling makes this an ideal large-scale sculpture court for long-term installations; adjacent to it is a smaller gallery for more rapidly changing shows (about six per year). Philip Morris has underwritten the entire program. The Whitney outpost furthest from home base is in Stamford, Conn., at the corporate headquarters of Champion International. There, too the sponsor provides full funding.

Willem de Kooning.
Woman and Bicycle,
Oil on canvas, 1952-1953

The Whitney's lateral growth has been matched in recent years by major gifts of art that have recalled attention to the museum's permanent collection and its importance within the museum's larger scheme. In 1970, Edward Hopper's widow bequeathed the artist's entire estate to the Whitney; in 1978, 850 works by Reginald Marsh entered the collection in similar fashion; and in 1979, a gift of Morgan Russell's works and papers made the Whitney the leading public repository of that artist's work.

Although the museum owns exemplary pieces by many outstanding twentieth-century Americans, it has never had an endowed acquisitions fund and has occasionally been accused of exercising insufficient discrimination in accepting gifts of art. Until 1981, the museum had no space reserved for showing works from the permanent collection. Quipped former *New York Times* critic Hilton Kramer, "it is probably a mercy that we almost never get to see most of them." With the inauguration of such a space (the entire third floor, where the current installation of seventy-three paintings and sculptures will remain until 1986), the public can view the cream of the Whitney's holdings arranged roughly chronologically and thematically: Hartleys, O'Keeffes, Hopper's *Early Sunday Morning,* Gorky's *The Betrothal,* de Kooning's *Woman and Bicycle,* Pollock's *No. 27,* a drip painting from 1950, four David Smith sculptures (1951–61), Abstract Expressionists and 1950s Color Field painters, Jasper Johns's *Three Flags* (1958), Stella's *Die Fahne Hoch* (a black painting from 1959), 1960s Minimalist paintings and sculpture, Pop and Photo Realism.

Other portions of the collection, too, are soon likely to be aired, thanks to a recent grant in support of exhibitions and publications based on the museum's own works, and the overall collection itself may be upgraded as a result of a new emphasis "on acquiring works of the highest quality in all areas of twentieth-century American art" and of building in-depth representations of certain pivotal artists (Georgia O'Keeffe, among them).

Anticipating the desirability of a full-scale installation of the collection, the museum is making plans for a Michael Graves–designed addition to its Breuer building. The future wing, which will house the permanent collection, will double the museum's current gallery space and extend the full length of the city block on which the museum now stands, incorporating commercial shops into its structure on the ground level.

CHAPTER SIX

PHOTOGRAPHY

by
STEVEN HENRY MADOFF

THE ART INSTITUTE OF CHICAGO
MICHIGAN AVENUE AT ADAMS STREET, CHICAGO, IL 60603.
Tel: (312) 443-3600
Hours: Mon–Wed 10:30 am–4:30 pm, Thurs 10:30 am–8 pm, Fri 10:30 am–4:30 pm, Sat 10:30 am–5 pm, Sun and holidays 12–5 pm, closed Christmas.
Admission: Discretionary. Suggested contribution $4 adults, $2 children, senior citizens, students, free to children under six; free Thursday.
Publications: None.
Reproductions: Selection of posters, postcards and slides from selected exhibitions.
Research: Library open to museum members, museum staff, students and faculty of the School of the Art Institute, visiting scholars and curators. Collection is strong in history of art and architecture.

In the grand Beaux-Arts building that houses the Art Institute of Chicago, four new galleries have opened recently; elegant rooms, varying in size from the spacious to the intimate, to exhibit photographs. This new wealth of space dedicated to photographic work will provide the Art Institute with an opportunity to display their excellent generalist's collection. Begun in 1949 with Georgia O'Keeffe's presentation of 150 vintage prints by Alfred Stieglitz and fifty of his contemporaries, the Art Institute had been exhibiting photographs in annual shows sponsored by the Society of Amateur Photographers from 1900 to 1938. But with the reception of the Stieglitz group, the museum possessed an important holding. In the 1950s, the Department of Prints and Drawings began to purchase photographs in a broad historical framework, and by 1959 the first curator of photography, Hugh Edwards, was appointed. Edwards bought Camerons and Fox Talbots, but also the images of Marie Cosindas, Robert Frank and Danny Lyon. This diversity is the hallmark of the collection. An inventory of the holdings is frustrating, if one seeks a particular strength. The enormous group of Francis Friths and Maxine Du Camps is matched by others of Stieglitz, Atget, Ulmann and Siskind. Both centuries of photography, here and in Europe, are represented in depth and with adroit comprehension of schools, movements and traditions. There are perhaps 15,000 photographs.

One group of special interest came to the museum in the late 1970s from Julien Levy. Levy, who had been studying at Harvard, went to Paris in 1927. There, Man Ray and the Surrealists had a strong effect on him. The volatile nature of the arts at this time, the continuing enthusiasm that combined myths and machines in the paintings of Picabia and Duchamp, encompassed photography as well. When Levy returned to the States and opened his art gallery in New York in 1931, his first exhibit was an homage to Stieglitz. In coming years, he was a great entrepreneur of Surrealism: putting on the first Surrealist exhibition in New York in 1932; giving Dali, Cornell, Matta and Gorky shows; publishing a Surrealist anthology and even translating for the Surrealists on occasion. But concurrently, he was collecting photographs by the most adventurous photographers of the day. Moholy-Nagy, Kertész, Man Ray, Brassaï, Outerbridge, Lucia Moholy, Alvarez Bravo and Cunningham were among his trophies. This collection of 250 images, largely dating from the 1920s and 1930s, forms an essential catalogue of the photographic aesthetic at the height of Modernism.

It has been said that the photograph began its existence as a copy of the painting and has spent much of its life in argument with that identity. Its "quotations from appearance," to use John Berger's phrase, are said to resemble the world more than any other art (except film, which uses photography as a transient medium). Yet in the images of Paul Outerbridge, another aspect of photography embraces the purely aesthetic not in the name of a retrograde pictorialism, but in the spirit of abstraction. Outerbridge had gone to Europe in 1925 and become friends with Man Ray, Picabia, Picasso and Brancusi. He had already been working with abstract composition, but in the photographs that followed his European acquaintance, the combination of Cubist and subconscious influences so important to Surrealism became patently clear. In his photograph *Consciousness* (1931), the picture's shallow space is predictably Cubist. Its ovals, cone, triangle and lines demand reception as a wholly aesthetic statement, refusing to refer to any representational whole. Yet the title inscribes a meaning, a metaphor that provides the image's content. It becomes fetishistic, a totem used to excite and repeat a state of being that is transferred from the object to the person through the idea superimposed upon it. The disturbance of the image is thus its *lack* of detail, its emphasis on what is not there. The decaying physical world, so popular in the modernism of Baudelaire and Eliot, is replaced by idea. And it is not surprising that Outerbridge's later work, none of which was shown in his lifetime, was fixated on visions of sexual festishism and decadence.

Outerbridge is a curious tonic here, for the majority of the museum's collection presents a more satisfied vision of the world as it is. The nineteenth-century holdings particularly delight in the discoveries of a world brought back to the salon. Frith's conquest of Egypt, the Bisson frères' magnificent views of the Alps and Cameron's portraits of the famous are all expeditions into regions generally inaccessible. The nineteenth century sought to captivate the palpable world through its cameras, and the dichotomy between its intentions and Outerbridge's is vastly instructive.

CENTER FOR CREATIVE PHOTOGRAPHY

UNIVERSITY OF ARIZONA, 843 EAST UNIVERSITY BOULEVARD, TUCSON, AZ 85719. Tel: (602) 626-4636

Hours: Mon–Fri 9 am–5 pm, Sun 12–5 pm.
Admission: Free.
Publications:

Helen Gee, *Photography of the Fifties: An American Perspective.* nd, $12.50.

Timothy Druckrey, *Reasoned Space.* nd, $5.

Guide Series:

Number 1 *Ernest Bloch Archive.* nd, $2.

Number 2 *Paul Strand Archive.* nd, $2.

Number 3 *Edward Weston: Photographs and Papers.* nd, $2.

Number 4 *Acquisitions, 1975–1977.* nd, $2.

Number 5 *Sonya Noskowiak Archive.* nd, $4.

Reproductions: Posters for some exhibitions, also slides, photocopies and Polaroids of the collection, with photographer's permission.

Research: Library open to public; volumes on all aspects of photography and photographic history.

The Center for Creative Photography is an archive and research center par excellence. It presents itself in a way different from the other major collections, which also have fine libraries, great masses of images and so forth. Perhaps the different orientation stems from the fact that the Center for Creative Photography is a division of the University of Arizona Library. Its function is thus pedagogical, and its purpose is hence neither purely aesthetic nor historical.

The center is formed around several major archives concerning such eminent twentieth-century photographers as Ansel Adams, Ernest Block, Wynn Bullock, Harry Callahan, Aaron Siskind, W. Eugene Smith, Frederick Sommer and Edward Weston, among others. Each archive contains a thorough coverage of prints and negatives, memorabilia, correspondence and miscellaneous manuscripts. As well, there are extensive holdings of nineteenth- and twentieth-century images by Félix Bonfils, Paul Caponigro, Alvin Langdon Coburn, Walker Evans, Giselle Freund, Emmet Gowin, Joseph Jachna, Eadweard Muybridge, George Tice, Carleton Watkins, Weegee (Arthur Fellig) and Gary Winogrand. In all, the center, founded in 1975, represents nearly 2,000 photographers with 30,000 prints and 500,000 negatives. A library comprising upward of 6,000 volumes completes the research facilities. Presently located in a single-story building of white stucco over brick, accommodating two spare, modern galleries lighted in part by sunlight streaming through a clerestory, the center is expanding into new headquarters that will provide greater storage space.

One of the significant archives at the center is the Edward Weston collection. Weston wanted to be a track star, a prizefighter, then a painter. But when his father gave him a Bulls-Eye No. 2 in 1902—Weston was then sixteen—he became an avid photographer. After a few desultory years of scrambling around in business, Weston opened a photography studio in Glendale, California. He was then taking pictorialist-style portraits, as was

Ansel Adams.
Canyon de Chelly Nat'l Monument,
Photograph, c. 1947

the fashion, but using a good deal of natural light. The singularity of these images brought him attention and even some prizes. But in 1915, upon visiting a show of modern painting in San Francisco, Weston became inspired to find new photographic means to capture the explosive energy and clean lines of the new technological era. In 1922, traveling east, he photographed the steel mills of Ohio in sharp focus, thus entering the ranks of "straight" image photographers. In New York, he met up with Stieglitz and Sheeler, who professed similar principles. And then he was off again, this time to Mexico, where he began a portrait studio with Tina Modotti. She would become a highly political, important photographer in her own right. During these years, Weston pared down his images to an elemental power and in 1927 returned to California to create his great studies of natural forms—shells, vegetables, fruit, rocks, kelp, dunes of sand and, later, the female nude. He was a founder of the Group *f*/64, along with Ansel Adams and Willard Van Dyke, propounding the notions of "straight" photography— though the group showed but once together. In 1939 he wrote: "The photographer's power lies in his ability to re-create his subject in terms of its basic reality, and present this re-creation in such a form that the spectator feels that he is seeing not just a symbol for the object, but the thing itself revealed for the first time." Nominally settled in Carmel, his peripatetic ways took him through the West, photographing and keeping detailed daybooks of his perceptions, activities and plans. In the early 1940s, he traipsed through the South and East on assignment for an illustrated edition of Whitman's *Leaves of Grass.* Toward the end of his life, his fame was finally secured. In 1947, Van Dyke made his movie about Weston, *An American Photographer,* and the Museum of Modern Art held a retrospective of his career. International exhibitions followed. Weston's Carmel home became a meeting place for young photographers who sat, as it were, at the master's feet. Stricken with Parkinson's disease, Weston had his son, Brett, take over the duties of printing. On New Year's Day, 1958, he died.

The Weston archive contains 3,000 vintage prints and the collection of every negative Weston left—an estimated 20,000 in all. There are boxes of correspondence: letters to Stieglitz, Adams, Beaumont, Newhall, Modotti, to his sons and to the great political muralist he met during his Mexican stay, Diego Rivera. The letters are an extraordinary history of Weston's evolution of ideas and an annal of the photography of his times, with numerous detailed critiques of his colleagues' works.

The archive is typical of the general collection. It is a primary source, an aggregation of materials designed specifically for the purpose of conveying a body of knowledge entire. The pedagogical aspect bespeaks a philosophical interest in photography as a kind of information that takes in the subject's aesthetic and documentary elements, but the exhaustive collection raises questions about the idea of the photograph itself. The center is a library of visual information. The photograph-as-text (to be read for its cultural, historical and personal content; to be read for its statements of composition, its principles of time and, beyond this, of ontology) is an issue that is particularly germane in this setting. More than half the staff is involved in cataloguing and in archival work, in creating the history of the photograph. But inside of this, they are involved in the transmission of the image, which has its own history.

FIRESTONE LIBRARY AND THE ART MUSEUM
PRINCETON UNIVERSITY, PRINCETON, NJ 08544. Tel: (609) 452-3788
Hours: Tues–Sat 10 am–4 pm, Sun 1–5 pm (academic year) 2–4 pm (summer), closed Mon and some holidays.
Admission: Free; nominal charge for groups.
Publications:
> *The Robert O. Dugan Collection of Historical Photographs and Photographic Literature at Princeton.* 1983, $4.50.
> *Record of the Art Museum, Princeton University,* volume 39, nos. 1 & 2. 1980, $7.
Reproductions: Postcards of many objects in the collection.
Research: No reference library. University library for use of university community and qualified scholars by appointment.

The Firestone Library and the Art Museum at Princeton University hold a very fine collection of photographs. The collections, begun as early as a century ago, cover the history of photography in the broadest way, with a catholic array of purposes, styles and photographers. There are significantly thorough holdings of William Henry Jackson, Francis Frith, Lewis Carroll, Eadweard Muybridge, William Henry Fox Talbot, Hill and Adamson, Timothy O'Sullivan and Alexander Gardner among nineteenth-century practitioners of the camera art. In the twentieth century, Berenice Abbott, Ansel Adams, Alvin Langdon Coburn, Edward Steichen, Alfred Stieglitz, Carl Van Vechten, Brett and Edward Weston, Clarence H. White and Minor White are well represented. But such a catalogue would give the impression that Princeton has primarily traced the history of aesthetic photography, and this is not particularly the case. There is a vast assortment of photographic materials in the Firestone Library: western landscapes (for geological surveys), theatrical personalities, political figures, literary figures such as Thomas Mann, Sylvia Beech and F. Scott Fitzgerald, and Princeton history. In the Rare Books collection, one can find Fox Talbot's *Pencil of Nature* complete, along with albums by Lewis Carroll, Edward S. Curtis and Francis Frith. The library has also amassed nearly 1,000 books that have been illustrated with photographs. The publications *Camera Notes* and *Camera Work* are on hand.

The rather large bodies of work by individual photographers mentioned above could be the subject of lengthy discussion in themselves. Yet there is one holding that deserves special commentary: the Minor White Archive. Minor White was a poet in his youth who was given to the discernment of nature. In college, he studied botany as well as English, and we can trace his spirit to this marriage of the analysis of mind, which is at the heart of literature, and the examination of organic form. When he turned to photography in the late 1930s, he was influenced by Stieglitz's principle of "equivalents." In the "Equivalents" series, Stieglitz aimed his camera at the clouds, seeking in the transitory formations of the sky the mirror of his psyche. This Romantic aspiration, which has its roots perhaps in Baudelaire's *Correspondances,* affected White strongly and became the banner of his vision. He was later to be influenced by Zen philosophy and by Jung's discussion of the archetype. He wrote: "Surfaces reveal inner states— Cameras record surfaces. Confronted with the world of surfaces in nature, man, and photographs, I must somehow be a kind of microscope by which the underlying force of spirit are observed and extended to others." In the photograph *Moon and Wall Encrustations* (1964), we are meant to penetrate the evident material of what is pictured in two ways at once. The first metaphor is of a night sky that is imaged in the cracks and dirt of the wall darkening as one glances upward. The second shift, predicated on the realignment of material into metaphorical vision, is no doubt more personal: What equivalent lies in this shattered vault of the night, with its oval, spattered moon? That is a matter of circumspection and choice. We are urged to look through matter to a private and immaterial condition of the spirit. It is an abstraction, and at the heart of equivalence is the willful dislocation of what is pictured, exchanging the effect of what is *looked at* for what can be *seen.*

White was a teacher, a writer and an editor of considerable influence. He was founder of the magazine *Aperture*. And one comes to look at his oeuvre metaphorically as well. The photographs were a platform, as it were, for his philosophical beliefs. His techniques were an extension of these beliefs and his images have offered the doctrines of Romanticism to photography as much as they have offered photography Romantic doctrines. All of this is available to the public through the bequest of the archive to Princeton. There are as many as 75,000 prints, negatives and color transparencies gathered. All of White's work is included, as well as his own collection of photographs by colleagues—which comprise a superlative holding of images from the 1950s and 1960s. White's publications, letters and library complete the archive.

Other holdings include an important selection of photographs by the pictorialists and post-photo-secession image makers spanning the period 1890–1941.

INTERNATIONAL CENTER OF PHOTOGRAPHY
1130 FIFTH AVENUE, NEW YORK, NY 10028. Tel: (212) 860-1777
Hours: Tues–Thurs 12–8 pm, Fri–Sun 12–6 pm, closed Mon.
Admission: $2 adult, $1 senior citizens and students, free Tues eve, and to school groups at all times. Groups must make appointment.
Publications:
    Roland Freeman, *Southern Roads/City Pavements*. 1981, $12.
    Japan: A Self Portrait. 1979, $10.
    Gjon Mili: Photographs and Recollections. 1980, $13.95.
Reproductions: Posters, postcards and some original prints from exhibitions available.
Research: Library open to students and interested public by appointment.

The International Center of Photography is a *kunsthalle*, an exhibition space, now gradually building a collection of twentieth-century images. ICP was opened in 1974 with two primary intentions: to provide a permanent location devoted to the photographic medium where exhibits would regularly occur, and to create a meeting place for photographers, a place to compare notes, give lectures, teach technical workshops and generally develop a milieu for creativity. There is something very much of the Stieglitz spirit about ICP. Like his gallery, 291, and later An American Place, the center has a liberal intelligence willing to engage every aspect of experiment, craft and theory. ICP is a laboratory. It is a place of practical ferment, where history is a foundation on which new work is built.

Of course, as an exhibition hall, ICP's intention is to display photography to the public and thereby increase popular understanding of the medium. Located in the old Audubon House, built of red brick in the Federal style, there are two main floors of galleries. The rooms are high-ceilinged, with parquet floors and tall windows. There have been over one hundred exhibitions at the center since its opening—thematic, one-person, historic, geographic and generic in kind. A sampling of shows over the past few years includes: "Henri Cartier-Bresson: Photographer"; "Japan: A Self Portrait"; "Fleeting Gestures: Treasures of Dance Photography"; "Photography of the Fifties: An American Perspective"; "Frederick Sommer at Seventy-Five";

"Spain, 1936–1939"; and "The New Color: A Decade of Color Photography." To complement its exhibitions, the Screening Room has been established. A continual program of films and videotapes are shown here, giving biographical and artistic insight into the photographers' work or providing a cultural context for it. While the exhibition of Alfred Eisenstaedt's pictures was displayed, for instance, the Screening Room ran a nine-week series of German films from the 1920s and 1930s, as well as the film entitled *Eisenstaedt: Germany.* Many of the exhibits travel afterward—some internationally—and the program is extremely ambitious. Indeed, it is a crusade. There is, then, a further distinction to be made concerning ICP's educational principles: It is a public *and* a professional center with a global outlook, informing an increasingly large and receptive populace about the many issues and personalities of photography while maintaining its identity as a place of work and discussion.

In the past few years, the center has gone about creating an archive and permanent collection. Its typically ambitious objective, to quote a recent annual report, "is to compile the most comprehensive visual history of the twentieth century, the first century to be documented by the camera." There is little question that the activities of the center and its burgeoning museum collection will have increasing influence in the years to come.

THE INTERNATIONAL MUSEUM OF PHOTOGRAPHY AT THE GEORGE EASTMAN HOUSE

900 EAST AVENUE, ROCHESTER, NY 14607. Tel: (716) 271-3361
Hours: Tues–Sun 10 am–4:30 pm, closed Mon, Thanksgiving, Christmas.
Admission: $2 adults, $1 students, $.75 senior citizens, free to members.
Publications:
   Janet E. Buerger, *The Era of the French Calotype.* 1982, $15.
   Robert A. Sobiescek, *Hedrich-Blessing: Architectural Photographs, 1930–1981.* 1981, $15.
Reproductions: Postcards, a few of collection. Photographic print service will reproduce from collection; inquire, as fees vary according to use.
Research: Reserach library temporarily open to staff curators only. Collection has large selection of rare books and periodicals.

In 1881, George Eastman introduced the Kodak camera. An advertisement for it read: "It is the smallest, lightest, and simplest of all Detective Cameras—for the ten operations necessary with most Cameras to make one exposure, we have only 3 simple movements. *NO FOCUSSING. NO FINDER REQUIRED.*" The Kodak made one hundred exposures, using the new gelatin film that came in rolls and could be loaded easily by anyone. It was the first truly popular hand camera, and with it the Eastman Kodak Company began to amass a fortune for its founder. And yet forty-four years later, sick and depressed at age seventy-eight, Eastman took his own life. In memoriam, the International Museum of Photography at George Eastman House (IMP/GEH) opened in 1949. And today, the Eastman mansion, a national landmark in Rochester, houses one of the world's preeminent photography collections.

Ten acres of gardens and fountains frame the fifty-room Georgian home built in 1905, with its great columned portico and first floor of marble and teak, its pipe organ and paintings by Corot, Daubigny, Reynolds and Gainsborough. But the visitor climbs to the second floor to find the museum's greatest wealth—selections from its archives of 500,000 fine art photographic prints and 100,000 negatives. In eight modern galleries, the history of photography unfolds. A special room is dedicated to the daguerreotype, the first practical photographic process, perfected by Louis Jacques Mandé Daguerre in 1837. The museum is reported to hold up to half of all the extant daguerreotypes in the world. In the two other nineteenth-century galleries, the first decades of photography are described by the prints of such masters as Julia Margaret Cameron; the eminent Civil War photographer, Matthew Brady; Eadweard Muybridge, whose stop-action images of horses running at Leland Stanford's Palo Alto farm are considered the predecessor of motion pictures; Lewis Carroll, with his portraits of Alice Liddell (*Alice in Wonderland*) among others; Timothy O'Sullivan, photographer of the untrammeled West; and Hill and Adamson's calotype impressions of Scottish society.

There is a striking calotype by the Frenchman Félix Teynard in the collection. Teynard was a civil engineer by trade, living from 1817 to 1892. In the years 1851–52, he traveled to Egypt and Nubia to record the architecture and landscapes. The image *Nubia: Island of Philae* (1851) would seem simply enough to record a grand structure eroded by time. The picture proposes nothing exceptional in its composition, being a symmetric frontal view taken from a distance, presumably to ensure the least distortion of angle. Yet the most interesting feature—what one might call the *disturbance*—of the image is the small grove of palm trees in the background to the left. Architecture of stone and crumbling columns were nothing new to the French. But palm trees were otherworldly, and this quality is reinforced by the emptiness of the site. On examining the decrepit facade, we see a broken lintel hanging precipitously, making us think: "People ought to be careful over there," and then, "but there are no people." It is a world without human traffic; a world become abstractly historical. The simple information the picture gives us is thus deepened by its indication of another history: the history of French sensibility during the period, which interpreted the past, and particularly the gone empire of Egypt, in terms of Romantic imagining as metaphor and symbol. Teynard's image uses the architecture as a site for this imagining, which tells all in its absense of contemporary figures, in its blank shadows and exotic grove.

The five galleries of twentieth-century images continue the display of photographic concerns over the years: landscape and aesthetic scenes; abstraction and other compositional experiments; temporal studies; the political statement; the social record and historical instant. Of course, they are often intertwined. Every familiar name from Atget to Kertész to Weston and Winogrand is here. A formidable offering of Stieglitz, Adams, Lange, Moholy-Nagy and Minor White is impressive, but so is the enormous variety of pictures by lesser-known and anonymous practitioners. The twentieth-

Frith.
The Pyramids of Dahshur, Egypt,
Photograph, 1858

century collections would seem to rehearse many of the issues proposed by photographers of earlier days. Yet emerging notions of the medium and societal change have had their evident effects.

How different from Teynard's image is Henri Cartier-Bresson's famous photograph *Hyres* (1932). Shot from the top of some winding stairs, with the dark banister spiraling down to a curving street of cobblestones, a bicyclist darts past, blurred by speed. Cartier-Bresson has caught the form of circularity as it moves inward to the final circumference of the bicycle's wheels. There, at the base of the narrowing vortex, these wheels become a statement of racing time, like two clockfaces awhirl. In his book *The Decisive Moment,* Cartier-Bresson writes: "At the moment of shooting, [composition] can stem only from our intuition, for we are out to capture the fugitive moment, and all the interrelationships are on the move." But it is not the technology of the medium alone that has changed these interrelationships. This dedication to the fugitive moment suggests a radical change in the *perception* of the moment as a divisible unit to be analyzed. The positivist's specificity, the sensibility of the scientific mode, the fragment specimen that will yield up the secrets of the organism have replaced the Romantic reconstruction of an idealized past.

Such comparisons are casually observed here, as the chronological layout of the museum's second-floor galleries helps us construct a comprehensive knowledge of the world viewed by photographers. To bring this up to date, the Corridor Gallery regularly shows the latest works of contemporary photography. And back on the first floor, the Mees Gallery exhibits items from the Technology Collection, numbering 8,000 pieces of camera apparatus—including a Giroux Daguerreotype camera signed by Daguerre himself. Adjacent to the Mees are the Brackett Clark Galleries, which display changing exhibitions of genres: industrial, fashion, xerographic.

LIBRARY OF CONGRESS, PRINTS AND PHOTOGRAPHS DIVISION

THOMAS JEFFERSON BUILDING, ROOM 1051,
2ND STREET AND INDEPENDENCE AVENUE, SE,
WASHINGTON, DC 20540. Tel: (202) 287-6394
Hours: Mon–Fri 8:30 am–5 pm, closed Sat, Sun and legal holidays.
Admission: Free.
Publications:
>   Alan Fern, Milton Kaplan, and staff, *Viewpoints: A Selection from the Pictorial Collections of the Library of Congress.* 1975, $9.20.
>   *Photographs by the Wright Brothers.* 1978, $4.
>   *The Prints and Photographs Division in the Library of Congress.* 1979, free.
>   Renata V. Shaw, *A Century of Photographs, 1846–1946, Selected from the Collections of the Library of Congress.* 1980, $9.

Reproductions: Pictures not copyrighted or otherwise restricted copied to order by photoduplication service. Also photographic copies, photostats, microfilm, slides and blue line prints available.
Research: Prints and Photographs reading room open to public. Curators available for special consultation; researchers should make appointment to study original materials.

There is no American collection of photographic images more diverse and numerous than that of the Library of Congress. The collection is so vast that no actual count of its prints and negatives has yet been made. By estimate, there are some 10 million images in 800 separate collections that range from the six daguerreotypes by John Plumbe, Jr., reported to be the earliest known architectural photographs of Washington, D.C., to the *Look Magazine* Collection, which numbers several hundred thousand images.

The Library of Congress began gathering photographs in 1846, when the copyright deposit law pronounced that a copy of each "book, map, chart, musical composition, print, cut, or engraving" be sent to the library. Without mention of the medium, so notable a number of photographs and stereotypes began to appear in the mails of the library that the law was rephrased in 1865 to include photography. By 1895, the mountains of every sort of visual material caused the library to reorganize into two separate departments, and thus did the Division of Prints come into being—with a gallery specially designed for the exhibition of graphic art opening shortly thereafter. At the beginning of our century, photography began to be appreciated by collectors for its incidental quality: people had been taking pictures of *everything* for more than fifty years. The flood of images being sent to the Library of Congress recorded everyday life in minute historical detail. The recognition of the photograph as historical document—the library was offered "Mr. Brady's Historical *Gallery of Portraits*" in 1871 and refused it—became a major issue in acquisition. In 1920, the Army War College gave the library 300 daguerreotypes of important New Yorkers and Washingtonians that were done in Mr. Brady's studio during the late 1840s and early 1850s. In the 1930s, over 10,000 negatives were sent to the library for its Pictorial Archives of Early American Architecture. By the mid-1940s, the library had changed that name to the Prints and Photographs Division, and 1944 proved to be especially remarkable. During this year, the division received the Farm Security Administration (FSA) files of well over 100,000 black and white photos and negatives documenting American life during the Depression. This is by far the library's most celebrated collection, for its massive spectacle of excellence seemed to join as never before the ideals of "straight" aesthetic photography and the documentary image.

The photographs of the Farm Security Administration document in themselves the development of photography. The past and the future are told in the contingencies of these images, which combine the instantaneous picture making that we now identify with the snapshot and the meditative study of composition that is essential to aesthetic photography. In Walker Evans's work, for example, we see again and again the delight in architectural scale and in the dynamic relationships of compositional arrangement: the way his *Negro Shop, Vicksburg, Mississippi* centers upon the classical aspects of symmetry and the balance of a lightened foreground to a dramatically darkened background. Capturing a classical tableau with little manipulation of the picture's elements was the hallmark of straight artistic photography that came to light after the First World War. Before that time, the most popular sort of photography was exemplified by the pictorialism of Clarence White, F. Holland Day, and Arnold Genthe, whose soft-focus scenes were arranged and then manipulated during development and printing to create works more like lithographs than photographic prints. After the Great War, the photographer Edward Steichen, and later Charles Sheeler and Edward Weston among others, popularized images of sharper delineation that celebrated the natural light and composition of their subject matter. This style naturally complemented the documentary interest of the Farm Security Administration photographers, who worked at an extraordinary level of aesthetic concentration, rather than recording whatever necessity or circumstances prescribed. Such photographers as Evans, Dorothea Lange, Ben Shahn and Russell Lee had come to work for the FSA, at any rate, from backgrounds in painting and portraiture. The marriage of artistic and documentary styles was so perfectly realized that it not only encompassed the influences of the past but influenced the photography of following generations. It is impossible to think of Robert Frank, Bruce Davidson, Diane Arbus, or William Klein—all exemplary aesthetic documentarians of society—without recognizing the superlative example the FSA photographers set. At a radical tangent, the snapshot aesthetic made known by Lee Friedlander, in which the seemingly arbitrary subject and viewpoint ironically capture the skewed angles and patterns of urban life, is itself based upon the contemplative compositional approach to the American scene that is the cachet of the Farm Security Administration Collection.

Walker Evans.
Negro Shop, Vicksburg, MS,
Photograph, 1936

Also in 1944, the library received another collection of great documentary and humanitarian interest. The American Red Cross gave 50,000 photographs recording its activities here and abroad, notably during the First World War and the European reconstruction in the 1920s. The collection puts one in mind all the more of what seems to be the Photography Division's orientation over the years: it perceives its holdings in the encyclopedic tradition. Despite certain splendid collections, the holdings do not reveal a particular interest in aesthetics. Rather, in the French philosopher Michel Foucault's phrase, they represent an "archaeology of knowledge" that seeks to categorize all human labor and existence and the landscape in which humankind has dwelled since the first daguerreotype could permanently fix its "archival" image. No photographic record is without its place in the library. Its curators are stewards of contemporary history, and within the Division's store rooms one may find examples of every passion and every place. Consider its collections of Nazi photographs, cowboy life, the Crimean War, the Spanish American War, the Civil War, pictures of Washington and San Francisco and Jerusalem, and, indeed, its superb "Master Photographs" organized in the 1960s to trace the history of photographic artistry.

So enormous are the holdings of the Prints and Photographs Division that it seems equally miraculous to find so comprehensive a record of the infinitely varying images around the planet. To meet its continual growth, the curators of the division are planning a possible system of retrieval for its viewers that Borges would have wished he'd imagined. The entire collection is to be placed on video discs—54,000 images on each side—that visitors will use to locate the photographer and subject they want to study in this most diverse of all American photographic collections, this visual encyclopedia of modern times.

UNIVERSITY OF LOUISVILLE
PHOTOGRAPHIC ARCHIVES
EXTROM LIBRARY, LOUISVILLE, KY 40292. Tel: (502) 588-6752
Hours: Mon–Wed, Fri 8 am–4:30 pm, Thurs 8 am–8 pm.
Admission: Free.
Publications: None.
Reproductions: Archives will print photos to order, provided they are not protected under copyright.
Research: Reading room and archives open to public.

One of the country's more impressive collections of documentary photographs can be found in the University of Louisville's Photographic Archives. There are more than 750,000 images, books, exhibition catalogues and equipment in-house, primarily documenting the scenes of American life. The collection is local to a certain degree. Among the thirty-one most significant groups of photographs, the majority report the faces, houses, streets and industry of Louisville and its surroundings over the past century or so. We are taught by such regional collections—and Louisville's is one of many exemplary collections often found in historical-society museums throughout the country—that there is a hunger for history in its guise as a *collector,* a magnet for the infinite details of existence.

The commercial photographers Caufield and Shook, Inc., have given the Archives over 400,000 pictures of life in Louisville from 1903 to 1972, and one can read a multitude of identities (personal, political, sociological, historical) in this warehouse of images. *Orphan's Home* (1921), for example, would seem at first a rather taciturn picture, only vaguely interesting in its homogeneity of detail. A frontal view of twenty-three children holding out their arms to the viewer is an instrument of sentimental rhetoric. We know the photographer has said that they must strike this pose of need and yearning, that they must assume this imposed similarity. Then we notice the *condition* of their homogeneity. They are all wearing the same short gowns, dark stockings and lace-up shoes. This is still a relatively harmless identification: the impersonality of a uniform does not run very deep and is easily enough changed. But then we see that each child's hair is the same. The intimacy, the singularity of the body has been refused, and we look more closely at these faces to see how this has affected them. It is impossible to know enough, our hunger having grown; disturbed not by the rhetoric but by the incidence of detail.

The same question may be asked of the erotic collection of photographs in the archives, for detail is a product of rhetoric, a *submission* of information in the genre of erotic/pornographic imagery. Yet the historical character of the collection changes this detail. We are not meant, presumably, to be aroused, but to be observers of fashion: the changing figure of what is erotic; the decor; the clothes dropped "casually" aside; even the images that hang on the walls of boudoirs. But in so doing, in becoming sociologists, semiologists, we see how like the voyeur the historian is. And in turn we see that photography is always consuming, acquiring its material subjects; producing by the graphic strength of its two-dimensionality the power of shape and the illusion (the fantasy) of volume, depth, weight.

The two fine arts groups, the Fine Print Collection and the Clarence John Laughlin Collection, are notable additions to the archives. The former is a smattering of aesthetic photographs emphasizing twentieth-century image makers—Stieglitz, White, Weston, Meatyard, Caponigro, Coburn and Adams, among others. The Laughlin Collection is an archive in itself, containing 17,000 prints, negatives and other materials by the Louisiana photographer who has used the premises of "straight" photography to create images of natural surrealism (see other discussion of him in New Orleans Museum entry). The Laughlin Collection is a primary resource for scholars of historical as well as aesthetic subjects. For besides the highly personal photographs for which Laughlin is well known are his architectural pictures of Louisiana, which are considered superb examples and add to the documentary orientation of the archives.

The most significant attribute of the Louisville holdings is the Roy Emerson Stryker Collections. It is comprised of three separate collections: the Roy Stryker Papers, which include 1,500 vintage prints from Stryker's days (1935–42) as the chief of the Farm Security Administration's photography division and the subsequent projects that form the two other holdings; the Standard Oil of New Jersey Picture Library, which Stryker supervised from 1943 to 1950; and the Jones and Laughlin Steel Corporation Picture Library, under his direction during the years 1952 to 1958. The Standard Oil collection is particularly interesting, as it is a vast visual diary of American life in the postwar years. The project was designed to give the public a favorable image of the activities of Standard Oil (now Exxon). And Stryker, following the same tenets of documentary propaganda and rigorous aesthetic standards that succeeded in the FSA program, sent his photographers across the country and beyond—wherever Standard Oil was affecting industry and the land. The 85,000 images that have come from this detail homelife, fashion, consumer goods, the distant rural reaches of America and the streets of towns and cities. Esther Bubley, Harold Corsini, Russell Lee, Gordon Parks, Edwin Rosskam and John Vachon are among the photographers Stryker used, and they adhered to the principles of formal composition that tended toward static symmetry—though Corsini's more dynamic composition suggests the influence of Moholy-Nagy. The overtly propagandistic quality of these collections describes the rhetoric of the documentary image in a relentless way. We are inclined to call Stryker's group benign or humane because the focus is on individuality rather than on the monolithic uniformity of the corporation. The documentary provides the detail of history, and in the mode of authentification attempts to conjoin propaganda with visual facticity. It is an instructive lesson from which we benefit. For we have before us an extraordinarily thorough record of a time and a people already distant, and we learn something about photography as a mechanism of power.

THE MUSEUM OF MODERN ART

18 WEST 54TH STREET, NEW YORK, NY 10019. Tel: (212) 708-9400
Hours: Sun–Tues, Fri–Sat 11 am–6 pm, Thurs 11 am–9 pm, closed Wed.
Admission: $3 adults, $2 students, $1 senior citizens, children; free to members; pay what you wish on Tuesdays.
Publications:
> Peter Galassi, *Before Photography: Painting and the Invention of Photography.* 1981, $10.
>
> Dennis Longwell, *Steichen: The Master Prints 1895–1914.* 1978, $40.
>
> Beaumont Newhall, *The History of Photography: From 1839 to the Present Day.* 1982, $18.95.
>
> John Szarkowski, *Looking at Photographs: 100 Pictures From the Collection of the Museum of Modern Art.* 1973, $14.95.
>
> Garry Winogrand, Tod Papageorge, *Public Relations.* 1977, $9.95.

Reproductions: Posters, prints, postcards and slides of works from the collection and special exhibitions.
Research: Library open to public by appointment Mon–Fri 1–5 pm. Study center in each department for use by appointment.

The photography collection of the Museum of Modern Art, though not the largest, is surely the most influential in the country. Its curators over the years, Beaumont Newhall, Edward Steichen and John Szarkowski, are established as three of this century's most powerful figures in photographic history, practice and theory. One may go so far as to say that under their tutelage American taste in photography has been generally trained.

The musum opened in 1929 with the intention of bringing the most advanced European art before American eyes. And hence, though its principles may have been historical in nature, its subject was the aesthetic of the new. The first acquisitions in photography were made in 1933, though there was no department yet and no curator of photography. But already there had been a show including photographs, "Murals by American Painters and Photographers" in 1932; and the following year, the museum's first one-man photography show was mounted: Walker Evans's "Photographs of 19th-Century Houses." In 1936 the director of the museum, Alfred Barr, asked Beaumont Newhall, who was then the museum's librarian, to curate an exhibition. The great survey, "Photography 1839–1937," was the fruit of Newhall's labors. But its greatest blossom was the *History of Photography,* the seminal text of American photographic study that Newhall generated from his exhibit and its catalogue. Through its many editions, Newhall's book has shaped our perception of what photography is. So thoroughgoing is its influence that it has become nearly impossible to consider photography without taking it into account. Newhall's concerns are formally aesthetic, with an emphasis on "straight" creative photography, which is in its most basic impulse documentary and compositionally rigorous. Newhall's predilections were influenced to a degree by Roy Stryker's Farm Security Administration photography team that popularly established the "straight" aesthetic as a hallmark of great American picture taking. It comes as no surprise that two of Newhall's largest curatorial enterprises were "Paul Strand: Photographs 1915–1945" and "The Photographs of Edward Weston" (1946), for both photographers were famous practitioners of the strongly composed, sharply focused image. In all, Newhall's tenure was short. Appointed director of the newly formed Department of Photography in 1940, he stayed on till 1947—mounting thirty shows—when he was forced to resign by the appointment of Edward Steichen.

By this time, Steichen had become one of the world's best-known photographers. He had gone from earlier pictorial, soft-focus work to "straight" imagery. He had been a founding member of the Photo-Secession, which brought together the most advanced photographers at the turn of the century. He helped design *Camera Work*, the leading artistic journal of its day (1903–1917), and became a celebrity in his own right as the photographer of the famous for *Vogue* and *Vanity Fair* in the 1920s and 1930s. During the Second World War, Steichen became the director of the U.S. Navy Photographic Institute and was ultimately placed in charge of the Navy's combat photography units. His celebrated shows at the Museum of Modern Art (MOMA), "Road to Victory" (1942) and "Power in the Pacific" (1945), were national propagandistic triumphs. Thus, his appointment to the photography department's directorship seemed an extraordinary victory in itself. Newhall had established the scholarly respectability of the field, and now Steichen made the Modern's department a magnetizing force. From the years 1947 to 1962, when Steichen retired at age eighty-three, the collection had tripled in size. But his own triumph as director came in 1955, when he curated "The Family of Man"—the most popular photography exhibit (and photo book) ever done. He put on fifty-four shows during his stay, mostly in the same vein as Newhall's, but turned to the more generally popular and spectacular.

The holdings of the department also continued to support the tenets established by Newhall. As the museum had largely fixed its sight on the modern, Steichen, as Newhall before him, focused on twentieth-century work. Of course, nineteenth-century images are represented, but the great strengh lies in photography from the present century. A. D. Coleman notes in "The Impact on Photography: No Other Institution Even Comes Close" (*ARTnews*, October 1979) that Steichen obtained the great number of prints free of charge or for minimal fees from the photographers, who considered "themselves lucky to be asked by Steichen to give their work away.... This precedent has done as much damage to the economic structure of creative photography as the existence of the MOMA collection has done good in that regard, for Steichen's example has long been accepted and followed by curators around the world." What this statement declares, beside its interesting accusations, is first that Steichen was collecting a good deal of contemporary work and second how very public his actions were. One can assume that if his acquisitions procedures were universally watched, so were his exhibitions. Photography during Steichen's reign became public in a new way: as an acceptable art form, an art form of the present. For the delight expressed by spectators viewing "The Family of Man" and the patriotic shows "Road to Victory" and "Korea: The Impact of War in Photographs" (1951) was a delight in the recognizable. Exploiting the democratic ethos in the humanism of "The Family of Man" and the work ethic in the war photographs, where the photographer is seen as a patriotic worker in the field, the most general audience could identify ingrained demotic principles with photography. The photographer as workman (whose tool is so much more accessible than the paraphernalia and techniques of painting) appealed in the most general way and was, in any case, borne out by the identification with the worker in the celebrated Farm Security Administration photographs. Steichen's success in this regard made his more theoretical aesthetic exhibitions more palatable to the populace roundly won over. In "Seventy Photographers Look at New York" (1957), the spectator was encouraged to corroborate the images in the most intimate way, having just stepped into the museum from the streets of the city. And in Steichen's own retrospective, "Steichen the Photographer" (1961), the viewer was induced to validate the principle of the photograph as public vision. For here the viewer stood before Steichen's work-as-spectacle to be attended to, judged by the opinion of the public.

When John Szarkowski replaced Steichen in 1962, the shift in emphasis was logical. Having established the broad appeal of the photograph, the question of aesthetics could be dealt with in good faith, considering the receptivity of the audience. Since his arrival, Szarkowski has mounted over one hundred shows, numbers of which are dedicated not to the recognizable but to the reformation of our visual knowledge. In the works of Diane Arbus, Gary Winogrand, Jacques-Henri Lartigue and E. J. Bellocq, the demi-monde is brought to light; the obscure, the freakish, the childlike vision lost to adulthood are all recovered and memorialized.

The photographs of Eugène Atget form another world, extensive and detailed, of their own. The museum purchased 4,000 of Atget's images from Berenice Abbott in 1968. A great admirer of Atget's, she preserved his photographs and printed a great number from deteriorating plates after his death in 1927. Atget had decided in his late forties, searching for a means of income, to photograph Paris and its environs in every aspect. The museum's holding represents a vast part of the 10,000 pictures that the brilliant and seemingly inexhaustible Atget took. We see in *Avenue des Gobelins* (1925) an example of Atget's extraordinary sense of detail that transcends its immediate subject without any apparent pretension of doing so. The shopfront of mannequins is at once isolated and still, while the figures seem caught in movement. The play upon the imitation of life that the mannequins portray and the intrinsic reference to the photograph's normal activity of freezing motion combine in an image of surreal reflection. For the world of the still life is here inverted, and the dark reflection of trees and a domed building across the way increase the inverted perception of which world is behind glass.

A. D. Coleman observes Szarkowski's predilection for the urban scene and the social landscape, complaining that much else has been ignored ("multiple exposure, post-exposure darkroom exploration, photojournalism, serial imagery, directorial imagery, color imagery"). And while the observation may be valid in a broadly quantitative way, most of these categories are represented in some degree. The collection could evidently expand, but what is most important is the sociological character of Szarkowski's taste. That the other arts (painting, literature, music, dance and even criticism) show the same direction toward more vernacular imagery and more self-referential explorations suggests that photography will continue to assert its vanguard intellectual position, but in the most public medium. The balance of intellect with populist perceptions of photography has apparently been Szarkowski's mission.

NATIONAL MUSEUM OF AMERICAN HISTORY
CONSTITUTION AVENUE BETWEEN 12TH AND 13TH STREETS, NW, WASHINGTON, DC 20560. Tel: (202) 357-1300
Hours: Winter: daily 10 am–5:30 pm; summer: May 28–thru Labor Day daily 10 am–7:30 pm; closed Christmas Day.
Admission: Free.
Publications: None.
Reproductions: Museum will reproduce photographs to order.
Research: Library open to staff and outside researchers by appointment.

The photographic collections of the Smithsonian Institution are scattered among many museums and divisions: National Air and Space Museum, National Museum of Natural History, National Museum of American History, Joseph H. Hirshhorn Museum and Sculpture Garden, National Collection of Fine Arts, National Gallery of Art and National Portrait Gallery, all in Washington D.C., plus the Archives of American Art in New York. Estimates of the collections' total holdings run to over 800,000 images, and they include every kind of photographic process and every genre of photography created since the inception of the medium. The different divisions have gathered interesting collections specific to their curatorial directions. Notably, the National Gallery of Art has acquired the most complete set of images by Alfred Stieglitz extant. One thousand six hundred photographs span his career in platinum, palladium, carbon, gum bichromate, silver prints, autochromes and photogravures. But the most comprehensive collection is held by the Division of Photographic History, occupying a part of the third floor in the National Museum of American History.

The collection is dedicated to the medium of photography in a way that is matched only by Rochester, New York's George Eastman House and the Humanities Research Center at the University of Texas in Austin. The apparatus of photographic image making, the various processes of printing and the applications of photography are the foci here. These are the subjects of the main exhibition room, a vast space divided into sixty units.

An example of the itinerary might include: balloon photography, photographic plates, flexible films, enlarging, stereo photography, Victorian parlor, shutters, lenses, panoramic photography, aerial and space photography, microphotography, William Henry Fox Talbot Laboratory replica, tintypes and early photojournalism. The mechanical production of the images as a technological history is interesting in its own right. And it has been paid little attention, particularly in the general run of aesthetic concerns. Beside its own properties, this technology points to the workings of the photograph itself.

When we look at a photograph, we step immediately into the picture plane, into the illusion of a world represented there, as is our habit from viewing representational painting in the Renaissance mode. But the image is, of course, materially inert; a paper sheet darkened by chemicals and light. Its fixity is a paradoxical transformation of movement, mass and volume. What is it, then, that animates this static thing? First there is the condition of time called retrospection. The photographic portrait, as Roland Barthes says, shows a face that *is* and that *has already been.* The concurrent appearance of these states is an oscillating force. It is a force of reference utilizing the energy—the retrospective energy, we might call it—of what is represented: a face, a historical scene, a landscape. But we must next step outside of the internal references of the image and consider the mechanism of reference at work. In this way, the photograph is a depository of references. Yet it is more than this, for it is perpetually manipulating its references as signs of history and of spectacle. The photograph is, hence, a machine of references, but its technology produces—by various manipulations of its pictorial elements (choice of subject, composition, printing process, cropping)—a rhetoric transforming reference into *inference.* The inert object of the photograph, this paper thing, is thus set into motion by the continual play between reference and inference.

The extreme diversity of the collection in the Division of Photographic History attests to the referential and inferential functions of the photograph. There is some resemblance here to the Library of Congress photographic holdings in the orientation away from mainly aesthetic concerns. Though the division has a great assortment of images by the practitioners of aesthetic photography, the intention is more encyclopedic—as the units in the exhibition hall suggest. There are approximtely 350,000 images all told, many of which are still unsorted and uncatalogued.

The Underwood and Underwood Illustration Studios gave the division an enormous archive of images in the 1960s. It is the sort of collection typical here. Comprised of 8,000 stereo and 13,000 glass and film negatives, the subject matter is truly encyclopedic: anthropology, art, archaeology, biology, botany, entomology, nuclear energy, mineral sciences, manufacturing, musical instruments, costumes, sports, military history, cultural history (Chicago and New York studio files), transportation, dogs, horses, naval history, agriculture, postage stamps and mining. The Ira Hill Collection devotes itself entirely to another category of knowledge: the portraits of celebrities. There are tens of thousands of portraits here taken from 1905 to

1920—Fred Astaire, Gloria Swanson, Anna Held, William Powell, Talullah Bankhead, Anna Pavlova and so forth. These images direct us to a cultural history. They are the outward symbols of the films, the dances, the era and ethos that are the absent context supplied by the viewer. Once again, the energy of reference is retrospective, and we recognize in the gala air, the voluptuous costumes and slick coiffures the inference that the photographer has imposed.

The very fine group of glass-plate negatives by Matthew Brady, best known for his documentary images of the Civil War, provides yet another collection of references, so to speak. Portraits of General Custer, President Grant, Grant's secretary of state, Hamilton Fish, and various senators, congressmen and cabinet members in the Grant and Lincoln administrations are markers, ciphers filled in by contexts appropriated elsewhere. Yet we learn more here than the face of a congressman, which can only be of use to the specialist. The details emerge as we turn away from the inference that is meant to attract us. It is not the face that we linger over much longer, but the way the hair is cut, the cloth of a jacket, the way the tie is knotted. The "unofficial" references capture us—each image a sensualist's delight bending beneath, disturbing the intentional veil of context.

This is the power of the photograph: to operate against the implications of its rhetoric; always to implicate something else, something at first unseen. By using the technology photography has given us, namely the cropping of the image, the process of separating out, we find the disturbances of detail that tell another story, and often a story of multiple values.

This is surely the case of Eadweard Muybridge's serial photographs that ultimately formed the album *Animal Locomotion* (1887). The division has some 800 images by Muybridge. In these studies of animal and human movement, sequentially photographed by as many as twelve cameras, the fluidity of motion as it affects stance and musculature provides much scientific information.

This is the implication, the original reason that we are supposed to look at the series. But we are moved as often by the references outside the scientific frame, the oblique inferences gathered there. A child walking to her mother half-draped in white cloth; a woman in Greek costume dancing; men boxing. The affects of culture, particularly the Greek Revival sentiment evident in gestures, dress, atheleticism and even the friezelike serial composition are details of vast wealth. The romanticism, the avowal of an organic vision of motion, is all the more fascinating as it underlies the scientific intention to dissect phenomena and fragment them in a way that would come to be a hallmark of High Modernism's refusal of just this romantic organicism.

The division's collections cover a great deal more territory. There are over 3,000 photographs of New York by photographer Sam Falk, for example. A complete edition of W.H.F. Talbot's *Pencil of Nature* is in house. And then there is an array of amazing and tantalizing aesthetic work by Nadar, Atget, Stieglitz, Käsebier, Cunningham, Weston, Adams, Brassaï, Feininger, Walker Evans, Frank, Capa, Lange, Kertész, Outerbridge, Minor White, Callahan, Uelsmann, Siskind, Uzzle and 1,082 prints and negatives by Avedon.

PHILADELPHIA MUSEUM OF ART

BENJAMIN FRANKLIN PARKWAY, PHILADELPHIA, PA 19101.
Tel: (215) 763-8100

Hours: Wed–Sun 10 am–5 pm, closed Mon, Tues and legal holidays.
Admission: $2 adults, $1 children under 18, students, senior citizens.
Publications:

Lobsang Lhalungpa, *Tibet: The Sacred Realm. Photographs 1880–1950.* 1983, $15.95.

Beaumont Newhall, *August Sander: Photographs of an Epoch.* 1980, $14.50.

Joel Snyder, *American Frontiers: The Photographs of Timothy H. O'Sullivan 1867–1874.* 1981, $18.95.

Reproductions: Large selection of posters, prints and postcards.
Research: Library, print and study collections open to those with professional interest by appointment.

It is particularly interesting that the Philadelphia Museum of Art houses the Alfred Stieglitz Center for photography and many of Marcel Duchamp's major works, including his last: *Étants Donnés: 1) La chute d'eau; 2) Le gaz d'éclairage (Given: 1) The Waterfall; 2) The illuminating gas)* of 1968. There are more than a few coincidences of artistic attitude between the two that bear on photography, and they are worth considering.

Stieglitz, who has been called the father of photography in the twentieth century, was a great proselytizer. He thrust his titanic energies on the world in a series of influential magazines under his editorship, in a series of galleries under his direction and, of course, through the lifelong intelligence of his photographic projects. His monumental editorial achievement was *Camera Work,* published in fifty numbers from 1903 to 1917, in which the most advanced photography, painting, sculpture and writing appeared. He was dedicated with a bottomless passion to artistic excellence but specifically to the inventive excellence of the Modernist sensibility. That is to say, he sought art that analyzed its own procedures with an eye for the reformation of aesthetic means—means that described the effects of a new age upon the psyche of the individual. During 1915–16, Stieglitz saw Duchamp, Francis Picabia and Marius de Zayas in New York. Under his auspices, de Zayas published the periodical *291,* named after Steiglitz's gallery at 291 Fifth Avenue. Picabia brought out a series of "object portraits" in *291,* showing Stieglitz as a camera, himself as an auto horn, and a nude woman as a spark plug. *291* manifested the tenets of Dada and Surrealism, European aesthetic movements that purposefully deranged the premises of conventional art making and presentation and advocated the expression of irrational perceptions excavated from the subconscious mind. Duchamp turned to mechanical abstraction to relay an ironic, psychological reconstruction of humankind in the technological age. Steiglitz, who was ultimately Romantic, turned to abstraction for his own psychological aesthetic in the "Equivalents" series, which depicted cloud formations as "an *equivalent* of the artist's most profound experience of life." His work and his influence were both crucial.

But there are more particular and startling coincidences here. Duchamp's last work, completed in the year of his death, was shortly afterward installed at the Philadelphia Museum. At this same time, Dorothy Norman, Stieglitz's biographer and friend, donated 500 images by the photographer, along with memorabilia and two sets of *Camera Work*. This was the inauguration of the Stieglitz Center in 1968. And with photography so powerfully present at the museum, it is more than a little remarkable that Duchamp's *Étants Donnés* should also enter the scene, relating brilliantly though obliquely to Stieglitz's medium.

At the far end of a bare room, a bolted antique door stands in a brick portal. Two peepholes give on to the outrageous scene of a naked woman on a bed of twigs. She holds a gas

Alfred Stieglitz.
Equivalent, Mountains and Sky,
Photograph, 1924

lantern aloft. Her nudity is detailed and her face is veiled by a sweep of blond hair. She is seen through the break in a brick wall, accenting the voyeuristic attitude suddenly forced on the viewer, and behind her a mechanical waterfall rushes in a painted landscape of cloudy azure sky, pond, hills and forest. The confluence of realism and the pictorial are charged with erotic involvement, which draws the viewer in but leaves no possible alternative view, no possible reimagining. This willful mediation of reality, indicting the authenticity of picture making, brings up all the paradoxes of photography: always voyeuristic, peering into the world that it reconstitutes as image through mechanical processes; distancing, objectifying and finally conflating the life of the subject with the imposed appearance, the constraining attitude of the frozen photographic take.

The Alfred Stieglitz Center stands in relation to Duchamp's profound questioning. Its collection, prominent for its holdings of Paul Strand, Stieglitz, Edward Weston, Minor White, William Klein, Robert Frank, Robert Adams and Danny Lyon, vies with difficulties and aspirations of the photograph's realism. Stieglitz, though intellectualy adventurous, had particular ideas about the nature of photography, and the collection seems to follow. Each of these photographers relies on the "straight" image, the direct relation of the viewer through time to the subject. Though Strand and Robert Frank, for example, are opposed in technique (the former composing each aspect of the image and the latter choosing the chance images of the instant), yet they both have little interest in technique for itself. Both uphold the belief that the process's mediating power is subservient to the content, the power of the subject, which comes *through* the image. The work of Stieglitz takes this premise to a remarkable point. His rejection of pictorialism early in his career, his preference for a *less* mediated photograph, and his attraction to serial imagery—the cloud equivalents, the cloud "music" series and the portraits of his wife, Georgia O'Keeffe, detailing every aspect of her body over the years—demonstrate the obsessiveness of his vision to describe everything the subject offered until it yielded the spiritual core of its physical appearance. The image is at once sharply focused and metaphorical, seeking a symbolism of transcendence through the highly articulated description of the physical. This is the *mobility* of the image, one might say; the celebration and demand for insight's reimagining that is the antipodal response to Duchamp's suggestion of visual constraint.

The Duchampian view, at least of the irrational element, has its advocate in another photographer well represented in the collection: Jerry Uelsmann. Uelsmann has been actively cavorting with the imagery of the irrational since the late 1950s. His composite photographs of a solarized brick maze mysteriously placed before the positive image of an ivy-covered wall, his Magritte-like rooms with ceilings of clouds and other unlikely scenes bespeak an alternative appearance that, like Duchamp's *Étants Donnés*, confounds our notions of the apparent, the reportorial and the mediated perception of the picture.

The Stieglitz Center, in its rectangular room of wooden floors, white walls and incandescent lighting, is no larger than Stieglitz's last gallery, An American Place. The seriousness of the collection originates in that place, known for its excellence and its questioning spirit. The center's rotating exhibitions generally focus on one photographer's oeuvre, and the major exhibits every year and a half result in exemplary catalogues published by Aperture. While the strength of the collection is clearly oriented toward bodies of work by masters of this century, there are also holdings of nineteenth-century photographs from America, Britain and the Continent.

UNIVERSITY ART MUSEUM

UNIVERSITY OF NEW MEXICO, ALBUQUERQUE, NM 87131.
Tel: (505) 277-4001
Hours: Tues–Fri 10 am–5 pm and 7–10 pm, Sat–Sun 1–5 pm, closed Mon, university holidays; reduced hours in summer.
Admission: Free.
Publications:
Van Deren Coke, *19th Century Photographs from the Collection.* 1976, $3.
Elizabeth Anne McCauley, *Catalogue of 20th Century Photographs.* 1980, $9.50.
Beaumont Newhall, *The History of Photography in New Mexico.* 1979, $3.
Reproductions: Prints from the collection, if in public domain, available on fee basis.
Research: Print and Photography Rooms open to public for study purposes; appointment recommended.

This superb collection surveys the entire realm of photography. No process is without example. No attitude is without its proponent. No style is missed or period left undocumented. When the museum first began gathering photographs with its opening in 1964, the nineteenth century seemed to take the upper hand. At least quantitatively, a greater number of images was collected from the first century of photography. In the most general way, of course, this historicism seems appropriate to a university museum whose primary clientele are students of art history. The holdings include the major photographers: Adam-Salomon, Annan, Baldus, Barnard, Beato, Bonfils, Cameron, Carjat, Lewis Carroll, Du Camp, P. H. Emerson, Frith, Gardner, Hill and Adamson, O'Sullivan and so on. Looking at this great array that has so many intentions (commercial portrait, landscape, war document, family scene, the worker and the simulacrum of genre painting), there is some sense that the photograph has no end or beginning.

In its first century, the revolution of the photograph is its *return* through other pictorial media, such as the painting, the lithograph, the engraving, the Japanese woodcut, to itself: an inherently precise record of the world that must be manipulated in some way to become different from the world it automatically copies as it is, to become, in a sense, less precise. Thus the photograph works backward through the other pictorial arts, picking up on its way traces of the human. So radical is the nature of mechanical representation that we are only now beginning to comprehend the philosophical ramifications of photography's material being. The 1970s' art of minimalism, in which the art object is drained of any evident content and is left without trace of human intervention, is a belated explication of what photography had created more than a hundred years before but did not or could not yet see. For the bright metal sheen of the daguerreotype, with its thin coating of an image, seemed to refer to Renaissance notions of perspective depth and chiaroscuro because Renaissance painting had intended to do what photography did naturally. This inversion belies the intrinsic property of the photograph as referent. Any inferences into the character of the photograph's references come afterward. They are the investments in the image that the *painter*, not the photograph's chemical creation, cannot help but make.

As well, the photograph holds within it a principle characteristic fundamentally feared and deplored by romanticists—and Niepce's heliograph of 1826 was born at the height of romanticism. For the human figure is contained by the mechanical frame of the photograph. The psyche is captured; even nature is subjugated, held against its will, as it were, by the anonymous powers of industrial science. Baudelaire saw in the precision of science the hateful component of photography, mimicking the enthusiasts of his day: " 'I believe that Art is, and cannot be other than, the exact reproduction of Nature.... Thus an industry that could give us a result identical to Nature would be the absolute of art.' A vengeful God has granted the wishes of this multitude. Daguerre was his Messiah."

Yet we see in the university's nineteenth-century collection that the attraction was not simply for a precision that would improve on painting's verisimilitude. Photography could not help its own precision. And anyway that was its selling point. Yet the mechanical genius of the new image was not in itself sufficient, for painting was still the reigning pictorial form of the day. The humanizing process of the painter's brushstroke had to find its way

Alfred Stieglitz
Scurrying Home,
Photogravure, 1897

into the photograph. Traces of the human, of course, do not necessarily mean traces of the human hand. An imitation of painterliness in the soft-focus images of P. H. Emerson, for example, are but one sort of intervention, one kind of manipulation to neutralize the mechanical nature that might otherwise dominate the photograph. Van Deren Coke, who was director of the university's museum and has a powerful interest in the relation of painting and photography that is all too clear in his present curatorial work at the San Francisco Museum of Modern Art, has written interestingly about the Italian photographer Giorgio Sommer. In an untitled image, circa 1870, Sommer shows a woman sitting with two boys at her feet. One child is leaning back against the woman's knees and her hands are in his hair, picking, it would seem. Coke brings to our attention the convincing likeness of Sommer's photograph to Murillo's seventeenth century painting *Old Woman and Boy.* The same geometric (a window, a door) form, the same table with domestic objects are presented. The woman is engaged in the same activity with a boy in somewhat the same pose. The albumen print does not imitate the painting in any tactile way. Rather it refers to the painting's *pose,* the invention of the figures, that defuses the autonomy of the purely mechanical reproduction. For unlike painting, the photograph does not need to invent its compositions. Such invention is an addition, a reference not to the subject matter but to image making itself.

The photograph thus seems to turn without end or beginning through the various influences that it swallows and continues like the snake swallowing its tail. In the twentieth century, we have seen the photograph begin to investigate its means more independently. In the past few years, the museum has built up its twentieth-century holdings considerably. Its emphasis is on aesthetic imagery, though it represents a number of documentarians, and it is a very fine collection indeed. Both the pictorial and "straight" styles, as well as later manipulations of the materials and processes unique to photography, are seen in a great range of expressions. The museum has an aggressive acquisitions policy, frequently adding new photographers and other images to deepen present holdings. As it is, there are upward of 2,000 twentieth-century images by Abbott, Arbus, Atget, Barrow, Alvarez Bravo, Bruehl, Cartier-Bresson, Larry Clark, Curtis, Doisneau, Frank, Gibson, Gilpin, Heinecken, Hosoe, Krims, Lynes, Lyon, Mertin, Moholy-Nagy, Man Ray, Sander, W. Eugene Smith, Steichen, Strand, Sudek, Uelsmann, Van Dyke, both Westons and both Whites, among others.

CHAPTER SEVEN

PRIMITIVE ART

by
Wendy Schonfeld

AMERICAN MUSEUM OF NATURAL HISTORY
CENTRAL PARK WEST AT 79TH STREET, NEW YORK, NY 10024.
Tel: (212) 873-1300
Hours: Mon, Tues, Thurs, Sun 10 am–5:45 pm, Wed, Fri, Sat 10 am–9 pm. Closed Thanksgiving and Christmas.
Admission: Suggested contribution $3 adults, $1.50 children; free on Fri–Sat 5–9 pm.
Publications:
  American Indian Art, Form and Tradition. 1972, $8.
  Walter A. Fairservis, *Asia: Traditions and Treasures.* 1981, $50.
  Allen Wardwell, *Objects of Bright Pride: Indians of the Northwest Coast.* 1978, $15.
Reproductions: Some posters, prints and postcards of objects in the collection.
Research: Library open to public.

The American Museum of Natural History currently displays objects from Africa and selected regions of North and South America. A new Andean Hall is planned for 1986, and the Pacific Hall is scheduled to reopen in the future.

African objects on display are from all major style and culture areas. From the Western Sudan is a large Bamana Koma Society helmet headdress. A small group of Benin pieces from the Guinea Coast style area includes a bronze plaque fragment with a woman, one of the very few female images known from the corpus of plaques. Two Kongo power figures from Central Africa are on display, one an anthropomorphic n'kondi and the other a zoomorphic carving.

The collection of Northwest Coast materials from this hemisphere is installed in a hall that evolved between 1900 and 1924 and has remained *in situ* since then as a tribute to a great period of American museum collecting. The Museum's Northwest Coast collection is probably the best of several strong collections in this country, and the range and quality of objects defies mention of only a few pieces. Other Native American culture areas represented ethnographically are the Eastern Woodlands and the Plains.

American archaeological objects include a segmented ivory mask and

Northwest Coast, Native American
Canoe-The Main Group
Diorama

baby walrus from the Eskimo Ipiutak culture dated from around A.D. 300 that are on display in a gallery that includes ethnographic Eskimo pieces including twentieth-century masks in a range of materials such as wood and leather and ivory animal figures from this century. From the archaeological Northeast is a copper bird from the Hopewell period exhibited along with other ornamental pieces of copper and mica.

The Mesoamerican collection contains many outstanding pieces, including Mixtec gold ornaments such as a labret, or lip ornament. Among the pieces in the strong preclassic Olmec collection is perhaps the only object of perishable material known from this culture, a wooden mask with jade inlay. The largest piece of pre-Columbian greenstone known, the Kunz ax is eleven inches high and weighs fifteen and a half pounds and is on display with smaller pieces. The ceremonial ax originally weighed more, but pieces have been cut away from the back probably to make other objects. The deep blue-green color of the ax was one especially prized by the Olmec. Classic period Mesoamerica is represented by several regional cultures. There is a wide range of ritual ball game regalia from the Classic Veracruz culture and two genealogical stone slabs from Monte Alban in Oaxaca. The Maya collection includes several outstanding pieces, a vase with a kneeling figure wearing a jaguar headdress, a carved wooden lintel from Tikal, Guatemala dated from A.D. 741, and a stone relief collected by John Lloyd Stephens near the Yucatecan sites of Kabah and Uxmal in 1840. The Postclassic period is represented by a lifesize Toltec ceramic Xipe Totec, one of the few ceramic images known of this size. There is also a collection of Huastec stone sculpture. The Aztec, the group in control of the Mesoamerican culture area when the Spanish made contact, are represented by rare pieces such as three wooden drums and a human mask of greenstone, demonstrating the continued preference for this material throughout Mesoamerican prehistory from the time of the Olmec. Among Central American objects on display is a collection of Costa Rican stone sculpture. South America is represented at this time by gold pieces displayed in a small adjoining gallery.

THE BROOKLYN MUSEUM

EASTERN PARKWAY, BROOKLYN, NY 11238. Tel: (212) 638-5000.
Hours: Wed–Sat 10 am–5 pm, Sun 12–5 pm, holidays 1–5 pm, closed Mon–Tues.
Admission: Suggested contribution $2 adults, $1 students; free to children under 12 and senior citizens.
Publications:
   Elizabeth Kennedy Easby, *Ancient Art of Latin America*. nd, $6.95.
   Norman Feder, *Art of the Eastern Plains Indians*. nd, $2.50.
   Michael Kan, *African Sculpture*. nd, $2.
   Jane P. Powell, Martin L. Friedman, *Primitive Art of the Pacific Islands*. nd, $.50.
Reproductions: Numerous posters, prints, postcards and slides from the collection and special exhibitions.
Research: Art reference library open to those with specific need by appointment only.

The Department of African, Oceanic and New World Cultures is one of the country's oldest such museum departments, created in 1903. The Brooklyn Museum first displayed African material culture as art in 1923. The African collection is particularly strong in Central African ethnic groups. A wooden portrait of the Kuba king Bom Bosh may date to the seventeenth century and is one of only five portraits of the early Kuba kings to survive. From the Guinea Coast style area is a small but fine collection of Benin objects, including a bronze hornblower and a carved ivory gong, both dated from the seventeenth century. The gong is one of only five to survive and is the only one in this country. The undamaged side shows the Oba, or divine king, with his arms being ritually supported by his war chief and his heir. The aristocratic court art of Benin is juxtaposed with masks from village-level traditions. The prize of the African collection may well be a small terra-cotta head from fifteenth- to sixteenth-century Ife, one of the few on public display in this country.

The pre-Columbian collection of Peruvian textiles is especially good. A Paracas mantle from about the first century A.D. is one of the two finest pieces known. The border is a double-faced procession of small, three-dimensional figures who would have numbered about 100 if the cloth were intact. The Mesoamerican collection is strong in many areas and has several outstanding pieces, such as an Olmec standing greenstone figure holding a were-jaguar child. Perhaps the finest life-size Huastec figure known, a Quetzalcoatl, is supported by other images of Huastec stone sculpture.

The Native American holdings are extensive and many pieces are the result of museum expeditions and are accompanied by strong documentation. A collection of Plains materials is dated from the early nineteenth century, and there is a fine collection of feather ceremonial regalia from California ethnic groups.

BUFFALO BILL HISTORICAL CENTER

PO BOX 1000, CODY, WY 82414. Tel: (307) 587-4771.
Hours: Mar–April, Oct–Nov 1–5 pm; May & Sept 8 am–5 pm; June–Aug 7 am–10 pm.
Admission: $4.50 adults, $2 children 6–12, free under 6.
Publications: Free brochure.
Reproductions: Posters and postcards of the museums.
Research: Reference library open to students by appointment.

The Plains Indian Museum of Buffalo Bill Historical Center is devoted to preserving and interpreting the traditions, art and material culture of the Plains Indian. Full-size tipis are included in the exhibition area, along with clothing, pipes, weapons, horse decorations and cradleboards. In an adjoining complex, The Whitney Gallery of Western Art, are paintings by George Catlin and Karl Bodmer illustrating the use of many objects by the Plains peoples in the nineteenth century.

DALLAS MUSEUM OF ART

1717 NORTH HARWOOD, DALLAS, TX 75226. Tel: (214) 421-4188.
Hours: Tues–Sat 10 am–5 pm, Sun 1–5 pm, closed Mon.
Admission: Free.
Publications:
Anne Bromberg, *A Guide to the Collection: Dallas Museum of Fine Arts.* 1979, $3.95.
John Lunsford, *The Arts of Ghana.* 1978, $17.50.
——, *Schindler Collection of African Sculpture.* 1975, $15.
Merrill C. Rueppel, *Stillman Collection of Congo Sculpture.* 1969, $6.
Reproductions: Posters, prints, postcards and slides of works in the collection and special exhibitions.
Research: Reference library open to public by appointment.

The Dallas Museum of Fine Arts displays art from Africa, the Pacific and the pre-Columbian Americas.

The African collection is strong in figural sculpture from the Central African style area. The number of examples from a single people, such as the Songe, allows the observer to see the range and variation of style within a given ethnic group. Kongo sculpture, noted for its representational qualities and interest in asymmetrical poses and gestures, is also strongly represented in the Dallas collection. There is a fine example of a Senufo rhythm pounder from the Western Sudan culture area.

Pre-Columbian objects from the Americas are from both Mesoamerica and the Andes. An incised stone tablet has been studied as an example of an Olmec writing system, possibly an invocation to the rain god. A gold mask for the mummy bundle of a Chimu king is an outstanding piece from Peru.

DUMBARTON OAKS RESEARCH LIBRARY AND COLLECTIONS

1703 32ND STREET, NW, WASHINGTON, DC 20007.

Tel: (202) 342-3265.

Hours: Tues–Sun 2–5 pm, closed Mon and national holidays.

Admission: Free.

Publications:

> Elizabeth P. Benson, *The Handbook of the Robert Woods Bliss Collection of Pre-Columbian Art*. 1963, $5. Supplement, 1969, $1.
>
> Michael D. Coe, *Classic Maya Pottery at Dumbarton Oaks*. 1975, $25.

Reproductions: Slides and postcards of works in the collection.

Research: Library for use of scholars who hold appointments at Dumbarton Oaks or who present evidence of recognized academic or professional affiliation. Especially strong in Mesoamerica and Andean South America.

The Collection at Dumbarton Oaks consists of pre-Columbian art and ranges from Mesoamerica through Central America and Colombia to the Andes. The holdings are small but exquisite, concentrating on objects in stone and metal that make strong aesthetic statements.

The collection is especially notable for two of the earliest time periods in both Mesoamerica and the Andes. From the Olmec of Mesoamerica are three stone transformation figures, part human, part feline; and a superla-

Pre-Columbian, Teotihuacan.
Wall Fragment,
(detail) Fresco

tive greenstone head that may represent a female. The Chavin culture of Peru is represented by textiles and steatite cups and gold ornaments.

Other outstanding Mesoamerican pieces in this jewellike collection are a wall fresco fragment from Teotihuacan, one of the few on exhibit outside of Mexico, that is reinforced with a case of Teotihuacan ceramics in the same technique; a Mixteca-Puebla necklace and earrings of gold hummingbirds and a turquoise mosaic mask. An exciting Aztec stone human mask and a fire serpent both bear the same date, the Aztec year *Two Reed,* or 1507, the last New Fire Ceremony before the Spanish conquest. The snake also bears the name glyph of Montezuma II, the last Aztec ruler, adding a certain touch of pathos to its beauty. Outstanding Andean objects include Tiahuanaco ear ornaments and an inlaid mosaic mirror. An Inca tunic, considered to be prehispanic, contains one of the most complicated patterns known and may represent a system of writing.

HAFFENREFFER MUSEUM OF ANTHROPOLOGY

TOWER STREET, MOUNT HOPE GRANT, BRISTOL RI 02809.
Tel: (401) 253-8388.
Hours: April–May, Sept–Nov: Sat and Sun 1–5 pm; June–Aug: Tues–Sun 1–5 pm, closed Mon; closed Dec–Mar.
Admission: $1 adults, $.50 senior citizens, children, free to members, affiliates of Brown University and Rhode Island School of Design.
Publications: Three volumes of a continuing series on the collection are:
>Susan G. Gibson, *Burr's Hill: the 17th Century Wanpanoag Burial Ground in Warren, RI.* 1980, $60.
>Barbara Hail, *Hau, Kola!* 1983, $20.
>Kenneth N. Kensinger, *The Cashinahua of Eastern Peru.* 1975, $14.

Reproductions: None.
Research: Research library open to public by appointment. Anthropological research in the collection available to any scholar by appointment.

The Haffenreffer Museum of Anthropology has gathered objects from all parts of the primitive and pre-Columbian world, Africa, the Pacific and the Americas. The Native American collections are the strength of the holdings, with an emphasis on the Artic and the Plains.

THE HEARD MUSEUM

22 EAST MONTEVISTA ROAD, PHOENIX, AZ 85004.
Tel: (602) 252-8848.
Hours: Mon–Sat 10 am–4:45 pm, Sun 1–4:45 pm, closed holidays.
Admission: $1.50 adults, $1 senior citizens, $.50 children over 7, free to Native Americans.
Publications:
>*The C. G. Wallace Collection of American Art.* 1974, $15.
>*Dancing Katchinas.* 1968, $4.

Reproductions: Posters, prints and postcards of the collection.
Research: Library open to public.

The Heard Museum usually displays only objects from the region of the Greater Southwest, although its holdings include objects from other parts of the world. Permanent galleries include an introduction to the prehistory of the Southwest and objects from the historic pueblos, the strength of the museum along with contemporary Native American art. The historic installation includes weaving, pottery, basketry [the provenance of women] and silver. Objects are changed periodically in order to cover the broad range of the museum's collections.

THE METROPOLITAN MUSEUM OF ART
FIFTH AVENUE AT 82ND STREET, NEW YORK, NY 10028.
Tel: (212) 535-7710.
Hours: Tues 10 am–8:45 pm, Wed–Sat 10 am–4:45 pm, Sun and holidays 11 am–4:45 pm, closed Mon, Thanksgiving, Christmas, New Year's.
Admission: Suggested contribution $4 adults, $2 children and senior citizens, free to children under 12.
Publications:

Paul Gebauer, *Art of Cameroon*. 1979, $14.95.

Julie Jones, *Art of Empire: The Inca of Peru*. 1964, $3.95.

——, *Masterpieces in The Museum of Primitive Art*. 1965, $4.95.

Douglas Newton, *Masterpieces of Primitive Art: Selections from the Nelson A. Rockefeller Collection*. 1978, $19.95.

Michael C. Rockefeller, *The Asmat: The Journal of Michael Clark Rockefeller*. 1966, $30.

Susan Vogel, *For Spirits and Kings: African Art from the Paul and Ruth Tishman Collection*. 1981, $35.

Brief Guides, various dates:

The Art of Africa, the Pacific Islands, and the Americas. $3.75.

North American Indian Painting. $2.50.

Sculpture from the South Seas. $.75.

Reproductions: Extensive selection of posters, prints, postcards and reproductions of sculptures and other works from the collection.
Research: Library open to staff of the museum and other qualified researchers and graduate students with appropriate identification. Most comprehensive art and archaeology collection in Western Hemisphere, including 210,000 books and 1200 periodicals subcriptions. It covers all areas in which museum has holdings.

The permanent installation of primitive and pre-Columbian art, which opened to the public in February 1982, includes the art of Africa, the Americas and the Pacific.

The African collection is particularly strong in ethnic groups from the Western Sudan, the Dogon, Bamana and Senufo. A surprising time depth is documented in the installation. An archaeological terra-cotta figure from the area of Djenne in Mali has been thermaluminescent-dated to the thirteenth century and an overlifesize Dogon wooden figure to the fifteenth century by carbon-fourteen dating. Perhaps the most important African piece is a rare ivory pendant mask that dates from between 1485 and 1550. The face may be that of a sixteenth-century Queen Mother and is one of only five ivory pieces in a similar early style from the Benin of Nigeria. A

Court of Benin, Nigerian.
Belt Mask,
Ivory

wooden figure of a Bangwa king from Cameroon is worth noting for the many ways in which it breaks many commonly perceived canons of traditional African aesthetics such as the cool, bilateral symmetry and motionlessness. From the Fang of Gabon is the largest and aesthetically the finest reliquary head—once owned by sculptor Jacob Epstein. Works from two of the earliest recognized individual African carvers' hands are represented in the collection by a neckrest from the Master of the Cascade Hairstyle and a stool by the Buli Master, from the Luba and Hemba peoples of Zaire.

The Pacific gallery covers Australia, is particularly strong in the Melanesian island groups, especially New Guinea, has a small fine Polynesian holding and represents Micronesian art with a displayed female architectural carving from the Palau or Caroline Islands. Again, a surprising time depth is found in the galleries. Two tortoiseshell masks from the Torres Straits area of New Guinea belong to a tradition documented in the Pacific to the seventeenth century by Spanish navigators. The Sepik River area of New Guinea is well represented, and some wooden hook sculptures may predate the Torres Strait tradition. The New Guinea Asmat collection is one of the most comprehensive known and was, for the most part, collected by Michael C. Rockefeller, for whom the galleries are named. Several of the Polynesian objects are rare. A wooden male figure from the Gambier Islands is one of only six large figures known. A stone fragment of a human head from the Hawaiian Islands is one of only eleven such pieces known and probably dates from ca. A.D. 1000. A small ivory female pendant from Hawaii is unique, the type documented by the late-eighteenth-century expedition of Captain James Cook.

The Americas galleries cover the hemisphere geographically and have pieces that range in time from terra-cotta and stone figurines from the coast of Ecuador dating from 2000 B.C. to Eskimo wooden masks of this century. The museum's collection of metal, gold, silver, copper and alloys is particularly strong, and a special exhibition space has been created for it within the galleries. The earliest metal pieces are personal ornaments of gold dating from the Nasca culture of Peru ca. the first century B.C. The largest gold-alloy funerary mask known from the Lambeyeque culture of the North Coast of Peru is on display along with another mask that still retains the red paint that once covered the gold surface. A wooden sculpture of a supernatural is among works from the Taino culture of the Caribbean on display. The Mesoamerican gallery contains outstanding examples of sculpture in various media, ranging from a terra-cotta "baby" figurine from the Olmec, the area's earliest widespread culture, to a seated standard-bearer of stone from the sixteenth-century Aztec. The prize of the entire installation is very likely a wooden figure from the Maya, which has been carbon-fourteen dated to ca. A.D. 527. The kneeling male is unique, the only three-dimensional, free-standing sculpture of wood known from the Maya.

THE MUSEUM OF THE AMERICAN INDIAN
BROADWAY AT 155TH STREET, NEW YORK, NY 10032.
Tel: (202) 283-2420.
Hours: Tues–Sat 10 am–5 pm, Sun 1–5 pm, closed Mon and national holidays.
Admission: $2 adults, $1 senior citizens and students; free to Native Americans.
Publications: Free brochure.
Reproductions: Prints, posters and slides of objects in the collection.
Research: Reference library open by appointment; research facilities open by appointment on a restricted basis.

The permanent installation of the Museum of the American Indian covers the hemisphere both archaeologically and ethnographically from the Eskimo to less frequently represented groups in Brazil and Chile and chronologically from Clovis hunters to modern Native American artists. It only begins to represent the range and depth of the collections, which are unrivaled in the world. Objects are often the earliest examples of their kind known and reinforced with strong documentation as a result of museum expeditions.

The North American ethnographic holdings contain rare examples from Northeastern ethnic groups. A wampum belt given by Lenni Lenape, or Delaware chiefs, to William Penn as a result of the signing of a land treaty dates from 1683. One of the earliest known Iroquois False Face masks, dating from about 1775, is on display in a group in which the most recent False Face was made and used in 1950. The Northwest Coast material is extensive, the result of early collecting by George Emmons, among others. Ritual regalia and masks from Southwestern ethnic groups were collected in the late 1890s. Material from the Plains is also early, in many cases from the early nineteenth century, and is often associated with known historical figures such as Tecumseh and Geronimo. The holdings in personal ornamentation are especially strong in early pieces that are done in traditional materials such as porcupine quill and moosehair embroidery and other natural materials and in the muted vegetable and mineral pigments of the forests and plains. The ethnological objects from South America are rarely represented in American museum collections.

North American archaeological holdings range from stone objects from the Northwest Coast and California through a feather and fiber duck decoy

Kuskokwim, Eskimo.
Dance Mask,
Carved wood

found in Nevada and dated ca. 1400 B.C. to the crown of the holdings, the Southeastern collection. Mississippian pieces include a stone burial figure, stone figurated pipes and, from the important site of Spiro Mound, Oklahoma, which was destroyed by vandals in 1936, incised conch shells showing eagle dancers and evidence of a trophy head ritual and a rare wooden deer mask inlaid with shell. Mesoamerican art is not currently exhibited except as it relates to a thematic gallery on the jaguar. Central American groups are well represented, which is one of the most extensive in this country, as is the culture of the Caribbean. The Ecuadorean material is the best in this country. Among the Andean objects are a Chavin gold crown and earspools, which were found together, and are among the earliest complete artifacts of metal known.

PEABODY MUSEUM OF ARCHAEOLOGY AND ETHNOLOGY

HARVARD UNIVERSITY, 11 DIVINITY AVENUE, CAMBRIDGE, MA 02138. Tel: (617) 495-2248.

Hours: Mon–Sat 9 am–4:30 pm, Sun 1–4:30 pm, closed Thanksgiving, Christmas, New Year's, July 4th.

Admission: $1.50 adults, $.50 children 5–15, free to children under 5.

Publications: Department of Anthropology publishes scholarly works by research staff and faculty.

Reproductions: Some postcards of objects in the collection.

Research: Reference library open to Harvard affiliates and other persons who register with the library attendant. You must have a reason to use the collection. It is a superior library in anthropology and related areas.

The Peabody Museum of Archaeology and Ethnology is currently undergoing renovation until the fall of 1984. Its holdings cover all areas of the primitive and pre-Columbian world, many pieces the result of early collecting and museum expeditions.

The African collection includes pieces from all style areas but is especially notable for masks from the Guinea Coast culture area, Liberia and Ivory Coast collected by the medical missionary George Harley. Dr. Harley studied these masks in terms of their function as agents of social control, such as policemen and judges. Of interest to students of transatlantic diffusionism are a power figure from the Kongo people of Zaire and a similar piece made in Surinam by a Kongo carver brought to South America as a result of the Slave trade.

The Pacific collection has several early and rare pieces. Of three known tapa, or mulberry bark cloth, figures from Easter Island known to exist, the Peabody has two, both collected in 1899. A crested helmet and a cloak, both of feathers, from Hawaii are also rarely represented in collections. A wooden staff god from Raratonga is a fine example of its type. A painted shield from the Trobriand Islands, off the second-largest island in the world, New Guinea, is one of only a handful known to exist.

The ethnographic collection from North America features what may be the most extensive holding of Hopi material culture known and includes pottery, textiles and ceremonial objects. Objects from the Northwest Coast were collected as early as 1867 and an Algonquian wooden beaver bowl before 1795. The great naturalist Louis Agassiz made the Surinan feather collections in 1871.

The archaeological collections from the Americas are extensive. The Southwest is particularly well represented with a flint blade inlaid with turquoise, shell and lignite from a Classic Pueblo site in Utah. The Hopi holdings include a kiva mural fragment from the site of Awatovi, dating from the late fourteenth century. The museum has what is probably the finest collection of Mimbres pottery in the world.

From Mesoamerica are jades and gold dredged from the Sacred Cenote at Chichén Itzá between 1905 and 1910. A jade plaque shows a seated male in the style of the Mexican site of Palenque. Another jade, a carved head, bears an inscription dated to A.D. 681 and is in the style of the Guatemalan site of Piedras Negras. Also from Piedras Negras is a wall relief showing a ruler and warriors. A carved stone head of the young maize god is from the Honduran city of Copan, where the museum excavated in the 1890s. The gold of Panama is represented by pieces from the cemetery of Sitio Conte. Objects from the museum's 1930 excavation include a gold disc of a stylized, perhaps dead, face that was probably a textile ornament and leg armor of gold decorated with crocodiles, a power animal of the region. A wooden backrest from a litter from the Chimu culture of Peru is one of only six such objects to survive. It is decorated with imported Ecuadorian spondylus shells and tropical Amazonian bird feathers as well as silver. The collection of Peruvian textiles is the most important outside of Peru.

MILLICENT ROGERS MUSEUM

MUSEUM ROAD, TAOS, NM 87571. (505) 758-2462.

Hours: May 1–Oct 31: Sun–Sat 9 am–5 pm; Nov 1–April 30: Wed–Sun 10 am–4 pm, closed Mon–Tues. Also closed New Year's, Easter, San Geronimo Day (Sept 30), Thanksgiving, Christmas.

Admission: $3 adults, $1 senior citizens, $6 family groups, $2 on pre-arranged tour; free to members.

Publications: A quarterly newsletter is published, plus:

Hebras de Vision/Threads of Vision. 1982, $3.

Reproductions: Some posters and postcards of the collection and special exhibitions.
Research: Library open to members. Strong in Southwestern and Hispanic art and periodicals.

The Millicent Rogers collection focuses on the art of Northern New Mexico. The Native American holdings include a small Plains collection in addition to southwestern material. The unique Spanish colonial style that developed in the region is also represented by sculpture, furniture, textiles and metalwork.

The Southwestern Native American collection is strong in Navaho weaving, the work of women, with over 150 blankets, many unique and dating from the nineteenth century. The comprehensive display of southwestern metalwork, especially Navaho silver, traces the art from its beginning to the current day. Pottery, sculpture and basketry, as well as Rio Grande Pueblo painting, are also included in the exhibition space.

UNIVERSITY MUSEUM
UNIVERSITY OF PENNSYLVANIA 33RD AND SPRUCE STREETS, PHILADELPHIA, PA 19104. Tel: (215) 898-4000.
Hours: Tues–Sat 10 am–5 pm, Sun 1–5 pm, closed Mon, national holidays; closed Sun during summer.
Admission: Suggested contribution $1.
Publications:
> *Expeditions: The University Museum Magazine of Archaeology/Anthropology.* published quarterly, $3.25 each issue.
> Froelich Rainey, *Guide to the Collections: The University Museum, University of Pennsylvania.* (Africa, North America, Middle & South America, China, Mediterranean, Biblical, Oceania, etc.) 1965, $.75.

Reproductions: Posters, postcards, prints and slides of the collection; special selections for children.
Research: Library open to the public; hours vary seasonally.

The museum's permanent galleries display pieces from all areas of the primitive and pre-Columbian world, many the result of museum expeditions and fieldwork.

All culture/style areas of Africa are represented. From the Guinea Coast region is a collection of Benin objects ranging in time from the sixteenth to the nineteenth century. A sixteenth-century bronze Queen Mother head is in the group, with her characteristic tapering, conelike cap and four scarification marks over each eye that indicate her gender. Objects from Central Africa include a Kongo power figure and a Songe kifwebe mask.

From the Pacific is a group of objects from Australia's Melville Island, collected by the museum, that includes a set of carved and painted grave poles. From Melanesia, the "black islands," are a New Guinea Sepik River area suspension hook and from New Ireland a fiber and wood mask worn during Malanggan ceremonies. The museum has a rare piece of sculpture from the Caroline Islands in Micronesia, a men's house gable ornament of wood. From Polynesia are two rare pieces from Hawaii, a carved wooden figure on a staff and a red and yellow feather cloak worn by the Hawaiian nobility.

Archaeological pieces from North America include a wooden deer head that was once painted and inlaid, from the site of Key Marco, Florida and probably dating from Mississippian times, which has survived only because it was submerged in a swamp before discovery in 1895. From the Southwest is a Great Pueblo period bifurcated basket, perfectly preserved in the dryness of a southwestern cave. Historic or ethnographic pieces from North America include a carved pair of wooden beaver bowls from the Northeast, made before 1795. Objects from the Tlingit people of southern Alaska were collected by Louis Shotridge, a museum staff member and himself a Tlingit. The museum also has pottery by Nampeyo, whose husband worked on the excavation of a fifteenth-century Hopi pueblo. Nampeyo saw the pottery excavated from the site and became interested in reviving styles her people had made 500 years earlier. Ethnological material from South America is also on display, again the result of museum staff fieldwork.

Archaelogical objects from North America include accession stela number 14 from the site of Piedras Negras in Guatemala, one of several Mesoamerican sites excavated by the museum. Also from the Maya is a Chama style vase that is a fine example of the naturalism and eloquence of the Maya vase painter. There is also a fine collection of white marble vases from the Ulua Valley in Honduras. Central American objects include gold from a

Meso American.
Stela,
Stone

pre-Columbian cemetery excavated by the museum in Panama. From Peru is a stone mortar carved in feline form that is a good example of the complicated, punning, metaphoric imagery of the early Chavin culture.

APPENDIX 1
MUSEUMS BY REGIONS
NORTHEAST

SOUTHEAST

APPENDIX 2

MUSEUMS BY SUBJECT CATEGORIES
KEY TO THE CODES

AM American Art	**AN** Ancient Art	**AS** Asian Art
EU European Art	**PH** Photography	**PR** Primitive Art
	M/PM Modern/Post–Modern Art	

Addison Gallery, Andover, MA **(AM)**: *11–12*

Albright–Knox Museum, Buffalo, NY **(M/PM)**: *121–22*

American Museum of Natural History, New York, NY **(PR)**: *171–73*

Art Institute of Chicago, Chicago, IL **(AS, EU, M/PM, PH)**: *59, 85–87, 122–24, 145–46*

The Art Museum, Princeton University, Princeton, NJ **(AN, PH)**: *41–42, 149–51*

Asian Art Museum, Avery Brundage Collection, San Francisco, CA **(AS)**: *60–61*

Barnes Foundation, Merion, PA **(M/PM)**: *124–25*

Brooklyn Museum, Brooklyn, NY **(AM, AN, AS, PR)**: *12–14, 42–43, 61–62, 173–74*

Buffalo Bill Historical Center, Cody, WY **(PR)**: *174*

Center for Creative Photography, Tucson, AZ **(PH)**: *147–49*

Cincinnati Museum of Art, Cincinnati, OH **(AS)**: *62*

Cleveland Museum of Art, Cleveland, OH **(AN, AS, EU)**: *43–45, 62–64, 92–95*

Corcoran Gallery of Art, Washington, DC **(AM)**: *14–15*

Dallas Museum of Fine Arts, Dallas, TX **(PR)**: *174–75*

Denver Art Museum, Denver, CO **(AS)**: *64–65*

Des Moines Art Center, Des Moines, IA **(M/PM)**: *125–26*

Detroit Institute of Art, Detroit, MI **(AM, AS)**: *15–16, 65–66*

Dumbarton Oaks, Washington, DC **(PR)**: *175–76*

Fine Arts Museums of San Francisco, San Francisco, CA **(AM)**: *16–17*

Firestone Library and the Art Gallery, Princeton University, Princeton, NJ **(PH)**: *149–51*

William Hayes Fogg Art Museum, Harvard University, Cambridge, MA **(EU)**: *87, 90–92*

Freer Gallery, Washington, DC **(AS)**: *66–68*

Frick Collection, New York, NY **(EU)**: *95–97*

Isabella Stewart Gardner Museum, Boston, MA **(AS, EU)**: *68–69, 87, 89–90*

J. Paul Getty Museum, Malibu, CA **(AN, EU)**: *45–47, 98, 101–03*

Thomas Gilcrease Institute, Tulsa, OK **(AM)**: *17–18*

Solomon R. Guggenheim Museum, New York, NY **(M/PM)**: *126–29*

Haffenreffer Museum, Bristol, RI **(PR)**: *176*

Heard Museum, Phoenix, AZ **(PR)**: *176–77*

Hirshhorn Museum and Sculpture Garden, Washington, DC **(M/PM)**: *129–30*

Huntington Library, Art Gallery and Botanical Gardens, San Marino, CA **(EU)**: *98*

International Center of Photography, New York, NY **(PH)**: *151–52*

International Museum of Photography at the George Eastman House,

INDEX

PICTURE CREDITS

Page 13. The Brooklyn Museum: A. Augustus Healy Fund B
Page 17. The Fine Arts Museum of San Francisco, Gift of the M. H. de Young Endowment Fund
Page 20. The Metropolitan Museum of Art, Morris K. Jesup Fund, 1933 (33.61)
Page 24. Courtesy, Museum of Fine Arts, Boston, M. and M. Karolik Collection
Page 28. Courtesy of the National Gallery of Art, Washington, D.C. Gift of The W. L. and May T. Mellon Foundation, 1943
Page 31. The New Britain Museum of American Art, H.R. Stanley Fund
Page 38. Worcester Art Museum
Page 40. Yale University Art Gallery
Page 43. The Brooklyn Museum: Charles Edwin Wilborn Fund
Page 46. The J. Paul Getty Museum
Page 52. Courtesy, Museum of Fine Arts, Boston, William Francis Warden Fund
Page 56. Virginia Museum
Page 58. Walters Art Gallery
Page 60. Courtesy of The Art Institute of Chicago
Page 61. Asian Art Museum of San Francisco
Page 64. The Cleveland Museum of Art, Gift of Mrs. A. Dean Perry 62.279
Page 67. Courtesy of the Freer Gallery of Art, Smithsonian Institution, Washington, D.C.

Page 69. Isabella Stewart Gardner Museum
Page 70. Kimbell Art Museum
Page 71. Los Angeles Museum of Art. From The Nasli and Alice Heeramaneck Collection, Museum Associates Purchase
Page 76. Courtesy, Museum of Fine Arts, Boston
Page 79. William Rockhill Nelson Gallery of Art. Atkins Museum of Fine Arts
Page 81. Philadelphia Museum of Art: Given by Wright S. Ludington in memory of his father Charles H. Ludington
Page 82. Seattle Art Museum
Page 83. Walters Art Gallery
Page 86. Courtesy of The Art Institute of Chicago
Page 89. Courtesy, Museum of Fine Arts, Boston, William W. Warren Fund
Page 91. Fogg Art Museum, Bequest: Grenville L. Winthrop, 1943.251
Page 93. The Cleveland Museum of Art, Purchase, Leonard C. Hanna Jr. Bequest 76.2
Page 96. The Frick Collection
Page 99. Los Angeles County Museum of Art, Gift of the Ahmanson Foundation
Page 100. Norton Simon Museum of Art at Pasadena
Page 102. The J. Paul Getty Museum
Page 104. The Metropolitan Museum of Art, Purchased with special funds and gifts of friends of the Museum, 1961 (61.198)
Page 108. National Gallery of Art, Washington, D.C.
Page 112. William Rockhill Nelson Gallery of Art. Atkins Museum of Fine Arts
Page 114. The John G. Johnson Collection, Philadelphia
Page 117. Ringling Museum of Art
Page 119. The Toledo Museum of Art, Gift of Edward Drummond Libbey
Page 127. The Solomon R. Guggenheim Museum
Page 130. Hirshhorn Museum and Sculpture Garden
Page 131. Milwaukee Art Museum Collection, Gift of Mrs. Harry Lynde Bradley
Page 133. Collection, The Museum of Modern Art, New York
Page 135. Philadelphia Museum of Art: The Louise and Walter Arensberg Collection
Page 136. The Phillips Collection
Page 138. San Francisco Museum of Modern Art, Gift of the artist
Page 140. University Art Museum, Berkeley
Page 142. Walker Art Center
Page 144. Collection of the Whitney Museum of American Art, New York
Page 148. Center for Creative Photography, University of Arizona copyright © 1983 Ansel Adams
Page 155. International Museum of Photography at George Eastman House, New York
Page 157. Courtesy, the Collections of The Library of Congress
Page 167. Philadelphia Museum of Art: Given by Carl Zigrosser
Page 170. University Art Museum, University of New Mexico Albuquerque
Page 172. Negative no. 329786, Courtesy, American Museum of Natural History (Photo: Rota)
Page 175. The Dumbarton Oaks Research Library and Collections, Washington, D.C.
Page 178. The Metropolitan Museum of Art, The Michael C. Rockefeller Memorial Collection, Gift of Nelson A. Rockefeller, 1972 (1978.412.323)
Page 180. Photograph courtesy of Museum of the American Indian, Heye Foundation
Page 183. Copyright © University Museum, University of Pennsylvania

---

ABOUT THE CONSULTANT EDITOR

Tom L. Freudenheim became Director of the Worcester Art Museum in 1982, after serving for over three years as Director of the Museum Program at the National Endowment for the Arts in Washington, D.C. He served as Director of The Baltimore Museum of Art from 1971 through 1978. Prior to that he was Assistant Director of the University Art Museum, University of

California, Berkeley. From 1962 to 1965 he was first Assistant Curator, then Curator, of The Jewish Museum in New York City.

He has written numerous articles and catalogues, ranging from topics on Islamic art through the decorative arts, modern art, and museums; in addition, he lectures frequently on those subjects.

ABOUT THE CONTRIBUTORS

KARLA KLEIN ALBERTSON has an M.A. in Classical and Near Eastern Archeology from Bryn Mawr College and is completing a Ph.D. dissertation in her specialty field, Greek votive terracottas. Archeology is a pursuit shared with her husband, and their research provides frequent opportunities for travel in the United States and abroad. In addition to scholarly writing, Mrs. Albertson contributes lighter articles and poetry to a variety of publications.

CAROL BIER, formerly a Smithsonian Fellow at the Freer Gallery of Art, received her M.A. in Art History from the Institute of Fine Arts, New York University, where she is currently completing her doctorate. A specialist in Islamic Art, having taught at Georgetown University and the University of Maryland, she has published articles in scholarly journals and has lived, worked, and conducted archeological research in several southwest Asian countries. She has helped organize major exhibitions for the Asia Society, Smithsonian Institution, Royal Ontario Museum, and Metropolitan Museum of Art.

PETER FRANK is a critic and curator living and working in New York City. He is currently Senior Editor at *Metro*, responsible for the weekly newspaper's arts coverage, and is Editor of *Re-Dact*, an anthology of art criticism. Frank has served as Art Critic for *The Village Voice* and *The SoHo Weekly News*, and is at present the Critic-at-Large for *Diversion Planner* magazine. He has taught at the Pratt Institute, Columbia University's School of the Arts, and Tyler School of Art at Temple University, among others, and has served in advisory capacities to several arts organizations.

STEVEN HENRY MADOFF writes regularly for *Art in America, Arts, Artnews,* and other publications. He is currently working on a book about American painting and poetry in the 1950s and 1960s.

SARAH McFADDEN is a critic and contributing editor for *Art in America.*

WENDY SCHONFELD is a doctoral candidate in Primitive and Pre-Columbian Art History and Archeology at Columbia University. She teaches Art History as Adjunct Lecturer at Baruch College of the City University of New York (CUNY). She has also taught at Arizona State University (Tempe, Arizona). While there she organized an African art exhibition with pieces from ASU and the Heard Museum in Phoenix. She has just organized an exhibition at the Bronx Museum of the Arts, concentrating on Africa, the Americas, and the Pacific.

GILBERT VINCENT holds degrees from Harvard College and Cambridge University, as well as an M.A. degree in Early American Culture from the Winterthur Program and a Ph.D. in American Art History from the University of Delaware. He currently teaches courses in painting, sculpture, architecture, and decorative arts at the Cooperstown Graduate Program.